FOLLOWING ON
IN THE FOOTSTEPS OF CRICKETING FATHERS

JAMES BUTTLER

GREAT N-ORTHERN

Great Northern Books Limited
PO Box 1380, Bradford, BD5 5FB
www.greatnorthernbooks.co.uk

Every effort has been made to acknowledge correctly and contact the copyright holders of material in this book. Great Northern Books Limited apologises for any unintentional errors or omissions, which should be notified to the publisher.

ISBN: 978-1-912101-00-9

Design and layout: David Burrill

CIP Data
A catalogue for this book is available from the British Library

To Dad – an excellent example of what
a father should be.

To Sam – a son I'm very proud of.

To all the sons and daughters – please
pick up a bat & ball and write your
own chapter.

CONTENTS

INTRODUCTION 5

CHAPTER ONE: THE COWDREYS 12

CHAPTER TWO: THE SIDEBOTTOMS 31

CHAPTER THREE: THE EALHAMS 44

CHAPTER FOUR: THE BAIRSTOWS 56

CHAPTER FIVE: THE LEHMANNS, LLOYDS
and STEWARTS 68

CHAPTER SIX: EVERYONE HAS A FATHER
AND A STORY 87

CHAPTER SEVEN: THE BRADMANS 100

CHAPTER EIGHT: THE BOTHAMS 110

CHAPTER NINE: THE RICHARDS 120

CHAPTER TEN: THE BAADER-MEINHOF
PHENOMENON 130

CHAPTER ELEVEN: THE BUTCHERS 141

CHAPTER TWELVE: NATURE v NURTURE,
IS THERE A CRICKET GENE? 153

CHAPTER THIRTEEN: THE HADLEES 172

CHAPTER FOURTEEN: THE HEADLEYS 185

CHAPTER FIFTEEN: THE D'OLIVEIRAS 195

CHAPTER SIXTEEN: THE TREMLETTS 204

CHAPTER SEVENTEEN: AROUND THE WORLD
IN 56 FAMILIES 214

CHAPTER EIGHTEEN: THE FINAL OVER 248

INTRODUCTION

*"If you cannot get rid of the family skeleton,
you may as well make it dance"*
George Bernard Shaw

Does having a famous father make life easier? Does a well-known surname create additional pressure, expectation and unwanted attention? Do you inherit a key to doors others have to work hard to open? Is it tougher to impress people who perceive you've experienced an easy ride?

All children want to please and impress their parents. Every one of us has had to fight to establish our own role in the world. Who are we? Where do we fit? What makes us unique?

Establishing a personal identity poses varying degrees of difficulty for average Joes with average Josephs for fathers. When your father has stood in the spotlight as the applause rattles around the auditorium, the flowers landing at his feet, it must be dazzling and daunting to step out and attempt to share that stage with him.

The human mind is capable of instilling confidence, visualising a path to glory and memorising previous triumphs for positive effect. It can also allow doubt, insecurity and demons to dance on one's dreams.

Playing professional sport, indeed life, is hard enough for people without famous parents. I had long considered the added pressures placed on cricketers attempting to follow in the vast footsteps of their fathers. Sports supporters can be an unforgiving bunch. Is the pressure of expectation ever too much? Is gaining the acceptance of sports fans a family right?

The questions were mounting up as fast as the surnames. Cricket is a sport that keeps it in the family more than most. I'd scribbled an A4 sheet full of surnames spanning at least two generations before I'd blinked. An all-I-could-eat buffet of food for thought.

* * * * *

Away from cricket for a moment, have you ever heard of Eric Douglas? If you have you are one of the few and it is probably for all the wrong reasons.

Eric was the youngest son of Hollywood A-list actor Kirk Douglas. Kirk's eight-year marriage to Diana Dill spawned two children. The eldest, Michael, would become a famous movie actor and Joel became a film producer. With his second wife Anne Buydens, Kirk had two more children. Peter also went into film production and then there was Eric, the youngest child.

There can be no doubt the Douglas surname had its advantages. Michael forged a career as illustrious as his father's. Joel and Peter succeeded behind the camera. They were not hampered by their lineage.

As for Eric, he had nine main film credits to his name after growing up in an environment where his family routinely socialised with major movie stars. He made his first appearance in films aged nine. It was all he knew. But the success of the rest of the Douglas dynasty weighed heavily.

Even his most renowned foray into acting saw him play his own father as a young man in a 1982 television film *Remembrance of Love*. There was no escaping his surname and the resulting, usually uncomplimentary, comparisons. He gave up on his acting dreams in the early 1990s.

There is more to a person's identity than a surname. Who was the real Eric Douglas? Would he ever be able to find out?

As the least professionally successful sibling he went off the rails. Countless run-ins with the law brought him infamy. The black sheep appeared in the media as 'the disgraced son of Kirk' and 'shamed brother of Michael'.

In the early 1990s, his attempt to become a stand-up comedian gave him fresh direction. Eric naively chose to centre his routine on his family and his struggles therein and took to the stages of New York's comedy clubs. At his first gig he was riotously heckled for being drunk, but it was an infamous trip to London where he cemented his name in folklore.

At The Comedy Store he had one of those nights all comedians dread. He "died on his arse," recalled club co-founder Don Ward. The harder he tried to elicit laughter, the louder the hecklers mocked. It wasn't how it was supposed to be.

Increasingly agitated, Eric rounded on the audience and pleaded into the darkness, "You can't do this to me, I'm Kirk Douglas's son!"

A quick thinking wag stood and responded, "No, I'm Kirk Douglas's son!"

A couple of rows further back another man did the same, "No, I'm Kirk Douglas's son!"

Gradually, one-by-one, the audience rose to their feet and said, "No, I'm Kirk Douglas's son!"

As Eric's comedy career fell through the stage floor he was

being taunted once more by his father's deeds. The Douglas elephant was in every room he entered.

In 1960, Kirk had starred in *Spartacus* which had included the iconic "I'm Spartacus", "No I'm Spartacus" scene. If you are too young to remember, put 'Kirk Douglas I'm Spartacus' into YouTube. The audience had mocked poor Eric cruelly and, it has to be said, rather brilliantly.

The family had been a meal ticket, a door opener and a source of inspiration. But he had found them impossible to live up to and a constant reminder of his own inadequacies.

"The pressures of being the youngest son in a famous family sometimes got to me," Eric said. "I used to feel I had to compare myself to them."

Through the 1990s he struggled badly as he developed problems with alcohol, drugs and the law. He was arrested for kicking a police officer in 1991. Three years later, he was detained for possessing cocaine and only weeks later he crashed his car after being involved in a fight in West Hollywood's Comedy Store.

In May 1996, he pleaded guilty to accepting and possessing 11 vials of crack cocaine and 1,085 Xanax pills and was placed on probation and ordered to complete a drug rehabilitation programme.

The hits just kept on coming. More arrests, then he mooned at the audience of a New York club as he mocked his brother Michael's acting in the *Basic Instinct* movie. He was sued for attacking the driver of his limousine and later had let his dog run amok on an American Airlines flight while being abusive and throwing blankets at flight attendants.

Eric's life was out of control.

In 1999, he accidentally overdosed on Xanax, fell into an eight-day coma and subsequently found his speech became permanently slurred and his gait affected. By 2001, Eric was suing his former psychiatrist for $50,000 claiming prescribed drugs had made him suicidal and caused heart problems when mixed with alcohol resulting in significant medical bills.

Kirk was not oblivious to Eric's struggle, telling *The Early Show* in 2009 that he had taken Eric to "twenty rehab centres" over the years and "nothing helped".

Eric died of a drug overdose on 6 July 2004, aged 46. An autopsy determined his death "accidental" and caused by "acute intoxication" from the combined effects of alcohol, tranquillisers and painkillers. The tortuous struggle for his moment in the sun, his desire to feel equal and important in his own right was finally over.

"Eric Douglas died as he had lived: disappointing people because he was not one of his more famous, more successful family members," Aida Edemariam wrote in *The Guardian*. Not a kind epitaph, but one Eric had been penning his entire existence.

Eric had studied acting at Lamda in London. One of his teachers, Helena Kaut-Howson, said shortly after his death, "Acting is a cruel profession and doubly cruel if you come from a family like the Douglas's. I know other such kids, like Laurence Olivier's daughter. It's always a problem, rather than a help. It takes somebody really insensitive, with a thick skin. I know some who can use it as an advantage, but sensitive ones really suffer. He was doomed by the fact that he was expected to develop in a certain way."

Kaut-Howson insisted that Eric had genuine acting talent. "I remember him phoning his dad", she recollected when he had been cast to play the role of a father. "He was talking to him about the part, and his father being so happy about it. Eric was so sweet, and so hopeful."

Kaut-Howson remembered a message Eric had sent her a few years earlier: "I start the day in a happy mood, feeling positive about life, but I see a hole in front of me. I know I should avoid it, but I know I will fall into it. And I do."

And that, usually to a lesser extent, can be what families do to us all. A need to live up to, be better than, not to embarrass, to achieve, to love, live and do justice to the family name. It's not easy.

* * * * *

Supporters often expect cricket sons to be clones of their fathers. I see similarities in myself to my own parents, but I am not an exact replica of either. It would be foolish to expect cricketers to be so. A supporter carrying those expectations is likely to be disappointed when the son is not as flamboyant, attacking or talented as his father.

To find answers I decided to chat with some of cricket's father and son pairings to tap into their opinions and experiences. But before I did that I gave Simon Hartley a ring. He'd been working across numerous sports as a psychologist for many years. I hoped his insight might push me in the right direction.

Simon's recent work with Yorkshire CCC had achieved notable successes.

Adam Lyth, the county's left-handed opening batsman had been a source of frustration. Everyone knew he had heaps of talent, but he often got in, looked amazing and then threw away a good start with a slack shot. Lyth, a keen golfer, was taken to a putting green by Hartley and given a concentration task that would appeal to his competitive instincts. He was asked to hole as many two-foot putts as he could. Professional golfers tend to manage between 50 and 100. Lyth's best effort was 213 consecutive successes.

Lyth took what he had learned into the 2014 season and scored more runs than any other division one batsman as Yorkshire won the first of back-to-back Championship titles in 2014 and 2015. Lyth was called up by England and scored a century against New Zealand at Headingley in early 2015. Unfortunately, the Australians got on top of him during the 2015 Ashes series that followed and Adam didn't bat long enough to require his enhanced concentration, but he remains far more consistent at the top of the White Rose batting order.

I hoped Simon would validate my choice of subject matter and give me a few tips on how to approach my task ahead.

"It's a really interesting area psychologically," he began. "It's hard to know whether the net effect of having a famous father is positive or negative. Life is not the same for them, they've got different challenges and they might also have more opportunities.

"One guy that might be really interesting for you to chat to is Liam Botham. I don't know whether you've managed to track him down or contact him?"

'Speak to Liam Botham' was scribbled on my notepad.

"I met up with Liam when he was at Newcastle Falcons," Simon continued. "I can't disclose anything that he said to me, but the fact that he had a very famous father had a big impact on him for a significant part of his life."

I was buoyed by Simon's initial response. I was getting the impression that he felt I was on to something. I asked him whether young cricketers with successful fathers faced potential problems?

"For many of these guys it will be an additional challenge when it comes to searching for their own identity and not assuming a pseudo identity from their father," he replied. "I think there is more expectation from fans and coaches. I think internally there tends to be an expectation too.

"I don't think this is just true of famous fathers. There's a desire with most boys as they are growing up and becoming adults, that whatever they do in life they exceed the point where their father got to," he continued. "For many it will be financial. I suspect that along with show business you'll also find the same with entrepreneurial fathers and sons. If Dad made a million, they need to make a billion kind of thing."

I wondered if that would translate to runs and wickets.

"There are kids with trust funds who probably don't need to put themselves through it. To look at the parallels in the experiences that they have had I think will be really interesting."

"I think you'll find that some embrace the opportunity and don't perceive the pressure, because pressure is not tangible. If you talk about pressure in terms of atmospheric pressure or water pressure, that's tangible. Psychological pressure isn't.

"Perception is key," he suggested. "Whether you experience pressure or not largely depends on whether you perceive it. Some people will deny there is any more pressure and think 'okay fine, people expect, big deal, so they expect, so what?' It's the person that dictates whether it is pressure or not. Equally the person dictates how they respond to it."

There is a perception that because a child comes from a successful family they have an advantage over others. To illustrate the point Simon told me about two swimmers. They didn't have famous parents, but one had everything laid on a plate while the other had to fight harder for his opportunities.

"They were in the same squad," he recalled. "When you looked at them externally and matched one against the other, one of these guys was naturally more talented. Also, he had parents who had bought him a flat in the city close to training and were paying his living costs so that he could concentrate on swimming. He was given everything he needed to be successful.

"The other guy didn't have any of that. He wasn't naturally talented, he wasn't given anything, he had to graft for everything, he had to get up early and drive into training because he didn't have a flat right next door and he had to make sure he earned himself a living so he could feed himself. But that guy became an Olympic finalist and the other one didn't."

I asked Simon whether a young Richard Hutton or Liam Botham would experience more pressure because their fathers were enormous in both reputation and statistics?

"If you are trying to match, or you think you are in competition with your father, then yes it's tough," Simon responded. "Some people would say it makes no difference whether they achieve or not, although again there is that tendency for some to want to better their father's achievements."

I tried to think about myself. How I would respond to perpetual criticism and comparisons. I knew I would really struggle. I gain confidence from reassurance. I doubted very much that's what Richard Hutton got. You'd surely have to be incredibly self-assured and secure as a person not to listen to the negativity of others and consequently doubt yourself.

"Yes, but it comes down to the person, their perspective and whether it bothers them," Simon countered. "In talking to lots of these guys I suspect there are quite a few successful fathers who are more critical than others would be, because they will have higher expectations of their son.

"One of the things that might go in a cricket son's favour is that their parents might not try and live or get their success through their kids as they've already achieved their own success. If you look at pushy parents syndrome, a lot of it is the parents themselves haven't had any success and this is the only way they are going to," he said. "If you look at Tiger Woods's dad for example. Why did he want Tiger to be successful? Probably because he never really had any success himself.

"In some cases it's because there are some real economic benefits to the family. In other cases I think it's about real vicarious recognition. The kind that Judy Murray probably gets because she wouldn't have got it any other way. No one would know who Judy Murray is."

The chat with Simon was extremely useful as I gauged how I was going to approach and structure this book. The last thing he said to me gave me heart. I told you I need reassurance.

"I think there are loads and loads of really great topics of conversation and areas to explore because it really does open up a lot, so from your point-of-view filling a book with interesting stuff will be no problem at all."

I'll leave you to judge whether or not Simon was right.

CHAPTER ONE

COLIN, CHRIS, GRAHAM and FABIAN COWDREY

*"Success is not final, failure is not fatal,
it is the courage to continue that counts"*
Winston Churchill

I saw my first live game of cricket in 1977 at the St Lawrence Ground in Canterbury and was immediately hooked. I collected autographs, ate and drank statistics and watched as many games as I could cram into an English summer. My Christmas and birthday presents took a welcome cricket theme. I would run up the drive at my family home in Lincolnshire and bowl anything remotely spherical at the garage door. The harvest from the apple tree in the back garden took a hit during my early teenage years. My bedroom mirror became Dennis Lillee and I'd hook, cut and cover drive England to countless Ashes victories.

Michael Atherton is roughly my age and played in very much the same style as I did. I sometimes wonder whether he enjoyed the career meant for me. In truth, I was enthusiastic, enjoyed some club cricket success, but Atherton not only grabbed my dreams and livelihood, but my talent too.

As those apples crunched against the garage door I never envisaged I'd work for Yorkshire County Cricket Club and become a cricket journalist. Being paid to watch matches from press boxes, asking inane questions to the best players in the world and calling it a job would have made the young me smile. It still does.

I looked up the scorecard for that 1977 match and was pleased that my memories of the Sunday League game between Kent and Yorkshire were pretty accurate.

Kent made 153 and bowled Yorkshire out for 102 to win by 51 runs. Boycott was dismissed early on in Yorkshire's reply, the crowd were friendly and I knew I wanted to return to watch another match long before my Great Uncle drove me home.

For most young people there is a moment when the door is thrown open to the complicated, rewarding, frustrating and beautiful world we call sport. Sat in the Frank Woolley Stand, the tobacco smoke tickling my nostrils, I was transfixed. My

Grandma had voiced concerns that I was too young to sit still all day. She was rarely wrong, but if it hadn't been for the game ending and everyone else going home I wonder if that eight-year-old would still be there.

I devoured newspaper reports, constantly refreshed scores on Ceefax, the world-wide-web on Mogadon for those too young to recall, and race home to the frequent disappointment that Chris Cowdrey had again been kept out of the England squad by Ian Botham. With less blinkered hindsight I could admit the selectors got that one right.

I returned to Canterbury every August for at least a decade. As Alan Ealham left the field of play, the Cowdrey brothers entered the scene and followed their ultra-famous father Colin into the Kent side. Mark Ealham, Alan's son, was not far behind.

I was loitering outside the dressing room after a day's play when a silver-haired woman tapped me on the shoulder. She smiled warmly as she asked if I could do her a favour. I began to fulfil my duties with trepidation. I climbed a flight of stairs and saw the Kent logo on the door to my left. It was being guarded by their head coach Brian Luckhurst who looked me up and down with suspicion, before asking: "What can we do for you?"

As I took a second to frame my response I glanced over his shoulder and saw England's wicket-keeper Alan Knott completely naked in the dressing room. Derek Underwood was also unclothed and Chris Cowdrey emerged from a shower, his modesty only covered with a white towel.

I had only just reached double figures in life's innings. I don't think I'd seen a grown man naked before and certainly not anyone I'd ever meekly ask for a scribbled autograph. Cowdrey was broad shouldered, suntanned and, as he stood mid dressing room running his hands through his dark wet hair, I've never wanted to be someone else more in my life.

"What can we do for you young man," Luckhurst repeated.

"Chris Cowdrey's mother has asked me to come up here and get his short-sleeved sweater," I mumbled. "She says she needs to wash it tonight so he can wear it tomorrow."

"Oh yeah," the gnarled old pro jabbed back. "That's what they all say. Have you got any form of identification?"

Luckhurst was jibing me. I was far from recognising his wit as my eyes realised that big Graham Dilley could have easily been rhyming slang.

I wondered whether I'd ever be good enough to shower in that room. People who tell you that anything is possible if you practise hard enough are not always correct. I practised like a lunatic, but never stood on that landing again. Cricket was certainly not in my genes.

Chris Cowdrey, the son of Colin, the brother of Graham, the man whose pictures I had cut out of *The Cricketer Magazine* and stuck on my bedroom wall, wandered towards me.

"Hi," he said brightly, after being beckoned by Luckhurst.

"Hi," I managed as I tried to smile.

"You need my short sleeved sweater?"

"Yes," I said, too intimidated to proffer anything multi-syllabic.

"Okay, thanks very much," he turned and was gone. A couple of seconds later a jumper landed on Luckurst's left shoulder. It was relayed to me and I descended the stairs, passed the sweater to Mrs Cowdrey who thanked me and departed.

I collected Chris's autograph many times after that. I wondered if we'd ever chat about our sweater moment. That common ground made me feel different to the other kids, but he never mentioned our bond, just wrote his usual squiggle and turned away.

It's bizarre how strong affinities can be developed with people you don't even know. I was incredibly excited when Chris was finally given international recognition and hugely proud of my clean-sweatered friend when he captained England in a solitary Test. And even then people still chirped that he'd only reached those heady heights because he shared his father's surname. I wondered what it might have been like to have called Colin Cowdrey 'Dad'.

Very few people are considered good enough to play for their country, let alone captain it. Chris skippered England in one Test against West Indies and earned six Test caps. Colin had 114 Test caps and captained in 27 games.

Colin's career was a large oak, Chris's a bonsai in comparison, but the latter had enjoyed a career that most kids, including myself, would chop their right arms off to enjoy for just one day.

Just because Colin was one of the all-time greats, did that make Chris a failure? For young Chris, and his brother Graham, who would also play for Kent, there was a great deal to live up to.

* * * * *

It was with excitement and a few nerves that I picked up the phone to have a chat with the Cowdrey boys. I'd heard you should never meet your heroes. I wasn't sure if the saying extended to telephone interviews.

Colin Cowdrey, or Baron Cowdrey of Tonbridge after he became the first English cricketer to receive a peerage, even had MCC as his initials. Michael Colin Cowdrey – nominative determinism for sure. He'd played 114 Test matches for England, hit 22 Test tons and scored 7,624 Test runs.

The respect he had garnered was for more than his sporting prowess. I met him briefly at an Old England fixture in the early 1980s. He had a twinkle in his eye that betrayed a complete and utter love of his chosen profession.

Colin had retired from the game in September 1975. His eldest son Chris entered the Kent dressing room the following summer, so hot on his heels that his father's seat in the changing room was probably still warm.

"It was an issue big time to begin with," Chris told me when I asked whether he'd encountered any struggles in those early days. "But I never felt bad about it because of the advantages I got when I arrived at Kent. Some really good players would come down for trials and get 20 minutes in the nets and were judged pretty quickly. Some of them never even got a 2nd XI game.

"I was given 2nd XI cricket at a young age. I didn't do very well and was given more opportunities and I ended up breaking through," he continued. "The advantages I might have had, and certainly some people thought I had, perhaps counteracted for the bit of pressure that I experienced when I first broke through.

"It was an unusual situation to be going into a dressing room that had nine or ten players that had played with the old man," Chris told me. "But it wasn't an issue once I'd got into the team and become established. I never gave it a second thought, except for the people that talked to me about it all of the time."

Chris revealed how despite his father's retirement, a season earlier, the generations had nearly been united for Kent during the hot summer of 1976.

"I got a lot of sledging about the old man," Chris had told ESPN Cricinfo, so I pressed him to elaborate.

"I got it most of the time," he confirmed. "More so going up north where there was a sledging mentality between north and south, although I got on brilliantly with the Yorkies. I think sledging was considered a northern trait back then."

I'd read that Chris had been playing against Leicestershire and Ken Higgs. Disgruntled that Colin had left him out of the England side when captain, Higgs made every attempt to put the youngster in his place.

"He never let me forget about it," Chris said. "He kept bowling bouncers and after every ball I got a tirade of abuse. I don't know how much Graham got, but there was more sledging in the game when he started anyway. You just lived with it."

Chris had always struck me as a confident individual and, whereas others may have balked at the scrutiny created by his father's legacy, he took it in his stride. When he got an England Test call-up the comparisons were inevitably reignited.

"When I got picked to go to India in 1984 it all came back

multiplied by 500," he recalled. "What happens is you have a bit of self doubt as you know people are talking about the old man all the time. He was a person that played over 100 Tests, got a hundred just about everywhere, won in India and therefore it all started again, but it didn't bother me for very long.

"It was a very strange one because I was appointed for the last two Tests against West Indies and then after that there was a one-off Test against Sri Lanka and then there was a tour to India. Although officially the whole world knew I was on a two-match contract, I knew that I was on a contract to take me through the whole of the India tour, whether we won or lost. Where that all changed was when I got injured, I didn't play particularly well in the game I got and then they had a change of thinking. That's water under the bridge. They can do whatever they want."

Chris seemed to have a 'say what the hell you like about me, I don't care' attitude to the knockers during his career, although he still got the 'you are only here because of your Dad' comments.

"I only really had it a couple of times when I was really young and was picked to captain Young England on a tour," he conceded. "One or two comments were made about me being captain. That's the only time I got that particular thing until I was made England captain. Then of course people like jumping on the bandwagon of nepotism with Peter May, Uncle Peter, being my godfather.

"I didn't really see that as a problem. I was a bit older then. The biggest problem you have is when you are a young player trying to prove yourself and people are more interested in talking about comparisons and whether you are going to be as good or whether you play the same way. You hear 'he played that shot just like his father'. You get a bit fed up with that every day of the week. If I'd ever played a drive like the old man, I would have been happy.

"Graham and I are different personalities. He was more sensitive to that kind of comment," suggested Chris. "He has a lot of personality but wasn't quite as gregarious as I was, so he would have found it hard."

And Graham, the younger brother, had indeed found it tough. Even brothers, cut from identical cloth, are very different.

Graham began: "I don't think Chris found the comparisons an issue, whereas I did. He had a very up and at 'em attitude with the way he played, more so than me and was more of a good time man off the pitch too.

"I'm glad I didn't have to follow Dad straight away because I think that must have been a burden. I think I would have really struggled playing with a lot of people that had been Dad's team-mates. But he made people think that he was very different to his Dad and they accepted him for that."

Chris intrigued me. Despite stating early in our conversation that he'd never had any problems, he'd proceeded to list quite a few. He then told me that to avoid comparisons with Colin he'd completely altered the way he played.

Chris told me: "I went into a side that the year before had one of the great classic players of all time in the old man and I was very conscious of people trying to compare me. I made probably the worst decision I ever made. When I was at school I played properly, an off-side player, but I decided, with one-day cricket increasingly prominent, that I would be totally different from Dad.

"I loved fielding away from the slips, I made a big effort to be a bowler as it was an important difference and I changed my batting to be a leg-side player. The comparisons ended pretty well as soon as I got into the 1st XI at Kent. I got picked as a No 8 batsman who was a good fielder and an extra bowler if necessary. I immediately became a bits and pieces cricketer, which suited my temperament but didn't make me a world-class player.

"I don't how much of that change was down to one-day cricket becoming increasingly important, but I think a very high percentage was down to my father," Chris added. "I also thought it wouldn't do me any harm to be a quick scoring player. I went into a Kent side with eight or nine internationals. I wasn't going to get in that top five or six too easily, I'd seen the big crowds coming in, those Sunday League games were awesome and that was my way into the team. If I had just gone and ground out scores in the 2nd XI to make my case I wouldn't have got in quite so easily and wouldn't have enjoyed it, but I might have ended up a better player. My temperament was more one of trying to entertain and really enjoy every day I played."

Despite seeing his opportunity coming down the order in Kent's one-day setup, Chris found himself opening the innings, and it paid off against Sussex in 1977.

"I wasn't in the side and arrived as a 2nd team player to do a bit of bowling at the 1st team in the nets before the game," admitted Chris. "It was a quarter-final of the Benson & Hedges Cup, a full house at Canterbury, and Asif Iqbal was captain.

"Asif came up to me 40 minutes before the start and asked if I'd got my kit in the car. He told me I was playing and they were going to make a change because the last time we'd played against Sussex, Mike Buss's slow left-arm swing bowling on a slow Canterbury pitch had caused real problems.

"So I was sent in like a pinch-hitter, to hit this guy leg-side and get us off to a good start. He was perfect for me because he used to drift it in to middle and leg and I just kept plonking him over midwicket and square leg. I got to about 40 and asked Bob Woolmer, 'Do I get out now?' We ended up chasing 264, which in those days was a pretty big chase and I got 114.

"I had a fair run opening, did a bit more bowling, dropped down to No 5 and was seen more as a finisher than a compiler of an innings."

I'd read an interview where Chris had admitted: "My father was the England captain, and because of that I thought I would rather not play cricket. When I was offered a contract by Kent I was still at school. It was then I stopped and thought, 'Well, I might as well play for a while'. I went through a spell of wanting to play golf when I was in my early teens. That all ended when a couple of pros had a look at me. They said I had no chance!

"I was playing off quite a big handicap aged 17," Chris told me. "It wasn't like I was off scratch or anything. It was getting towards a decision time on cricket, I had a contract offered to me, and I just didn't know if I wanted to go into that world.

"I wanted to be a flair player, so if I'd have been a golf pro I would have been exciting and aggressive and probably never won anything. If I'd played tennis I would have been a Monfils or a Nastase. That was the streak I had in me that probably made me a decent one-day player."

Graham told me that he'd often be asked whether his Dad had pushed him into playing cricket.

Graham told me, "It was quite the reverse really. We were very lucky that our sports cupboard was better than most people's with Slazenger bats, pads and everything. I'm sure Dad must have thought *where the hell has all my gear disappeared to*? Chris, Jeremy our other brother, and I used to raid it. We used to play Test match after Test match in the garden and loved it.

"I sometimes question now whether I ever thought of life without cricket," Graham pondered. "Did I ever think of doing anything different? The answer was 'no'. It was almost a destiny and, because of Chris probably, I was always better than my mates at school. I had balls thrown at me from the age of three, so you learned to catch and play.

"Dad was very proud of what we achieved. If he watched a game and I played another, typically awful slog and got out, he'd never mention a thing and always be hugely encouraging."

Graham had mentioned the middle sibling Jeremy. I'd known of his existence throughout their careers and often wondered whether he was a crying, bitter man in a dark room frustrated that he had been unable to step into the cricket light. Graham soon put me right.

"Unfortunately, it's the absolute opposite," he chuckled. "We are very jealous of him because he became a stockbroker and he made all the money. He's been a massive supporter of Chris and I during our careers and there was never any resentment.

"Jeremy was a leg-spinner at school, but he had a lot of back issues as a teenager, which caused him to miss a lot of sport growing up," explained Graham. "He couldn't play golf because of his back and never had the right constitution. He wasn't the same build as Dad, Chris and I. He was like a pencil. He loves playing, but never played enough."

Although, like most cricketer fathers I'd speak to, Colin had stepped back from his sons' cricket, Graham continued to tell me that his father was always there, if needed, with sound advice.

"In 1986, Michael Holding broke my jaw, and I think five of my teeth are still on the wicket at Derby," Graham winced. "I went to him then to get his help with facing the short-pitched ball.

"When asked, he would speak for hours. He'd talk about different ideas with the grip and about when he was facing Lillee and Thomson in 1974/75 and little things he'd tried to get through that initial five-over barrage. His idea was that surviving that period would see them slowing down a bit and you're through the worst.

"With spin I remember having loads of problems facing Mushtaq Ahmed, who was playing at Somerset at the time. I can assure you I was playing him worse than anyone else," he replied when I suggested most batsmen found 'Mushy' tough going. "I couldn't pick him and was a walking candidate for being caught bat pad. When I talked to Dad about it he'd talk me through the things he'd tried.

"Of course I was always going to listen to Dad," Graham underlined. "He was a real technician. He probably over-analysed his game but he did have amazing thoughts. I think I spoke to Dad more as Chris didn't really analyse his game as much.

"Dad was very conscious that he didn't want to step on the toes of coaches. Coaches would have found it difficult if I'd said 'look hold on I've spoken to my Dad'. Coaches would have found it a lot harder to say 'well stuff *your* Dad'.

"Dad was also very aware that we were, particularly myself, entering into a different game than the one he played. He would say silly things like 'I wish I could play some of the shots you play' and I used to say 'no, no, I'm sure you don't, I wish I could play some of the shots you played'.

Chris agreed: "I spoke to Dad about a lot of things but not on cricket. I loved one-day cricket and I think he found it quite hard to judge what he should say to me to make me a better player. He would never have played some of the shots I played, going well at 40 not out and getting caught at cover off a medium pace bowler was totally alien to him. He didn't really see the point of hitting the ball in the air.

"He just encouraged me to play," Chris added. "If I were to say to him 'I'm really struggling and keep edging the ball to third slip,' he would be brilliant technically, but I don't think he ever set out to teach me how to play or give me much more than little tips here and there.

"David Gower couldn't teach me that shot he played through cover - he probably didn't even know how he did it himself. The old man was the same. You bowled him a length ball outside off-stump and he'd wait, hit it through extra-cover for four and there'd be an awed silence, it would be the most extra-ordinary shot, but you can't teach it."

Graham held a bat when he was two and could remember playing regularly with his brothers from the age of five.

"The genes allowed us a head start," Graham said. "Without question both Chris and I had a good eye for the ball. One of the things that always makes me smile is when you hear coaches shouting down a net at a young lad, 'play the ball later'. And I always think crikey, how does a nine-year-old play a ball later? I've always believed that batting is in many ways God-given. Players like the old man, like Gower, the great players, had the ability to wait that bit longer. It was natural. It's amazingly difficult to try and play the ball later and I do believe you either have that inside you or you don't. That kid is going to leave it so late that he gets bowled and asks 'is that late enough coach?'

"That skill definitely wasn't passed down to me in the genes," Graham laughed. "Put it this way, by the time it got to me it had become very diluted. Having two older brothers benefited me without question. We were always playing. If it wasn't cricket, we were playing other sports."

Chris agreed that some aspects of cricket talent were passed down in the genes, but believed that early experiences of the game were even more crucial.

"If you are exposed at a young age you have the interest there and you are ahead of everybody else," he insisted. "By the time I was six or seven, I'd been playing cricket for two or three years, hitting a ball every day, had nets and everything. Then you'd go to a school where people were just starting – you are always ahead of them. But you have to have some inbuilt talent and have some hand-eye co-ordination, which I think is what our family had and what we inherited."

What must it have been like to have had Colin Cowdrey as your father?

Chris answered: "You don't know anything else. It's what you are. I remember aged around seven at school, I had this celebrity status for nothing I'd done except getting black marks, getting detention and kicking a ball through a window a few times," he sniggered. "The pressure you are under is unusual and one you shouldn't be under. You think I haven't done anything, I just happen to have a father who has just scored 150 in a Test match."

Graham added: "I found the comparisons very difficult when people came up to me with stories about Dad. When I was in my early 20s I didn't want to hear all of that stuff and it was only when I got to the end of my career that I loved guys coming up to me and talking about him."

At one stage Graham seriously considered moving away from Kent to start afresh at another county, a team not synonymous with his surname.

"In around 1989, there was a guy playing for Middlesex called Keith Brown. In early November Don Bennett, their 2ⁿᵈ team coach, called me and said he thought Keith was going to sign for Glamorgan in the next couple of hours. He said that as soon as that happened he would call me back and sign me for Middlesex.

"I was desperate for that to happen because I just wanted to get away from Kent and the whole Cowdrey thing, but would you believe it? The deal fell through. Keith Brown stayed at Middlesex and I stayed at Kent. It was fine, but I do sometimes think that if I'd played for Middlesex things might have been a bit different."

The question of finding one's own identity in a sport where a father has been such an imposing figure is a constant theme of this book. For Chris Cowdrey he consciously morphed into a player that could cope and never seemed to look back. For his younger brother the weight of that famous surname was a far more significant factor in his personal development.

"Early on I couldn't get my head around it," Graham admitted. "I am not my Dad and I will never be a player of his class and I almost wanted to shout out at these guys and say 'please don't compare me'.

"I think it took me far too long to be able to say 'it doesn't matter what people think' and stop worrying about people making comparisons. I should have been able to understand that this is just the nature of having someone like Dad was.

"The simple fact was that our life was dominated from such a ridiculously young age by cricket. We had Don Bradman to stay. We had Garry Sobers to stay. That was when I was very young and probably thought we just had some Aussie staying, but it was the great Don and looking back you think 'oh my God!'

And so to that impossible question, what would life have been like if you'd been called Fred Bloggs and still had a talent for cricket?

Graham admitted to thinking about it long before I prompted him for a response: "I've often reflected that if I'd been Graham Bloggs how good a player could I have been? If I'd had the talent that I'd been given but without any of the issues or concerns wondering what people think. That's one of the reasons that I would have liked that opportunity at Middlesex. Mike Gatting was captain, and I have a feeling the weight would have been lifted off my shoulders.

"I played one England Under-19 game at Trent Bridge against Australia. It was a bloody good team - there was Neil Fairbrother, Hugh Morris, John Morris, Paul Jarvis and Steve Rhodes. I remember getting out for hardly any and a bloke said to me as I walked back through the gate 'You're only playing because of your father'. If I'd had the character to think 'what a plonker' I'm sure I'd have been a better player. I was thinking too much and thinking 'is that what everyone thinks?'

"There was without question that undertone always that the only reason you've got as far as you have is because of your Dad. I had to process the fact that I'd done well enough at 2nd team level and scored hundreds there and paid my dues to get to where I'd got, but in a funny sort of way people don't really ever believe you. You almost have to work harder."

Chris added: "Another side is we didn't have to do very much to hit the headlines. The Cowdrey name was more of a story than someone with a simple name who was a very good player. The classic example of that was that game where I got a hundred against Sussex. Yeah, I probably stood a good chance of getting the man-of-the-match, but Alan Ealham scored 94 in no time at all and smashed them all over and took a great catch, but there was never any chance that I wouldn't get that award. I saw some of the stories and there was hardly a mention of Alan. 'Ealham chipped in with 94' one of them wrote.

"Other times when you only make 35 as a young player, and you've got these really good players around you, the media want to talk to you and not the others. It feels weird," Chris emphasised. "And if you played a cover drive for four, that shot will be written about because it was Dad's shot. If you plundered everything through the leg-side they'd write 'it was a totally untypical Cowdrey-like innings'. I saw once 'his father would have turned in his grave if he'd seen that shot'. It's a bit boring after a while and I know Graham suffered because of it.

"Your point – is there a difference pressure-wise in going in with a name rather than not going in with a name? There definitely is," Chris added. "I've said to you, I changed the way I played and changed the way I approached my cricket. If you like I became more of an entertainer than a guy who was driven to play for England. Playing for England was never something I thought I particularly wanted to do. I wanted to captain Kent and wanted to win the Championship with my county – that was my only real ambition in the game apart from to have a great time and enjoy it. If you ask most people at the age of 17, what is your ambition, most will say they want to play for England."

Graham had already said he found it hard to listen to supporters constantly mentioning his father in glowing terms. I asked Chris whether he welcomed that kind of attention or whether his response too was leave me alone.

"It's 50:50 because there wouldn't have been a day, and there aren't many days still now, where I don't bump into somebody who says 'I saw your father,' 'your father's a great friend of mine' and all that kind of stuff.

"I don't know how many grounds I must have played cricket on in the world, but there wouldn't have been a day where seven, nine, eleven people would come up to me and talk about the old man and when he last played on that ground, how many he got and how they saw him bat.

"The home grounds are a bit different," Chris continued. "You know the crowd to some extent and they couldn't come up to me every day and tell me the same story, although one or two did. I generally went the way of thinking that these people are really nice, they are well-wishers and they are not people trying to piss me off. It can get tiresome but all I did for many years was say 'thank you very much'."

Graham told ESPN Cricinfo in 1998: "Any time I visit Australia or India, where the old man was born, there are always reminders. In fact, I've lost count of the number of times in Bangalore or New Delhi someone has come up to me and said: 'Please say hello to your father. I was at school with him, you know'. And I say: 'No you bloody weren't, you're only about 26'. Everyone claims to know him."

Chris then explained how as a football fan he has often tried to see the other side: "I used to love watching Peter Osgood and Alan Hudson in that Chelsea era. If I bumped into Osgood's son somewhere the natural thing to say would be 'I saw him play in the Cup Final in 1970' or 'I saw him score in the Cup Winners Cup Final' and all that sort of business. So I probably would have said the same. You've got to put up with it.

"Where I slightly changed on it was when I said I happened to be seeing my father later in the day," continued Chris. "I got a guy once who came up to me and said he was a great friend of Dad and had known him for 40 years and they'd been shooting together. I mentioned his name to the old man later and he'd never heard of him in his life. So for five percent of these people it's an ego trip."

I asked Graham if he'd do anything differently if he could have his time as a cricketer again: "The mistake I made was that my initial way into the team was playing Sunday League and coming in at No 7. I would go in with five overs left and my technique changed over those early years to manufacture shots for those last few overs.

"We played at Northampton against Curtly Ambrose and Nick Cook, who is a good mate of mine," Graham said. "I got through against Curtly somehow and then thought I've had enough of this, I'm not in particularly good nick, I'm just going to play shots. It was a three-day game and everything came off. I remember Nick at the end of play saying to me, 'You're crazy, you should play like that all the time. That is the way you play'.

"A lot of the time I was agonising about making sure I didn't get out. I played with inhibitions and that comes back to your initial premise of being able to think 'forget about the Cowdreys'. What Dad did was amazing, but *that was him and this is me*!

"Where I probably struggled most was I was tee-total which was almost unheard of in those days. Even in the early 1980s the dressing room attendant took a drinks order and it would be seven pints of lager, three pints of bitter, a glass of white wine and I'd be the diet coke of the end. It took quite a while for people to get that. It certainly wasn't a fitness thing, just down to the fact that alcohol didn't particularly agree with me and I wasn't interested in going out for a long night clubbing.

"Ironically I shared a room with a great friend of mine, Steve Marsh, who was the Kent wicket-keeper, for 12 years on away trips. The reason it worked so well was that we hardly saw each other. Steve would get ready to go out at about 8.30pm every night we were away and I'd be settling down, watch *Inspector Morse* and go to bed. In the morning I'd go and have breakfast at 7.30 and Steve would be the sort of bloke that would get out of bed at 8.50, straight to the car and the ground.

"That took quite a few years for a lot of the Kent guys to understand. Wherever we went I used to try and find a music concert or something instead. I went to a lot of gigs over 15 years.

"I sound as though I cry every night about it and I certainly don't, but this subject is very interesting to me as I did think a lot about it throughout my career," Graham admitted. "I was always searching to get it absolutely right. I'm sure if I'd got a good sports psychologist he would have put me right very quickly. It sounds really weak that it should affect you, but unfortunately it did."

Graham also admitted that he wished he'd paid more attention to his father's career when he was young.

"If I have a regret, there were all of those times when I was six, seven, eight, nine, when summer holidays were either at Maidstone Festival or Canterbury week," Chris remembered fondly. "From the minute Dad got to the ground I used to play cricket all day behind those marquees and I'd climb into the car at the end of the day and ask Dad whether he'd got any runs. As a kid you have no idea what's going on."

I'd already shared with Graham my own nostalgic experiences of Canterbury Cricket Week. I told him about being asked by his mother to fetch Chris's short-sleeved sweater.

"There was no lady in the history of cricket who has washed more pairs of whites. God bless her, she loved cricket and God knows how many times she had to wash the old man's whites and as soon as Chris started she wanted to be in her deckchair at 10.55am to watch every ball. She got very nervous about it all, even to the day I finished."

Chris, seven years older than Graham, had watched his father play a lot.

"You could see that he was different and a class above everyone else," Chris enthused. "He had something, a touch player, like Gower got born with, Graveney too I suppose, but the game is different. If you had a little 2lb Slazenger and you've got to hit it over a grassy outfield, whoever had that timing was pretty special. Nowadays they just plonk it into the stand."

I asked Chris whether his Dad had watched him play. "They say a lot more than I knew. Apparently he used to hide behind trees and stay out the way to watch me. He used to ring me a lot and say 'well done' or maybe not well done. He never used to say he was going to come to watch me, more 'I was there,' or 'I had to pop in for lunch and saw you for half-an-hour'. Then someone else would tell me he'd been there all innings. I might have tried to play straighter and nicked it to slip if I'd known he was there (laughs)."

Graham had obviously struggled with having Cowdrey as his surname and his plight was not made easier with Chris as his captain.

"I found it very difficult either being left out or being picked in the team," Graham recalled. "There were always players who, when I was being picked in front of them, there was a lot of animosity because Chris was captain.

"I had some great times and always enjoyed playing under Chris because I liked the way he played, but it's not that easy when your brother is captain. If you are a very fine player, which I wasn't, it doesn't matter, but when you're always on the edge of playing or not playing, it was difficult."

Chris agreed that him being captain made things tough for his brother: "I think it stopped him being a hugely good player. If Graham was an 18-year-old now, the way he used to play, he'd be an unbelievable Twenty20 player. He was playing at a time where one-day cricket was getting stronger but it still wasn't quite as expansive as it is now."

Chris is a regular on the after dinner circuit. He has started his speech with: "Between my father, Colin, and myself, we captained England on 28 occasions, of which he captained...I can't quite remember...27 I think."

"I've been speaking at various things for years and I have a go at myself and it's given me another career. I've got something there that other people can't talk about.

"I don't feel bad about anything at all about the father and son thing. I feel bad for Graham because I think it did affect him and I feel that my game changed because of it, but who knows, it might have been for the better. I'm sure Graham would say the same, we didn't become the sort of players that people thought we might, but we had a good time."

Graham said: "I've told you a lot about how I think Chris felt and it will be interesting to see what he says to you," and then with a snigger added, "You can also ask him why he left me out so many times.

"In the end I used to say to him 'after you've done the toss and come back in I don't want a crappy two-minute talk telling me you are sorry, you've had to leave me out and I very nearly played and I should go back into the 2nd team and work hard. Just tell me I'm not playing, that is fine by me. You don't have to tell me I nearly played. I know I nearly played because I was in the 12'."

I asked Chris the question Graham had given me and with almost exactly the same snigger as his brother he told me: "I remember him saying that quite a lot. I think it was hard captaining a brother, but at the end of the day I wanted to make sure I got his career right.

"Graham was someone who in a one-day match would have been the first name on the teamsheet after Underwood, but when it came to the Championship I don't think he had a game we'd seen before. As somebody who played the shots he played, he was ahead of his time, and it wasn't until John Inverarity came as our coach in 1988 that he said that Graham had to go up the order. He said he was the best striker of a ball we had at the club.

"I didn't enjoy picking him or not picking him on a close call and he's right, he was always on a close call. The only way I could do it was just get on with it. The other players knew I picked him, or not, on merit."

Chris left Kent after 16 memorable seasons before playing one final summer with Glamorgan in 1992. Graham retired in 1998.

The Cowdreys are arguably the most famous cricket family in the world and the fourth generation is now gracing the field at Canterbury. I say fourth because Colin's father Ernest did play one first-class match in Madras for the Europeans against the Indians in January 1927 and now Chris's son Fabian, born in 1993, is pursuing Kent cricket as a career. There are high hopes for his future.

"There is quite a bit of water under the bridge between his career and the rest of us," suggested father Chris. "He's also a very different personality to Graham and me. He's always been a real fighter and someone who would never give his wicket away. He also claims to love any accolades he gets for being related to a grandfather who could play a bit. He loves it. He's not bothered.

"He was getting sledged when he was seven when playing against teams higher than his age group and he grew up with it and I think in the end he took it as a compliment. I actually think he does really like it. He always claims he's proud to be playing and proud to be a Cowdrey, which is quite an interesting approach. He welcomes the attention.

"If he's getting attention it means he's playing well and he's odd like that. I think it's great that he has that approach, but I think it does help that he's had quite a breather since Graham and I played. We're talking 15-plus years ago, whereas I played 15 weeks after the old man had retired."

Fabian told me: "It's been great to have had people in my life who I can confide with when I go through tough periods. My family have never pushed me, or put any pressure on me, to play cricket. It's been tough at times earlier in my career but I have no choice but to accept it, so I have done."

Fabian grew up with his twin brother Julius, who is now a musician. It was a fiercely competitive environment.

"It was a case of always trying to do better than the other brother," Fabian explained. "I used to wind Julius up, telling him I was a better singer, and he used to tell me he was the better cricketer. We're still competitive, but I think it's eased off as the years have gone by."

Fabian, the more intense and driven of the two brothers, always wanted to be a professional cricketer: "My mum told me at the age of three that I whispered the words 'I want to play for England' to her...I do remember it was all I ever really wanted to do."

Grandfather Colin died in December 2000. A year earlier Fabian had been playing in an Under-9s game at the age of six. "I was far too young, had no technique and was completely out of my depth," he remembered. "But I somehow managed to hit the winning runs. My grandfather was watching on, encouraging me. It's still one of my fondest cricketing memories. It was the only game he got to see me play in. It's quite surreal to think of it."

Fabian followed Colin as captain of Tonbridge School's 1st XI and in his final year scored over 1,200 runs, beating his legendary grandfather's record. After signing for Kent he admitted struggling with the step up into the professional game.

"I think the addition of the family name brought a lot of pressure with it, and it's easy to forget the adjustment you have to make from school to facing bowling in the mid-80s. It's one thing being able to play a cover drive off a 70mph half volley, but can you play a pull shot off a bouncer at 85mph? That's a different ball game entirely."

He made strides forward with his game at the University of Cardiff. After making 62 for Cardiff MCCU against Glamorgan on first-class debut in April 2013 he left university a couple of months later to focus solely on cricket with Kent. It's not all been plain sailing with first team opportunities at a premium, but many pundits that have watched him more than I feel he has what it takes to forge a long and successful career.

"Seeing my Grandfather's name on the stand, and practically every honours board put a lot of pressure on at first. Now I'm accustomed to it. At the moment I can't see myself anywhere but Kent, and it's a lovely place to be with all the history."

Fabian still has a pressure of expectation. A house at Tonbridge School bore Colin's name, they offered a Cowdrey scholarship, a stand at the St Lawrence Ground is named after his grandfather and a well-known figure from cricket gives an annual Cowdrey Lecture at Lord's.

And then just prior to the 2017 season, long after I thought the draft of this chapter had been put to bed, it all changed. Fabian announced his retirement at the age of 24, telling BBC Radio Kent that it was a "very difficult decision" to have made.

"It's been a decision that's been in the making for about a year-and-a-half," Fabian continued. "Things haven't been right for my personal happiness for a long time. To put a finger on exactly why is quite difficult, but the enjoyment and the passion for the game hasn't been there. And with that in mind, and those emotions present, entering into a new season wouldn't be fair, not only on the lads that I wish so very well, but also on myself."

Fabian, when questioned on the pressure to continue because he was a Cowdrey, said: "Absolutely, I've always tried to push it under the carpet so to speak, but it was not one of the reasons or a contributing factor to my decision at all. If anything I felt that I'd really come a long way in dealing with that pressure. Dad always wanted my best interests and never pushed me. I think it came as a shock because they'd seen me take so much enjoyment out of it and it has been all I've ever wanted to do since I was five-years-old. They've completely backed my decision and I think they understand why I've made it."

Fabian planned to go into sports media and also to join his brother Julius, also a star of the reality TV show *Made In Chelsea*, as a songwriter in the music industry.

I learned a number of things from speaking to Chris, Graham and Fabian.

Firstly, the pressure of expectation is a burden on every follower in someone's footsteps, but the degree they recognise it and allow it to affect them is very much down to the personality of the individual. I believe that it affected Chris more than he lets on, certainly in his younger days. But once established in the Kent side he let the different brand of cricketer he'd made himself into do the talking.

For Graham, a more sensitive and introspective soul, the pressure was there throughout and undoubtedly diminished his achievements. When he was a youngster he was tipped to be the best of the lot. That he didn't scale the heights some anticipated for him could only be because he played with doubt, inhibition and self-consciousness brought about by the Cowdrey comparisons.

For Fabian the journey is still in its relative infancy and perhaps Chris is right, the length of time that has elapsed between his Grandfather's exit and his arrival does dilute the expectation. But it certainly still exists.

It had also become evident, as Chris had stated, that the bigger the achievements of the forefather the harder the task for the youngsters that follow.

"With respect to Micky Stewart, who was a very good player, Alec Stewart went and played 133 Test matches and is probably one of England's greatest ever all-rounders," Chris voiced. "He wasn't under pressure following Micky. There was a bit of a gap between the two as well and I think the audience watching Alec didn't over-know Micky, so that wasn't so hard.

"I think someone like Liam Botham, trying to follow Ian Botham, well that really was tough," he went on. "You are coming into a game where your old man had been a legend for 15 years and will go down, almost certainly, as the greatest all-rounder of all-time. To be better than him in terms of charisma, batting, bowling and catching, you probably can't do it. He'd have to have been the best player ever pretty much.

"That shouldn't matter though, because you should be able to go into a career saying that you are going into it because you like it and want to play and I'm good enough to play. I wrote a book with a friend of mine called Jonathan Smith called *Good Enough?* Not enough people jumped onto the question mark and just thought I was saying that I was good enough. What I was saying was that I didn't mind if I wasn't as good as my father as long as

I was good enough.

"Unfortunately you are always going to be compared. Most people are interested in the comparison. It's fun. 'I saw his father play and now I'm seeing him play'.

"I played a lot with Butch [Alan Butcher], a lovely man, but his name is not ingrained with the greats," Chris added. "For Mark Butcher to come in, I don't think he should have been under too much pressure following big Butch, and I mean that nicely."

Graham finished with: "You better talk to that bugger Alec, because he was without question the best timer of a cricket ball I ever played against and I played against him a lot. He was a magnificent player."

And so I sent an email to Alec Stewart at Surrey County Cricket Club.

That first match I attended back in 1977 became pivotal to the start of my quest for answers. In addition to Chris Cowdrey, there were three other people on that scorecard that I wanted to talk to. David Bairstow had worn the gloves for Yorkshire that day and his son Jonny was now centre stage for Yorkshire and England. Alan Ealham had captained Kent and his son Mark had since come through to represent club and country.

Initially however, I opted to begin my quest with Yorkshire's Arnie and Ryan Sidebottom.

CHAPTER TWO

ARNIE and RYAN SIDEBOTTOM

*"Pressure can burst a pipe or
pressure can make a diamond"*
Robert Horry

Arnie Sidebottom would have known as he raced in to bowl that August day in 1977 that his wife was pregnant with son, Ryan, who would be born the following January. Arnie, a stalwart of the White Rose County's seam attack between 1973 and 1991, was the last of a rare breed. He excelled professionally at both cricket and football, playing in the winter months for Manchester United and then Huddersfield. As the rigours of each game grew and the spans of the respective seasons conflicted he opted to concentrate on cricket.

"I had nine years where I played both and never had a day off," he would tell me. "I had six-and-a-half years at Man United and then went to Huddersfield for a couple of seasons. When I'd finished with the football I'd play for Yorkshire for three months as there used to be 14 weeks in between the seasons, but that gradually got less until it got to a stage where Huddersfield said I had to make my mind up.

"Cricket was always my first love. Boycott, who's a friend, was the captain at Yorkshire and he said they'd give me a five-year contract if I packed in the football and concentrated on the cricket. It was a no brainer really."

I needed my interviewees to be honest. If it had been genuinely great to be born into a sporting family then fine, but if there had been any issues I needed them to surface. I was also acutely conscious that my external view of the families was potentially very different from their real experiences. For lads born with a famous father it was all they had ever known. Were these people going to be able to step outside of their own skin and see a bigger picture?

So, when I phoned Arnie, and then Ryan, I wanted to know how Dad's high profile Yorkshire career had impacted on his son's rise as a cricketer, and also their own relationship. I was hoping I'd not get a succession of 'it was fantastic' responses. I need not have worried. Arnie's a straight-talking Yorkshireman, and as we'll find out, Ryan is very much like his father.

"It was really difficult," Arnie began. "I always kept out of the way when he first started as a young lad. We had other parents at Yorkshire saying he only gets selected because of his Dad. If he bowled well they said 'well he should do he's Arnie Sidebottom's lad' and if he bowled badly they said 'oh, he's not like his Dad,' so he couldn't win. It was really tough for him.

"I've probably only seen him bowl live five or six times in his career," he continued. "I've just kept out of the way and his Mum and Granddad did everything for him and carted him here, there and everywhere. I just kept in the background."

Arnie then recalled a Yorkshire schools trial match where a 14-year-old Ryan had taken a couple of wickets and was hopeful he had impressed. The coach had other ideas.

"The coach said to him 'find something else to do, you'll never be a cricketer'. It was unbelievable. He came home in floods of tears and said 'I don't want to play cricket again, I'm done'.

"I said 'that's fair enough, no problems at all, but what are you going to do because you're not bright at school and you've got to find some work. Have a think about it Ryan, come back to me in a couple of days and we'll chat then'."

Ryan remembers it well: "I was playing for Yorkshire Schools B-team. I played the game, did pretty well and all you want to do at that age is go out, do well and make your family proud. The coach sat all the lads down. I think we'd lost and he said to us we hadn't played well, certain things should have been done differently, we weren't concentrating and then he singled me out in front of all the other boys.

"He said, 'You might as well give up playing cricket because you're never going to make it'. It really hit home.

"I remember going home in the car with my Mum who'd driven me miles to get to that game. I was sat in the front and I didn't say a word all the way back. One of the other lads was in the car, so I held it in and waited until I got home and then burst into tears. I knew what it was about, but you are still young, naïve and immature and it really hurt me.

"On the other hand I was very fortunate with Dad being who he was, a straight-talking Yorkshireman from Barnsley. My Mum was really angry, Dad was too and he simply said, 'you can either sulk and go work in Thomas Cook for the rest of your life, or work down the pit as my Dad did, or you can prove them wrong and work harder and shove it up 'em'."

Ryan made a decision that would ultimately see him take 79 Test, 29 ODI and 23 T20I wickets for his country.

"He came back and said, 'Dad I want to play cricket for a living' and I said 'right, that's great, what are you going to do about it?'

"He said, 'I've got to get fit' and I said 'you are going to have to sacrifice things' and he said he would.

"I maybe doubted him a bit thinking he was just a young lad, but he did it. He got up every morning at six o'clock and ran with the dogs in the fields at Holmfirth. He built a little gym in the garage and did everything himself."

At that stage the England caps and County Championship titles were a world away. But Ryan had turned a corner.

"I've never ever said it to this day who the coach that said that to me was, but if you want to know it was Tony Bowes. It was very disappointing. All I wanted to do was do right by my family and give it my best and to hear those words at that early age is pretty poor, but it made me the man I am.

"In some senses they were very harsh words Dad spoke, but good and choice words at the time. And it just made me think 'I'm going to prove people wrong'.

"I suppose that's the way it's always been throughout my career. I've always had criticism because I'm a bit different. I've had long hair like my Dad did when he played football and there's always been those comparisons with Dad."

I remember covering a Yorkshire pre-season tour to Barbados. As I sat outside my ground-floor hotel room Ryan wandered across and asked me if I was watching the Manchester United match. Rather boringly I was editing a video interview I'd done with him the previous day. I asked him if his love of the Red Devils was purely down to his Dad having played for them. His Dad kept the cuttings and team photos – he'd played alongside some of the all-time greats.

"Yes, pretty much," Ryan answered. "He's quite shy and doesn't really say a lot about it and what he's done. That inspired me, not to play football because I was an absolute donkey – my right leg was for standing on. But looking at who he played with and the games he played in inspired me."

Arnie played football and cricket in an era far removed from the riches on offer to the top players these days. He could be forgiven for feeling jealousy towards the current crop raking in the big bucks.

"No, not really, good luck to them. I played professional football at Manchester United and was on £22 a week as a professional. You can't believe they earn £200,000-plus a week these days. It's a different world. I've no envy about it, but it seems criminal when there are people starving in the world. I was really fortunate to play with George Best, Bobby Charlton and Denis Law. You'd have to sell most of Manchester to buy them today.

"When we played cricket we used to play hard during the day

and then go out drinking. We never thought twice about having a few pints and staying up until after midnight. Today it's totally different. There's no drinking hardly and players are in bed early and that's the way the game has gone. And the money is totally different. We played virtually for the love of the game. It's good money these days if you get to the top."

Ryan appreciates that he has played in a more lucrative time for cricketers: "I've been very lucky. Because of the money that Dad earned in the game, I think he always instilled within me that I had to look after my money and be sensible. You've got to live your life and enjoy it, go to parties, buy nice clothes, but also look after your money. I've done that in the right way I think. I've got a few rental properties and things like that so when I do retire I will have a little bit to fall back on. I won't be worrying about what I do next. So that was good advice from my parents."

At another trial for Yorkshire Schools Under-15s Ryan received a further glimpse that things were not the same for him as the other young players.

"I was walking around the boundary, with my Mum, eating a sandwich and getting ready to play. I think we were batting first. I remember some parents of three or four of the other lads that were trialling saying 'Oh, that's Ryan Sidebottom. He's only here because of his Dad'. Even at that age I found it bizarre and hard to take. Up until that point it had been just like any other game. I loved playing cricket and playing sport.

"I have all of those people that tried to make me look a fool to thank. The ones that tried to embarrass me. It made me the person I am today. It made me go out there and say 'I'm going to prove you wrong' and 19 years later here I am with all those international caps and a T20 World Cup winner.

"I've always been humble. I don't think I've ever been a bighead. I've always tried to treat people with respect and I'd expect them to treat me the same. I just love playing cricket and it's all I ever wanted to do. From a younger age, that has been the making of me."

Arnie remembers that early period in his son's career well: "He went through some times where people were really horrid to him. And that was because of me, because I was a player at Yorkshire. People would snigger and say that he's only playing because of his Dad and it was far from the truth."

Was being good at bowling something you could pass on in your DNA, was it a fluke, or was Ryan's exposure to his father's career always going to predispose him to follow suit? I was sure the nature versus nurture question would be one I'd ask time and again.

"When my wife came to the cricket at Headingley, Ryan used to play in the nets with the other kids when he was young," Arnie remembered. "So I suppose that is the way and he wanted to follow his Dad a bit."

Ryan remembered, "I grew up with Dad's playing career and saw how popular he was at Yorkshire," added Ryan. "To me it was just a game of cricket. My Dad played cricket, I used to go down and watch him and get all the autographs of the other famous players, like Greenidge and Marshall, and I've still got my autograph book now. I loved playing. I wanted to grow up and be like Dad. Or be like Botham.

"As I got older it became a little bit more competitive and you're playing for Yorkshire Schools and that's where the nepotism came in. I felt it first-hand and had to deal with it."

Arnie could empathise with Ryan's belief that he had to impress more than other youngsters in order to stand still in the pecking order.

"There's no doubt that was true," insisted Arnie. "That Yorkshire coach only said that to him because of jealousy. I don't know the reason, but he's still in a job now and Ryan walks past him every day and I think he just laughs really.

"I was a 2nd XI coach, but again I kept out of the way. He was with the 1st team and so he rarely came to me, thankfully. Other people always looked after him at the club."

Ryan recalls how his father, although always supportive, steered clear of his son's cricket development.

"Yes, he's right, he took a backward step. It was generally my Mum and my Granddad who travelled everywhere with me, watched me play and looked after me.

"Dad wanted me to toughen up," Ryan said. "I was lucky in that he'd been there and done it. He knew what I'd have to do to make it and when we spoke his words meant a great deal. They were quite harsh words sometimes and maybe I didn't always like them, but I think they made me hardened to the pitfalls of the 'you're only here because of your Dad' comments and the general criticisms. I took what he said on board and used to turn myself into a better player.

"I sacrificed my younger days," said Ryan. "I didn't know what girls were until I was 19 or 20. The lads were going out to youth clubs and going to people's parties and I sacrificed my teenage years to try and make it as a cricketer.

"George Batty was the Yorkshire Under-17s coach and he wanted me to play and was really right behind me. He saw a little bit of talent in me and I never looked back. I got invited to train with the Yorkshire 1st team at Headingley in the indoor nets in the winters and that was it."

The question of whether it would have been easier for Ryan to have grown up as Fred Bloggs is hypothetical speculation. I asked it anyway.

"It's a good and interesting question and I really couldn't say because you only know one way," he said to confirm my worries. "I know it may have been easier in my younger days, but it might not have made me the man I am today and I may not have had the same career. Again, because of the criticisms and growing up with that famous name in Yorkshire cricketing terms decided my future in the sport.

"Having another name, which wasn't associated with the club, I may not have been here now. I may have done something else. You just never know do you? I think with what happened to me in my younger days I may have just given up the game for good if it hadn't been for my Dad and the history of what he achieved."

Ryan's move to Nottinghamshire in 2004 was a career choice and nothing to do with the pressures of his surname.

"It was a real wrench leaving Yorkshire, but a big decision I had to make in my career if I wanted to play for England again. I owe a lot to Stephen Fleming's guidance there and to Mick Newell and Mark Ealham, who became a sort of second father to me at Trent Bridge. We talked about our Dads lots of times."

If Ryan's close friendship with Mark Ealham had been forged because of their fathers' cricket exploits it was subconscious and hadn't been the foundation of their friendship. "We still keep in touch now. We go down to visit them and they come up to us. I looked to him, at how he behaved as a pro, how he handled himself, what he did during training, because he was the age I am now. He still loved it and had huge enthusiasm for the game.

"We had chats about how to bowl on different surfaces, how to conduct yourself and I got a lot of wise words from him," Ryan continued. "We became very close and he's got a very dry sense of humour and he's a great man. He helped me realise what to do in different situations and learn more about the game."

Arnie revelled in his son's success at Nottinghamshire and admits he was reluctant to see him return to Headingley in 2011. "He had a fantastic seven years at Nottingham and it was amazing what he did for them. He made his own decisions and to be brutally honest I didn't want him to come back to Yorkshire who had never really treated the top players properly. I'm talking the legends of Yorkshire cricket like Boycott, Illingworth, Close, etc. They've never really been able to treat them with the respect they deserved.

"I was wary of him coming back, but he'd made his decision to leave Yorkshire when I didn't want him to leave. I told him to stay and tough it out and he said 'no I'm moving'. He went to Nottinghamshire, which was the best thing he ever did as they treated him fantastically.

"The New Zealander Stephen Fleming was the captain and he said 'Ryan you are going to be my opening bowler in every competition' and that gave him the confidence. Mark Ealham was signed from Kent and was fantastic for him. He'd probably seen the same problems as Ryan had and was a lot more experienced player and Ryan doted on him. So he had two great mentors there.

"Then he wanted a lengthier contract at Notts and they said they couldn't afford it so he decided to move," Arnie revealed. "He rang me up and said 'Dad, I'm coming back to Yorkshire'. It was great for us because of the grandkids, but I asked him if he was sure. He said that Yorkshire had a lot of talented young players and he thought he could help them. He said it would be good for him as he'd be back home. He was more mature then and knew his own game and it's been fantastic for him."

I'd interviewed Ryan when he returned to Yorkshire in 2011. I have to admit to being very wrong. I had been concerned his age would work against him and restrict the opportunities for some of the talented youngsters at the club. He couldn't have played better, given more or worked harder to stay on the park.

He told me in that interview his prime motivation, as well as winning trophies with his native county, was to pass his Dad's tally of 596 first-class wickets. He knew exactly how many he needed and how long he thought it would take him. His strong performances meant he bettered his prediction.

"When I moved away from Notts that was a big desire," he recalled. "Sometimes you need those goals to keep you hungry. I think going past Dad was one milestone I was definitely after. So to go past his tally and to come back to Yorkshire and win trophies has been wonderful.

"That goal has always been at the back of my mind. It wasn't to say 'I'm better than you are,' but to go past his tally from the career he had means I've had a half decent career too."

Ryan had told me that if he managed to overtake his father's record he would take him out, have a beer and chat about their cricket careers. Had that happened?

"Yes, but it wasn't like I was saying 'I've gone past your tally Dad'. It was more in homage and paying credit to him and the pride in what I'd done which has been similar to his career."

The glaring upshot of talking to senior and junior Sidebottom is the enormous pride the pair have in each other's achievements.

"I'm immensely proud," Arnie confirmed and you can hear it's genuine. "I don't really say that in front of people, but I'm immensely proud of what he's achieved. His CV is incredible. To win five County Championships, be a World Cup winner, have taken a hat-trick in a Test match, be England Player of the Year and *Wisden* Cricketer of the Year - you can go on and on. It's incredible and he's achieved it all himself.

"I'm the past and he was the future and it was always him that wanted to beat my records. When he passed it, it was brilliant. He's got over 700 first-class wickets now, and he's still going."

I relayed what his father had said. Ryan took a second before responding and, when he did, his voice displayed obvious emotion.

"What can I say? I suppose sometimes words can't really describe," Ryan began. "It means a massive great deal to me that to hear his kind words. And again, what he's achieved in the game and having played football too, a lot of people would give their right arm to play for Manchester United and play cricket for Yorkshire.

"All I wanted growing up was to be like Dad, to play for Yorkshire and England, so I suppose I'll look back with fondness, probably when I finish it will sink in a little bit more and I'll sit back and reflect. It means a lot."

Yorkshire supporters are a forthright and passionate breed. They'd happily castigate anyone not pulling their weight, but equally, they love someone that gives every ounce of effort. Arnie had always been an every ouncer. When Ryan entered the Yorkshire ranks the crowds would have been forgiven for hoping he was a chip off the old block.

"It is catch 22 isn't it," suggested Ryan. "I've had lots of wonderful comments about my Dad. I still get called Arnie now on a regular basis. They say 'are you alright Arnie?' and I laugh and say 'no, it's Ryan' and they laugh and apologise. I think it's quite funny and a compliment. For people to call me Arnie is a really nice thing.

"Every day I get someone come up to me and talk about my Dad. He's very well thought of at Yorkshire and people talk about how he was a grumpy fast bowler and that family history means a great deal. So coming back to Yorkshire and having that desire to go past his wickets was something to head towards, rather than thinking I'm just going to come back for a couple of years and have a knees up, which was never going to be the case.

"I met up with Martyn (Moxon) at a hotel in Brighouse. He spoke about this young generation of talented players – Joe Root, Jonny Bairstow, Gary Ballance, Adil Rashid, Adam Lyth – all coming through together, all hugely talented and improving every year. He said that he firmly believed Yorkshire would win trophies. I've always been a winner and have played to win and contribute."

And win Yorkshire have done since Ryan's return, with the now veteran linking up with the likes of Tim Bresnan, Steve Patterson, Liam Plunkett and Jack Brooks to lead a seam attack that has been instrumental in back-to-back County Championship crowns in 2014 and 2015. Add these two titles to a previous triumph with Yorkshire in 2001, and two with Nottinghamshire, he now has five on his CV. His Dad would have loved to have won just one.

"He chides me a bit saying 'did you win a Championship Dad?'" Arnie laughs, "He wanted to beat my records and he has done."

"I'm delighted with my achievements in the game," Ryan adds with trademark modesty, "But to do 20 years as a pro will probably show that I've put the hard work in away from the game, off the field with my fitness and the way I've looked after myself. And 20 years will be the icing on the cake.

"To be part of a winning team makes you want to contribute. To win the County Championship back-to-back was a special achievement by that group of players and I wanted to be part of it.

"I'll look back with great fondness. You etch your name in history, make your own legacy and it's for other people to decide how good you were."

Arnie may not have ferried him to games as a youngster, been in his ear throughout, but he'd definitely been available to his son when his input had been required even if, as Ryan says, his words had often been brutally honest.

"I never got involved but even now he will ring me up when they are playing somewhere and say 'Dad, it's not coming out quite right today, I don't feel right' and he'll send me a little video and ask me to look at it," said Arnie. "I'm there thinking that he's achieved everything in the game you could possibly want to achieve, but even now he still wants me to look at the video of his bowling."

There's often a natural assumption that father and son are built the same. The Sidebottoms were certainly made from very similar moulds. Both strong as oxen, passionate about winning, red-haired (when Arnie had a bit more) and willing to run through brick walls for their side, Ryan believes that never-say-die attitude is the biggest gift his father has handed down.

"Dad always said go out and give it your best and never give up because you never know what's going to happen," Ryan said. "Things can change in sport very quickly and I think I've always had that attitude. I may not have been the greatest bowler in the world, but I've always had that 'come on, let's show 'em, I want to beat you, I want to be better than you' attitude, even if I'm not.

"My Mum also said that even if people had a go at me, respect them and always treat people how you'd expect to be treated. I've always tried to be polite, approachable and well mannered and come across as a decent down to earth bloke.

"Martyn Moxon says you're just like your Dad. Umpires always say it too. If that wasn't how I am I don't know if I'd be where I am today. I've got that passion to always give my best, I like winning and if I didn't have that I don't know if I would have played as long as I have.

"People called Dad 'Red Dog' because when he got the red mist and didn't get any wickets he'd go bright red and get sweatier and angrier and that's a little bit like me when I'm playing. It's all come from him."

Ryan then reminded me about Paul Hutchison, a tall blond paceman who had been making his way at Yorkshire at the same time as him.

"Paul and I were close mates and he was also a left-armer. He was probably better than me and he took loads of wickets in a very short period of time. I could have sulked and given up. He just made me train harder and work harder in the gym and get stronger. Then he got injured, he unfortunately had quite a number of back injuries, and that paved the way for me to go in and prove I was good enough.

"I think I'm very determined and I think I've taken a lot of that from Dad's advice. I never ever give up and I never let anyone criticise me and, if they do, I don't like it but turn it around and make it into a positive."

As far as Arnie is concerned that inner strength and determination has been one of Ryan's major assets. I lost count of the number of times he repeated with pride, "And he's done it all by himself."

That resolve was something he consciously tried to instil in his lad from an early age and he believes it has helped his son bounce back from a disappointing Test debut and several years in the international wilderness.

"He always said that when he was first selected by England he'd hardly played county cricket. I think the atmosphere and pressure got to him a little bit and he didn't bowl as well as he could.

"He never gave up. And that's the thing about him. Even now on the field he still wants to do really well. He's very quiet and laid back off the field, whereas on it he's aggressive and in your face. That's why he's done so well.

"I think I've instilled in to him to never give in whatever because Yorkshire people will forgive you for anything if they know you are giving 100%. Even if you take 0-150 they will forgive you because they know you are trying every minute of the day. That's why he is popular because they see that.

"Off the field he's very quiet, doesn't say too much and doesn't get involved in too much, but on the field he's a Jekyll and Hyde character. He's aggressive and gets OTT if someone drops a catch and he's throwing tantrums or laying into them and that's part of his makeup. But he leaves the field and switches off and it's all gone."

Arnie has said on numerous occasions that he is a terrible watcher. He's missed many of Ryan's heroics live for fear that nerves would get the better of him. He did however choose an excellent match in early 2008 to watch his son play in the flesh for the first time.

"The first time I went to see him play he paid for me and his Mum to go to New Zealand and the first day there he got a hat-trick in the Test match.

"I was jumping up and down on the boundary and everyone was looking at me thinking 'who's that nutcase?' Ryan said, 'Dad you'll have to keep coming now'. But I don't. I just swear at the TV and kick it whenever he was bowling badly."

For Ryan it was a magical day: "It was lovely. I was 30 and had come back into the England side. People said I wasn't a great choice as I wasn't one for the future, but again that made me more determined to do well.

"Dad never really watched. He was always a nervous wreck. So I paid for my parents to come out to New Zealand to watch me play in that Test series. I remember meeting them in a hotel. They were on a group tour, so there were quite a few other ex-cricketers, lots of other people and they made some great friends.

"They were having a picnic, mixing with some of the Barmy Army fans and watching the game at Hamilton. The day Dad's watching with Mum I took the Test match hat-trick. Nothing better! It is etched in history and to have my parents there was absolutely amazing. To do something like that was very, very special."

Ryan may yet follow his Dad into coaching when he retires at the end of the 2017 season. For now, Arnie's only concern is that his son's transition into retirement is an easy one.

"It's a shock once you've finished playing. You don't realise and when it happens you don't know what to do. You've been going in training every day and suddenly it all stops. You've been staying in hotels all week and it stops. It will be difficult for Ryan, even though I've tried to say that he needs to start looking to the future now and prepare himself. It is still a shock and still hits you.

"It's been unbelievable that he's continued to perform so consistently. If you get an injury when you're 20 it might be a couple of weeks, but when you're 37 it's six or eight weeks on the sidelines and that's a third of the season gone. He's had a couple of injuries but come back bigger and stronger.

"He still loves it, still loves going training and loves it with the young lads at Yorkshire. They take the micky out of him and call him Granddad."

Ryan's 21st season in first-class cricket will be his last and those boots will be hung up at the grand old age of 39.

"Again, I've proved people wrong," Ryan told me. "12 month contracts have made a massive difference, the strength and conditioning, masseuses, ice baths and the all-round professionalism have helped my longevity," Ryan said. "Guys certainly don't go out drinking as much as they used to. Certainly when I first started you'd have five or six pints and you might go clubbing and you'd back it up by bowling all day the next day. But now I could never dream of doing that. You might have a glass of wine and sit back and relax and you definitely need to get yourself away from the game, but it really has changed so much now. It's far more professional. It has made me even more determined to keep up with the young lads. If they are lifting weights I want to lift bigger weights than them.

"They call me 'Granddad,' 'Uncle Siddy,' all sorts. All in nice ways," he insists. His Yorkshire team-mates are not shy in reminding the veteran of his advancing years. "Probably the biggest one was when Matthew Fisher said that when I made my debut he wasn't even born. It just shows how long I've played for. Again, I don't take that as a negative. It's a nice compliment and it shows what I've done, the career I've had and how I've managed to keep going so long."

Despite the obvious difficulties that Ryan seemed to have faced when he was coming through the Yorkshire youth system, it was obvious to me that he shared something special with his father. Arnie has stood back, let his son find his own identity, but been there with the advice and tough love as required.

"He's a great Dad," Ryan said warmly. "I've travelled the world, I went to South Africa, he used to take me to the games, I used to sit in the dressing room and listen to all the banter and the swearing and go round the back of the stands and play football and cricket with all the other boys and girls.

"Yeah, I've had a great life. I've been very lucky. It was a bit hard on me of course but sometimes you need that kick up the backside.

"I used to play football on a regular basis and I wasn't very good, but Dad used to watch me more at football. And God, he used to hammer me when I got home.

"He really used to be hard on me. 'Stop being so soft,' 'get stuck in'. It was upsetting but again it made me more determined.

"I was like 'I hate you Dad, I'm going to show you now that I can get stuck in and I can do better'. Some words of wisdom, a little bit hard on me, but what I needed.

"We've always had a good relationship," he continued. "When we won the Championship at Trent Bridge he bought me a bottle of wine. When I went past his tally he was very emotional and that was really nice. We went to the local pub and had some Sunday lunch and I bought him a whisky and he bought me a bottle of wine, so I don't know who won that day."

My reaction was that cricket had been the winner before mentally slapping myself for being a walking cliché. As I mulled over the conversations with Arnie and Ryan and looked down the long list of the fathers and sons I still wanted to talk to, I had a sense that I was on to something.

At the very least, I was going to get to have a chat to some of my favourite cricketers. At best, if Ryan had felt pressure, others would have too and there were going to be a few interesting tales to be told.

CHAPTER THREE

ALAN and MARK EALHAM

"There is no truth without responsibility following in its wake"
George Bernard Shaw

It was an interval in play some time in the mid-1980s. A gaggle of young Kent cricketers walked onto the outfield as their names were announced over the PA system. I settled down to watch a catching competition.

It was scary stuff. A bowling machine had been wheeled onto the square and was firing cricket balls high into the Canterbury sky as the youngsters took it in turns to make a great catch or shuffle away eliminated after one too many spilled opportunities.

My eyes were firmly fixed on one lad. It wasn't difficult to pick him out. Mark Ealham was built very much like his Dad. At 5 foot 10 inches (when he'd finished growing) he was a little taller than Alan, but he had exactly the same squat figure. To describe them as rotund would be cruel and inaccurate, but they were more orange than banana. It belied a high level of fitness, Alan being one of the best ground fielders I have ever seen.

So this was Ealham's kid, and he was good. Mark progressed through the contest as others fell by the wayside. My memory told me he'd been the winner that day, but Mark remembered it differently.

"I think I came third," he chuckled. "Although I might have won. The balls came down like sledgehammers in your hands, I know that much."

If I'd won something like that I would definitely have remembered. Mark had continued to play 21 summers as a professional cricketer and bigger days had edged the clarity of this one from his consciousness. I'd watched him closely because of his surname and he admitted to feeling a bit of pressure.

"I wanted to catch a few, otherwise everyone would have said I wasn't as good a fielder as Dad. Fielding was always very important to me because of that. Dad always said that you could influence games with a bit of brilliant fielding as much as with bowling."

Alan also remembered that catching competition and understood my tunnel vision on his son's participation.

"That's part and parcel of being a name," Alan told me. "You'll find in most sports, in acting and other public professions that a lot of them follow their parents and people will pay them extra attention."

After his retirement in 2009 he had followed his father again, this time as cricket master at King's School in Canterbury. Alan had worked there for just over a decade and enjoyed a part-time association with them for well over 30 years.

Mark was now going through it all again as a father himself. His two sons were keen cricketers with serious promise. It had gone full circle.

"My two boys are in the age group stuff," Mark explained. "The eldest George is playing Under-15s and and the youngest Tommy is Under-13s. The pressures these days in terms of selection, other parents and the stress of sport are a bit more than I think we had. So I talk to Dad a lot about how he managed it all so I can try and get it right with my boys.

"I'm trying to take a leaf out of Dad's book because I felt he got it pretty right with me," Mark continued. "I think 18 months ago I was a bit too technical and too involved, and in the last year I've said next to nothing and let them develop a little bit on their own.

"I spoke to Mike Atherton, because his lad Josh is in the same age group as my eldest. I took a picture of our lads tossing up as opposing captains and sent it to Athers. Josh is the spit of Mike and my lad is the spit of me and he had a giggle. I asked him what he did with Josh and he told me he throws balls at him but doesn't advise him technically. Athers said, 'If he's going to be any good he's got to find a way and work it out'.

"That really struck me as I'd been the opposite and I felt Athers was right," Mark admitted. "I was going down the route of too much information too young and so I've stepped back. I never felt there was a constant technical or mental bombardment from my dad and so I've let my boys talk to some other people.

"When you see they've got talent and they don't get runs you sit in your deckchair and worry, but like Dad tells me, it will unfold and whatever happens will happen. He always said to me, 'If you are good enough nobody will stop you'. It's far worse watching! I don't hope for millions of runs and wickets every game. I just hope they enjoy it. If they get a couple of noughts you can feel the pressure as *a son of* and I don't want them to have that, because I never really felt that too much. I just went out and played and enjoyed it.

"You don't want them to be under so much pressure that they stifle themselves and don't enjoy it. If you don't enjoy it there's no point doing it." Mark said. "The eldest is just like me, medium pacers and bashes it right-handed and Tommy is a right-arm off-spinner and a left-handed bat. My wife's brother is a left-hander so it wasn't that much of a shock and I instantly thought what a great thing because it's an advantage because his strength is in his top hand. They are very different, which is quite nice because they don't get compared too much. The little one gets loads more wickets because he's a spinner and in age-group cricket nobody plays spin very well, so he's had quite a successful start with the ball, but the bigger one has been a little bit better with the bat. The eldest one is pretty adamant that he wants to play cricket, but there's a long way to go and time will tell."

Mark laughed when I asked him how he would feel if either of his sons told him they didn't want to play cricket any more. "It would be a lot easier," was his instant response. "It wouldn't worry me in the slightest. George said to me last night after I'd picked him up from school and we were driving home from Beckenham at 10.30pm, 'Dad I don't know how you do this, all the running around you do and the coaching, taking us here, there and everywhere and your jobs'.

"I said, 'I enjoy it and it's nice watching you boys play, but it's up to you if you want to play. Whatever you want to do, just go ahead and do it. If you want to give cricket a go, then give it a go'. But I think they've known from day one that they can do what they like.

"But I say to them that the minute I feel that they haven't got the desire, or aren't playing it for the right reasons, then I'll soon let them know. It's got to be a passion. If you want to do it for a job, be good enough and give it your all, you've got to really love it. With all the distractions they have now and millions of sports at school it's important they have that desire for the sport they've got a bit of talent for.

"Dad said to me once when my mates wanted to drag me in to town, 'There's a tenner to go with your mates into town and there's a tenner and your supper money to get the train to Ashford and play your cricket'. I think one time I took the tenner and went off with my mates and never did it again. He made me make the choice and said he wasn't going to make it for me."

I suggested to Mark that the best a cricket father could give his child was the freedom to choose. How hard must it be for a child who felt pressured to play cricket? A kid who knew how important it had been to their father, who didn't want to disappoint, but didn't really want to play the game - trapped in their father's dream.

"It would be horrible wouldn't it? I chatted to Alan Wells about his son Luke," Mark said. "He'd developed pretty quickly and he'd got in and done really well for Sussex. Alan told me he was very proud of him and we talked about his younger son, Daniel. He told me that a couple of years ago he'd found him with his head in his hands in the dressing room one day and he turned to him and said, 'Do you mind? I don't think I can do this'.

Mark continued: "Alan replied, 'Boy, I've been waiting for you to say that. You know me, no worries at all'. And he had quite a long chat where his youngest told him he was trying to follow his brother, he'd got a bit of talent, but he felt he wasn't quite there and he'd just got out again. I think the pressure had got so much that he wanted to do something else and he said, 'I can't do this, I don't think I can follow Luke'.

"Alan said it was a defining moment with his time with his lads. And he felt a relief because he'd seen him struggling a little bit to live up to his brother. And when Alan was talking I was listening very closely because I might find myself in that same situation with one, or both, of my boys."

Mark's sons could make a go of it and become good county players, or even internationals. Would that mean more as someone that has done it himself?

"It's about stepping stones and not looking too far ahead," he stated. "You see they have a bit of talent and if they achieve something then fantastic. My mum said that when I played my first Test I visited my parents sitting in the crowd during one of the breaks. She said I had my England jumper on and, although Dad didn't say too much at the time, he was very emotional. He'd put a lot of time in through the years, the nets on a Sunday morning and getting me through tricky times, to see me put on an England sweater from his perspective was obviously a major thing.

"In terms of following in the footsteps, the major achievement for me was getting my Kent cap," Mark added. "I'd managed to do what Dad had done. He captained Kent as well, which I didn't do, but it was never a competition. I so wanted to get a cap and that was my main thing. England was a bit of a bonus and had been more of a distant dream.

"Robert Key once told me that he thought it was every kid's dream to put on an England sweater and that's what had driven him as a child, but I told him that my first dream had always been to get the Kent cap because that's what my Dad had done.

"So who knows? It would be lovely if the boys find their talent and succeed, but likewise, as long as they are healthy and happy and doing what they want to do, what will be will be."

Granddad Alan is keeping a close eye on George and Tommy's efforts on the cricket field too.

"They've got a lot of talent," Alan told me excitedly. "I said to

Mark that you've got to let them have their own head to a certain extent, but I've watched the older one in the Kent setup and he's easily the best fielder and that's a massive plus in this modern game. He reminds me very much of me as a little-un, running and tearing around and catching and throwing. His stature is quite low to the ground at the moment. Whether he's going to get much bigger, I don't know.

"Mark is a little bit taller than me, but we've all had good hands, his youngest has too, although he's a little bit more methodical in the field, but he's no slouch. If they carry on they'll probably have a little more pressure than Mark did, as their Dad played for England."

For Mark, having a cricket father provided an exposure to the game at an early age, although his participation wasn't at all forced.

"He was quite relaxed with me and without me realising it I was dragged around here, there and everywhere to do nets in the winter and stuff," Mark recalled. "I just loved cricket because I was following Dad around and playing with a lot of my mates with a tennis ball and the dustbin for stumps. I was brought up with it.

"Dad said he was relaxed with me to start with and I asked him how he coped with the age group stuff and the pressure. He said that there was a bit that went on in the background and there was always a conversation from somebody who said 'he's only playing because of his old man'. He did quite well to shield me from it. He just let me play and enjoy it.

"He didn't get too technical too early," Mark added. "Obviously he showed me a few things from time-to-time. But I think it started to take shape when he was 2nd team coach at Kent when I came on the staff. That probably made it a bit harder. He was involved in selecting who from the 2nd team would go to the 1st team."

Alan remembered that period of his coaching life well. His role at the club was to bring through the next generation and encourage them all regardless of whether they called him Dad or not. When one of your fresh crop of talent is your son the quest to show no favouritism can potentially create unfairness.

Alan said: "I was employed by Kent as the director of youth coaching and then moved on to 2nd XI cricket. It made it quite tough. One or two decisions that I made, when looking back, I felt I was a bit too hard on him.

"I took over from a chap called Colin Page when he retired and we had two or three years working together with youth cricket. I'd worked with him throughout my career when I was playing and we knew each other pretty well.

"Colin would sometimes say 'that's being a bit tough on the old boy mate' and we'd ease it out that way," Alan admitted. "Mark probably had to work a little bit harder and I don't suppose that hurt him too much.

"There was only one occasion where I feel I shouldn't have done something," Alan confessed. "We were playing in the final of the Bain Clarkson Trophy in the late 1980s and I didn't play Mark. I had seamers already in the side and although Mark had done reasonably well through the rest of the tournament, it came to the final and he probably should have played, but it would have left me a spinner short."

When I mentioned to Mark that his omission was his dad's one regret he could remember being 12th man for the game and his father's admission made him chuckle. He remembered Colin Page being an important figure.

"Colin was brilliant for me," Mark enthused. "Obviously with being in an environment where Dad was around, you don't want to be stuck to his side when you're trying to forge your own identity. Colin gave me that little bit extra I couldn't get from Dad at work because it was too close. He was a major influence on my development, not just as a cricketer, but also as a person. Colin was quite a tough character. You didn't step out of line and you learnt a lot quickly.

"Dad and I had a very good relationship and I trusted his eye and spent many hours with one-on-ones and hit balls from bowling machines," Mark recalled. "He showed me things from time-to-time but he just let me hit balls. You get to the teenage years and turn round saying, 'I'm not doing that,' and he'd simply say, 'It's up to you, I'm giving you the opportunity to do this and you make your own decisions'.

"I didn't feel under pressure when I first joined the Kent staff, but it was a couple of years in when I was making the jump into playing 1st team that I had the odd issue with a few grumblings or undercurrents with one or two players, guys I was competing with. I found that quite difficult, but if you spend a lot of time worrying about other people it takes away from your own game.

"I thought the characters around me were all pretty solid, but the pressure of wanting to be a pro and get an opportunity had a few effects on some. There were a few comments made in nets and a couple of little pointed chats on trips and things.

"Dad was there as 2nd team coach and pushing forward who he thought should play, but luckily your performances merit selection and when I went into the 1st team I was fortunate to do pretty well straight away, made a bit of an impact and then waited until a proper opportunity came up.

"I've got older and grumpier now and if I had my time again I'd probably tell them to do one," Mark said. "It was so out of the blue when someone leant through the nets and said 'come on lads let's have a look at a 1st team player'. I thought it was a joke to start with and then realised it wasn't. It didn't last very long and didn't affect me as I believed in my selection and went off and enjoyed what I did.

"Dad always told me to just let bat and ball do the talking and nobody could question what I was doing if I was performing. I was always quite relaxed and never too punchy a character. It was all very much a stepping stone for us and you got your 2nd team cap and then your Kent cap, you respected your elders and kept your mouth shut. I think sometimes now it can all be a bit fluffy.

"At the end of the day you are trying to be a professional," Mark asserted. "It's a tough existence as there are a lot of players after your spot. I spoke to Neil Taylor recently, who was at Kent at the time, and we were talking about my two lads. He asked me how I was going to deal with it. He said, "Your Dad was really hard on you. If it was a tough situation in the nets and somebody was bowling quickly, he'd point to you to bat next. Or somebody got called off to the 1st team and you'd suddenly go from No 8 to open the batting when Patrick Patterson happened to be playing at Old Trafford in the Lancashire 2nd team. You have baptisms of fire pretty regularly as a bit of a test I suppose'.

"I was surprised when Neil said that as I never felt that really," Mark continued. "I always trusted Dad and felt he was making the right decisions for me as a cricketer. In one season he asked me to open the 2nd team batting and I thought I better say yes. We came up against some very good bowlers and it gave me the opportunity to develop my batting.

"If he wasn't around at times later on, like when I started playing for England, I'd still call him and ask whether he'd seen anything and he'd give me a few pointers. He was my sounding board."

As a youngster making the transition from promise to professional Mark had one conversation with his father he always remembered.

"I never spoke to Dad about becoming a professional apart from when I was 15 when I said, 'Should I do this Dad?' He replied, 'Yeah, you are good enough,' and that was all I needed to hear. That made deciding to be a cricketer a little easier.

"It was quite nice that he called me into the office when I got picked to make my England debut," Mark remembered. "David Graveney had phoned and spoken to Dad and asked if he wanted to tell me the news. So he called me into his office and said, 'Well mate, you'd better get your gear organised because you're going to play in the Test at Trent Bridge'. I expected Jeremy Beadle to wander in. I think Dad enjoyed that and it certainly sticks in my memory."

One of the definitions of being a father is that you are from a different era. Part of the parenting conundrum is how to stick to family values while moving with the times.

"I kept getting it from his grandfather that Mark should be doing an apprenticeship, which is what I had to do before I was allowed to play first-class cricket," Alan recalled. He'd completed his own apprenticeship as a welder and panel beater before his first-class career took priority in the mid 1960s. "That era was gradually getting moved aside and youngsters were given more opportunity and were subsidised better. In my day I had to go and get a job."

I don't get star struck very often when interviewing sportsmen, but talking to Alan mattered somehow. Maybe it was because my Great Uncle Reg, who had introduced me to the game back in 1977, had a soft spot for him. He was captain of the Kent side between 1978 and 1980, but by no means the star in a dressing room of internationals. My Great Uncle thought he was the bee's knees because he looked like someone that would bust a gut for the cause. When it comes down to it, whatever sporting side we support, if we see one of 'ours' giving it the blood, sweat and tears routine, we can forgive them almost anything.

"We were very fortunate to have a side that came together like that," Alan remarked when the fan in me asked what it was like to play alongside Alan Knott, Bob Woolmer, Derek Underwood, et al. "We obviously had a couple of overseas players. We had Asif Iqbal and John Shepherd, although John was like a local anyway because he'd joined in 1965 and he'd been with us ever since. There was none of this mercenary thing you get nowadays where they flit from county to county.

"The toughest part for me was when I first finished playing was seeing other people carrying on," Alan admitted. "I was still playing club cricket back at Ashford and gave them six years, three as captain and three more to help Mark as he was coming through. Mark remembers his time playing with his dad at Ashford with great fondness.

"As a kid I was always playing tennis ball cricket with Asif Iqbal's sons and different lads around," Mark said. "So I didn't often watch Dad play that much. Occasionally Mum would stop me and say that he was on 49 or 99 or the Kent team were about to win, so we'd stop for a bit and then carry on playing.

"It wasn't until I was 15 and I played with him in a game for Ashford against a decent touring side from West Indies with some quick blokes bowling," Mark told me. "It was a bit hairy and watching him the other end pulling, hooking and driving, I suddenly realised how good he was. I'd never really seen him playing up close and never really taken it in. That makes you listen even more because you think *he knows what he is talking about* because he's pretty good. He was an attacking player, played on uncovered pitches with no helmets, so he was a lot braver than we were.

"It was amazing to play with him and fairly comforting to think you had that support and that he was keeping an eye on me," Mark suggested. "Without me realising it, he was there through all the important stages of my development."

The players I was speaking to were correct when they told me that the game had changed massively over the years. In many ways Alan played a generation too soon. His fielding would be an asset to any current Twenty20 side and his attacking game was ahead of its time.

"Colin Cowdrey once said to me, 'I'm amazed at how many shots you play,'" Alan recalled. "I suppose I was one of those innovative blokes. I could play the reverse sweep quite well, but in those days it was frowned upon. You'd never dream of doing things like that. You'd have probably got left out of the side. It's the same with wearing sunglasses – with some of our old coaches they'd have given you a right earful."

Alan had lilted through our chat mentioning a few times that Mark being his son had caused issues, but it wasn't until the stick of rock with Kent running through him told me he'd suggested Mark leave the county when still a youngster that I realised how seriously he'd viewed the situation.

"It got to the stage where I thought it might be better if he went and joined another county," Alan said. "I spoke to Graham Gooch about Mark going to Essex, which wasn't far away. And it was Mark who wanted to stay with Kent and aim for a 1st team place there.

"He'd come through the Kent setup from the age of 10 and he said, 'No Dad, I want to stay with Kent'. So I said 'Okay fine, we'll just muddle along and do our best. I told him he was probably going to get lots of people saying that he was only playing because of me and we'd deal with that if it cropped up.

"I was very fortunate to be in a position to watch the development of his career, without spoiling it and making it too tough for him," Alan said. "With the surname I thought he may have found it tough at Kent, but he said he wanted to do it his way and from my point-of-view I thought *well done, that's fair enough*. He had the mental toughness to put it to the back of his mind and not let it worry him. I think that's part and parcel of the make-up you need to be able to make the grade.

"When I put his name forward to take him onto the staff I did get opposition," Alan added. "People wanted to wait another year and I told them if they did that they might miss him. I backed him and said he'd got the talent. I'd told them about other players that had come through and I'd been right, so they should take my experience on Mark too.

"It was a bit of a fight to get him onto the staff, but when he was on there he never looked back. In those early days I looked after some of his money too. I said, 'You're earning good money now, you give me so much and I'll keep it for you and then you'll have a deposit for a house or something,' which he did. I'm not saying he'd have blown it all because he was quite a sensible lad, but it was just my way of doing what Dad used to do with me. That set him off with his first house."

Mark had recalled how a good start in the Kent side quashed any doubts that might otherwise have lingered.

"In his first match he got 45 at Old Trafford," Alan agreed. "He was an all-rounder, but he initially got into the Kent team because of his bowling in the one-day stuff. And I always said to him, 'If you get into the side as a bowler, you're always going to get a bat from time-to-time,' which he did. He got the experience and was then able to move up the order as time went by."

It had surprised me to hear that Alan had considered the dangers of Mark following him into the Kent setup were such that a move elsewhere might prove beneficial. By 2004 the Ealham roots within Kent cricket had got even deeper, so how did Alan react when Mark moved to Nottinghamshire?

"That was the changing face of cricket," Alan said. "If the lad wasn't going to get what he considered to be a reasonable deal, after he'd been a servant for them for 15 years.

"Mark said, 'Right if you are not going to back me and give me what I think I justify I'll have to go somewhere else'. He was a good mate with Adam Hollioake through the England setup and Adam told him not to mess about with Kent and he'd get his agent to have a look around if they were not going to play ball.

"I told him it was up to him," Alan continued. "There didn't seem to be as much loyalty then as in my day. I know he'd got to 33 but he asked for a three-year contract. He might have accepted two, but he wanted a bit of security after he'd been playing for England and one thing or another and they only offered him a one-year deal.

"He'd approached them quite early in the season and it had dragged on. He told them he didn't want to be doing a Nico [Paul Nixon] at Leicestershire, who had almost got his cards as he walked off the field after the last game of the season. He had so many meetings with them it was unreal and they never budged. In the end, he went in for his last meeting in September and they said so and so and we'll offer you a year and we can talk about it and he told them he'd done all of his talking through the summer, thanks very much and shook their hands, told them he was off and they were sat there with their mouths open."

So after the 2003 season the Ealham name stopped appearing on Kent scorecards. Was there an element of sadness in the family?

"Of course there was and quietly Mark was gutted, but it was a new experience for him going to another county and one that he really enjoyed. It opened his eyes to how other counties carry on and it was a Test ground as well. He had six seasons there and could have gone on for another season as they wanted him to sign for another year, but I'd got this job down in Canterbury at the school and I said I'd keep it open for him and carry on until he was ready as they wanted him to come in and do the same thing. He said, "No, I've had enough Dad, I'm 40, I don't want to be in and out of the 2nd team and I'll finish at the top.""

A first-class career spanning 21 seasons came to an end in 2009. Mark had played eight Test matches and 64 One-Day Internationals for England between 1996 and 2001. 210 Test runs at 21 with two fifties didn't quite cut it at the highest level but his Test bowling record of 17 wickets at 28.70 was more than respectable.

It is his one-day career that Mark will be most remembered for at international level with 716 runs as a late order hitter and 67 wickets at 32.79. His five for 15 against New Zealand in Kimberley on the 1999/2000 tour were the best figures for England on ODIs at the time. All five wickets were lbw, an ODI record.

Alan, who never made it to international cricket, despite being around the squad regularly as 12th man due to his notorious athleticism in the field, was as proud as punch to see his lad go further.

"I did do 12th man on four or five occasions so I was there for the atmosphere and got a taste of it, but for actually playing, no," he said. "So of course it was with great pride when me and the wife went up there on his first one at Trent Bridge against India. What can you say? When one of your own does it, it's great."

Was it a nervy watch as your son took his first strides as an international player? Any part of Alan ever wishes it had been him?

"I was nervous and from my point-of-view I'd been retired the best part of 15 years. So I wasn't thinking *I wish I was out there*. I wanted him to do really well and it's easier from the stands," he laughed.

It genuinely had been a pleasure to talk to Alan and his son.

Alan, now in his early 70s was exactly who I hoped he would be – someone who still sounds as if he genuinely loves the sport that has given his family so much.

I'd found the father and son, coach and player aspect, an interesting aspect of our chat. It's not uncommon for former players to turn their attentions to coaching. If their son decides to follow into the game there's every likelihood that their paths will cross, as had been the case with the Sidebottoms and Ealhams. That topic would crop again.

But before then, and to round off the 'first game at Canterbury' motif of these initial chapters, I turned my attention to the Bairstow family.

CHAPTER FOUR

DAVID and JONNY BAIRSTOW

*"I'd love to know how Dad saw me when I was six.
I'd love to know a hundred things.
When a parent dies, a filing cabinet full of all the
fascinating stuff also ceases to exist.
I never imagined how hungry I'd be one day to
look inside it."*
David Mitchell in 'The Bone Clocks'

The last of my quartet of players taking part in that first game I saw at Canterbury in 1977 had been David Bairstow. 'Bluey' as he was known was a flame-haired, robust character, loud, cheerful, committed to the cause and, in the best way possible, a fighter. These traits made him hugely popular with the Yorkshire public.

David appeared in four Tests and 21 One-Day Internationals for England in a career spanning two decades. For Yorkshire he scored almost 14,000 first-class runs and snaffled 1,099 chances with the keeping gloves. His 11 catches in a Championship match against Derbyshire at Scarborough in 1982 equalled the world record.

His Yorkshire career had famously begun in 1970 when he made his first-class debut against Gloucestershire after arranging to sit his A-level examination at 6am on the same day.

"There were better wicket-keepers but put in his temperament, enthusiasm, team spirit and never-say-die attitude and he was the best," said former Yorkshire and England skipper, Raymond Illingworth. Another former Yorkshire captain, Phil Carrick, wrote: "He wasn't a good wicket-keeper and he wasn't a good batsman, but he was a great cricketer."

Bairstow was the kind of player that writers dream about. The number of stories attributed to him are plentiful, my favourite being when he was batting against Australia in an ODI at the Sydney Cricket Ground. England required 35 runs to win and in walked Yorkshire team-mate Graham Stevenson at No 10, with only John Lever to follow. Stevenson on debut, himself a character, greeted Ian Chappell with the words "nice night for it, int'it" before Bairstow turned to his pal saying, "we can piss this old son!" Dennis Lillee, Len Pascoe, Jeff Thomson and Geoff Dymock conceded a barrage of boundaries and scampered singles as 'piss this' they did.

On the same tour against West Indies, also in Sydney, Colin Croft left the task of scoring three off the final ball. England captain Mike Brearley, allowed by the rules then to move all of his fielders on to the boundary, stationed his keeper in front of the sightscreen. With the crowd hurling abuse at Bairstow, he laughed back heartily.

The best example of his unquenchable spirit came in a Benson & Hedges Cup game at Derby in 1981. 80 runs short of victory, David was joined by Yorkshire's No 11 Mark Johnson, who was making his debut. Bairstow hit nine sixes in his unbeaten 103 as he led his side to an unlikely win. At the other end Johnson was four not out.

When David took his own life at the age of 48 it shocked the cricket world. The much loved, hugely respected and larger than life figure had been suffering from depression, financial worries and his wife Janet had cancer. He was also due to appear before magistrates the following week on a drink driving charge.

In January 1998, eight years into retirement, David committed suicide at his home in Marton-cum-Grafton, near Boroughbridge. His wife and their two children, Jonny and Becky, finding his body when they returned home from school. "Mr Bairstow was found hanging at his home," a North Yorkshire police spokesman said.

Fred Trueman, who had worked with Bairstow in the media after his retirement, told the BBC: "He was always positive, jovial, liked a story, liked his golf. I just remember his love of life. I can't believe it."

And that was cricket's conundrum. How could a man that loved life, end it when so many people loved him? Depression had been the cruellest of mistresses.

"We found Dad and, even aged eight, it was pretty obvious what happened," Jonny told The Guardian in May 2016. "We all found him. That wasn't easy to take because you don't really know what's going on when you're seven, like Becky, or eight. But we also knew mum had cancer at the same time because she'd lost her hair. It was a pretty intense form of breast cancer and she was going through chemotherapy.

"Having gone through two bouts of breast cancer and all the operations and treatments it's fair to say mum's a special human being – especially as she had to deal with the tragedy and heartache that went with Dad's death," Jonny added. "But the support we had, the amount of people who came to the funeral and memorial service, was very touching."

It's a horrific event for any family to deal with and one that could have ripped a lot of families to shreds. I worked as the Media Manager at Yorkshire CCC between 2007 and 2011. Janet worked there too, an impressive woman and incredibly protective and proud of her two children. With true Yorkshire grit and spirit she managed to galvanise her family and pulled them through the toughest of times.

It had been Geoffrey Boycott that suggested to the club that Janet was employed in the cricket department. Jonny had got to the age where he could drive himself to matches and Boycott had been concerned that Janet needed something to occupy her time. She had quickly become a matriarchal figure for the players and I remember having two thoughts. Boycott had a much bigger heart than people gave him credit for and it was a real testament to Janet how both of her children had turned out. Jonny was gifted, polite and well rounded. Becky was a lovely, smiley, intelligent young lady.

The day after David's suicide had been Janet's birthday. "Mum sent us to school that day as if saying: 'Right, OK, we've got to deal with it, carry on,' Jonny recalled. "The only thing I can't really remember is walking into school that day.

"Going through that adversity as a family has made us closer and stronger. Look at my sister – she's hard as nails as well. We're a special family and it's just that Dad's life was taken away from us far too early. Everywhere you go around the world he had an effect on people – in the Caribbean, Australia, South Africa or England. I've never heard a bad word said about him.

I often thought Jonny had built a *Bairstows against the world* scenario inside his mind. Just like his father he's wired to succeed, he's a fighter and fiercely protective of Mum and sister. Some elements of the media gave his mother an unnecessarily hard time after David's death. I could understand their mistrust, but I don't think as many people were out to get him as he sometimes thinks and certainly not in Yorkshire press boxes where everyone shared fond memories and a huge respect for his father. And amongst the Yorkshire public the Bairstow name gave him an enormous head start in their affections.

When former Yorkshire Post cricket correspondent David Hopps was tasked with picking his favourite cricketer for ESPN Cricinfo, he chose David Bairstow. He wrote: "In Bairstow's hands, cricket was at its most combative and rudimentary. He was belligerent, straightforward, hot-headed. He was right, he was wrong, although rarely wrong in his own head. He forever carried the fight. He brought colour to the dreariest day. He was endlessly interesting. It assured him a popularity that ranks alongside anybody in the county's history."

Jonny said: "That shows the amount of respect people had for Dad. He was very well liked and someone who is very sadly missed – even now. People still come up and say: 'I had a pint with your dad in X, Y and Z pub and we laughed and joked'. Those are the amazing things you want to hear."

Unfortunately for me, I worked at Headingley in a rather barren period for the club's trophy cabinet. The back-to-back County Championship wins of 2014 and 2015 came after I'd left, but there were three young talents that I was privileged to see mature into world stars. To watch Joe Root, Gary Ballance and Jonny Bairstow play for Yorkshire's Academy before making their 1st Team debuts and thriving was manna from heaven for a cricket badger like myself.

There were never any doubts in my mind that all three would play for England. In Jonny's case the transition took him a little longer to master than Root, now England Test captain. While Joe has invariably taken each step up in class in his stride and never looked back, Jonny has taken his time to settle. He's always been good enough, just found it harder to prove his worth as instantly as Root. When the dust settles I don't think that little bit of additional soul searching has done him any harm.

Jonny broke schoolboy run-scoring records and Yorkshire supporters knew for some years that he was on his way towards the 1st Team. His first senior appearance, in a County Championship match against Somerset at Headingley in June 2009, saw him make 28 and 82 not out, stranded short of a debut century in the second innings as the team were dismissed around him. On both occasions when he walked out to bat, and then when he passed fifty, the welcome from the crowd was different to that received by 'normal' debutants. There were a few more decibels and, if I could feel the warmth, I am sure he could. There seemed a genuine desire that this little ginger fella, whose Dad they had loved, would succeed.

Jonny signed his first professional contract ahead of the 2009 season and scored his maiden first-class century at Trent Bridge in May 2011. That innings against Nottinghamshire showed exactly why the England selectors would come calling. He'd already impressed on the previous winter's England Lions tour where, despite not playing every game, the coaches had noted his work ethic and attitude.

He'd passed fifty on 17 occasions prior to that innings at Trent Bridge, nine times of which he'd been not out, which added to the frustration. He entered the scene with the score 184 for three and was initially forced to bat within himself as he shared a stand of 119 with Root. He was 50 not out from 101 balls overnight and resumed on the second day as Yorkshire lost four wickets for 40 runs. Again he was made to work hard as he neared his first three figure score, which came in 184 balls and included 13 fours and a six. When the shackles were loosened so were Jonny's shoulders. His third fifty took 49 balls and his fourth came in 57. He dismissed the bowling with an impudent authority and it was appropriate that his partner for a ninth wicket stand of 151 runs was Ryan Sidebottom. Their fathers had shared so many moments for Yorkshire and it was their boys' time to shine.

I interviewed Jonny after his maiden hundred. At one stage he flicked his eyes up to the heavens and said: "Dad's here and I'm sure he's proud." That he mentioned his father surprised me. Moxon had always been keen to shield 'Young Bluey' from unnecessary scrutiny. It was commonplace for media outlets covering his embryonic career to devote a large chunk of the first paragraphs to his father. We'd adopted a policy that Jonny would only be interviewed if his performances warranted the attention.

Sometimes when milestones don't come easily it ultimately makes them worth more. The serious graft and psychological hurdles Jonny had to counter made him stronger and forged a better player. But it was tough at the time.

"I was out for 82 about five times, which is ridiculous," he recalled. He had actually been either dismissed or ended unbeaten in the 80s on six occasions. "I got 82 on my debut against Somerset and tried so hard to get over the line. It was the first time I'd come across the media and everyone doubting you. And then the first hundred I got was a double."

Having watched Jonny at close quarters for the first few years of his career he could often be a bit prickly in interviews. I wondered whether he was actually acutely aware of the attention his father's deeds brought him and that resulted to him being oversensitive to anything remotely resembling criticism.

He'd taken what many pundits viewed as the brave decision to continue as a wicket-keeper batsman, exactly as his father before him, when his batting was strong enough on its own to fulfil his international aspirations. He often got touchy when repeatedly asked whether he was determined to retain the gloves. Personally I admired his tenacity and the many hours of hard work he invested in his keeping. It's improved every season and vindicated his decision.

But his view that the media was critical and, at times, almost out to get him was extreme. Any county player with his quality that waited until his 35th first-class match before converting to three figures would receive media comment. The coverage he got wasn't personal. It was recognition of his immense potential. It was extraordinary that he'd not reached the milestone sooner.

The genie was out of the bottle and two more centuries came

in 2011 leading to an England tour to India in 2011/12. Jonny said: "I have some very fond memories of Dad, fond things that people have said. He was a great character and did a lot for the game. It's a very proud moment for the family now I'm on tour with England.

"I remember going to Barbados with Dad and playing cricket on the beach and also on the outfield at The Oval, things like that. They are fantastic memories and will always be cherished. We all pull together and I think that's made us a lot stronger as a family."

That family unit was threatened again in early 2012 while Jonny was still in India. "We were warming up and I got a tap on my shoulder from the security guy. He said: 'Your mum's trying to get hold of you'. I thought 'Oh no...' and sprinted to the dressing room. I couldn't get through to mum. I said: 'Tell me what's wrong, I can't get hold of her'. And then the words were uttered: 'Your mum's got cancer again'.

"I was in the middle of Pune, a five-hour drive from Mumbai. I had another five-hour wait at Mumbai airport before flying back to Manchester. I then got stuck in traffic from Manchester to York and arrived at the hospital 20 minutes before mum went into theatre. But I had to come home to look after her."

Thankfully Mum Janet has made a full recovery, was at Lord's when Jonny played his first Test in 2012 against West Indies at Lord's, and she continues to work at Yorkshire CCC. I know only too well that working at Headingley doesn't always mean you see a lot of the cricket played there, but Janet's career has given her a close proximity to her son's career and allowed her to witness many of his finest moments. Both Janet and Becky were in Scarborough when Jonny was awarded his County Cap in July 2011. Another proud family moment as the full bloom White Rose adorned his cap, as it had done his father before him.

The step up to England wasn't always smooth, often two steps forward and then one or two back. A new chapter and a new set of national journalists would question his ability to hold down his place. He was often dismissed in those early international days playing across his front pad and Sky Sports' pundit Bob Willis made himself unpopular in the Broad Acres by suggesting that Jonny "hasn't any sort of defence to play Test cricket", that he "looked like a rabbit in the headlights" and he "can't bat above No 8 in an England Test team in the future".

The former England captain's barbs would have hurt. Jonny responded in the best way possible by getting his head down, working on his game and producing a run of form that has established him as one of the best players in the world. Compare the tight, rigid, almost hunched stance he brought into Test cricket to the tall, raised, free stance he adopted in 2016 and you can see why he has played straighter and with more authority. That transition took dedication. Bairstow junior is certainly no quitter and in that respect he is very much a chip off the old block.

His Test career had begun a little like his early Yorkshire days. After making his debut in 2012 his 95 against South Africa at Lord's in his fourth game had remained his highest score. As he began his 22nd Test against South Africa in Cape Town the hunt for three figures was still ongoing. He had six fifties to his name in 36 innings, but as he had at Trent Bridge for his county, the monkey was flung from his back in dramatic style.

At 223 for five when Jonny joined Ben Stokes in the middle, England's innings against a world-class Proteas attack could have gone horribly wrong. The sixth wicket pair moved along unscathed to 317 for five at the close with Stokes 74 not out and Jonny unbeaten on 39. They'd played well, but there had been little hint of what was to follow the next morning.

Stokes and Bairstow resumed on day two in scintillating style to add 196 runs in the morning session. While Stokes went bananas and completed the second fastest double century in Test history, Jonny was tantalisingly poised on 95 when he chewed on his lunchtime sandwiches. He'd equalled his highest Test score, but was this to be his moment?

In the fourth over after the break he clipped Morne Morkel through backward square for a single to reach his highest Test score. Three overs later van Zyl dropped a bit short outside off-stump and the right-hander rocked back and cut to the fence and let out a raucous 'Yesssss' before raising his bat and eyes to the sky. The gesture was for the two most important men in his life. His grandfather had died a few months earlier and his father 18 years before. They were both very much with him in Cape Town. As were his mother and sister.

"I had a vague idea where they were," he remembered later, "but in that split second everything is a massive roar and pure emotion comes out. So trying to see my mum and sister was a challenge – even if Becky has bright red hair like me. We're like warning beacons but when everyone is standing, clapping, waving and cheering it's difficult.

"They played a massive role," he continued when asked about his gestures skywards. "Dad played (for Yorkshire) for 20 years, and for England, and that's a huge legacy. If I come close to emulating that I'll be happy. Then there's Grandpa. When Dad passed away, Grandpa took on that mantle of teaching me how to tackle at football or taking Mum and me to cricket.

"Lots of people doubted my ability for a long time and so I

thought: 'Right, you can stick that where the sun doesn't shine,'" he added. "'That's for everyone who doubted me. I've just scored a hundred against the number one nation in their own back yard'. There will be many challenges ahead but that one is embedded in my memory."

Janet and Becky gave an emotional interview to Test Match Special commentator Jonathan Agnew during the tea break. Aggers asked about Jonny's poignant celebrations.

"Well that was for Granddad and for Dad, all sorts of different reasons and it was all very emotional," said Janet. And on father and grandfather she added: "They'll be playing cricket upstairs somewhere. Or probably standing by the bar area."

When England declared on 628 for six shortly after Stokes had been run out for 258, Jonny had reached 150 not out. The pair had shared a world Test record partnership for the sixth wicket of 399 runs.

As with the maiden hundred at Trent Bridge, the Cape Town Test ended in a draw, but it wasn't for lack of trying! I remember having a chat with a couple of colleagues after his first Yorkshire century and we all agreed that the floodgates were now well and truly open. The same thought came to me when I watched him batting in Cape Town.

2016 turned into a stellar and record-breaking year. He would better his highest Test score with an unbeaten 167 against Sri Lanka at Lord's the following June to put the memories of falling short in 2012 behind him. Whatever follows his name was on the Honours Board at the Home of Cricket.

He had entered the top ten in the ICC Test Batting Rankings for the first time. His 1,470 Test runs had raced past Andy Flower's 1,045 in 2000 to set a new high for most runs by a Test keeper in a calendar year. Only Michael Vaughan (1,481 in 2002) and Joe Root (1,477 in 2016) had scored more in a calendar year for England. He also set a new record for dismissals by a Test wicket-keeper of 70, beating Ian Healy (1993) and Mark Boucher (1998) who had both dismissed 67 batsmen.

Probably, although he'd not say it, his most satisfying achievement was to have silenced Bob Willis and left egg firmly caked on his face. The debate was over for anyone who ever doubted him.

I'd discussed Jonny with Ryan Sidebottom. The pair had formed a strong bond like their fathers before them. "My Dad and David were great mates on and off the field and I think that's rubbed off on us two," Ryan said. "We sit next to each other in the dressing room. He's a bit of a fiery redhead and I try and give him little bits of advice and help him along.

"He asks me the odd thing, but he's his own person. He

sometimes asks me what he did wrong or what he could have done better. And sometimes he needs to chill out," Ryan added. "We do have chats about our Dads and there was no prouder moment than winning the Championship at Trent Bridge in 2014. His Mum was there and with his Dad's situation it was emotional. To win it having our Dads not having won it and with him now playing for England, I think was wonderful.

"Growing up couldn't have been easy without his Dad," Ryan suggested. "So great credit to him as a young man to have achieved what he's done. And he's ever improving."

I told Ryan that I thought it must be quite hard for both of them to have had the pressures that they face as sons of two well known and much loved characters at Yorkshire.

"I think that's made us both stronger and is maybe why we've made it," Ryan suggested. "You know about our fathers and their careers because people are always saying, 'Your Dad did well' or 'Your Dad was a great player'. Jonny has had that too and you have no option. You can either take a back seat or get out there and think 'right okay, I'm going to show you I can play too'. And that's what Jonny has done.

"Knowing the Yorkshire history and what our fathers have done, now when you walk into the dining room and our Dads are up there in the wall and their careers. It means a lot to be part of that.

"You are just playing," Ryan concluded. "You go out there to try and do well for Yorkshire. You don't always think 'my Dad played and his Dad played' but it will sink in at some point. Whether that will be when Jonny finishes, but people will know the Bairstow name and that he's now etched in history alongside his father's achievements."

Whether it's a natural maturity, or there is an element that he's now outgrown the 'son of David' tagline, Jonny appears more relaxed in interviews and more confident in his own skin. He will always be the son of David and proud of it, but he doesn't need telling who his father was. He knows.

Now he's his own person and I for one wish him well. I've been telling people he's the real deal since I first saw him hit a fifty for Yorkshire Academy back in 2007 and there's a lot more yet to come. I like to be proved right and Bob Willis wrong!

Without doubt he's withstood the pressures that expectation brought and done the Bairstow name proud. If there is a place where David has watched his lad grow into a man, he'll be supping a pint with a justifiably proud look in his face.

* * * * *

And so the initial part of my search for answers had ended. I'd dug further into, and spoken to most of the players and their families that had initially sparked my interest in Canterbury all those years before.

Ryan Sidebottom had admitted to really struggling with the surname when a youngster, Graham Cowdrey had fought an inner struggle with his perception of what had been expected of a Cowdrey for most of his career. His brother Chris had opened with a 'no it was never an issue' remark and then proceeded to tell me how he had completely changed his game to avoid comparisons with his father. Alan Ealham's experience showed how hard being a coach to one's son could be and his son Mark was now using what his dad had experienced to steer his own sons into the game. And Jonny Bairstow, denied a father in the cruellest of circumstances at the age of eight, was finally writing his own headlines after beating the doubters to become a world-class player.

I was chatting to a friend on the subject of sporting fathers and sons and he paused for a moment before saying, "Eidur Gudjohnsen". I recognised the name. I'd seen the Icelandic forward playing for Chelsea many times on Match of the Day. He followed with "Rivaldo". For a moment I wondered if my pal had developed some kind of sporting Tourette's. Just barking out names of random sportsmen in an intelligible basis, but not so, as he explained.

On 24 April 1996, a 17-year-old Eidur Gudjohnsen came on as a second half substitute for Iceland in their 3-0 win over Estonia in Tallinn. The man that he replaced was his 34-year-old father, Arnor. Although they were never on the field together in a professional match, they made football history by being the first father and son pairing to have played in the same international game. They seemed destined to play together in the next match, but Eidur broke his ankle in an Under-18 tournament and missed the next two seasons, during which time Arnor retired.

"It remains my biggest regret that we didn't get to play together," said Arnor, "and I know it is Eidur's too."

Arnor played 73 times for Iceland and scored 14 goals, while Eidur passed his father, who would become his agent and play a key role in a career that saw him play for clubs including Bolton, Chelsea and Barcelona and score a record 26 international goals for his country in 88 caps.

Rivaldo had been capped 74 times by Brazil, scored 35 goals for his country and won the World Cup in 2002, but shortly before his retirement he achieved something remarkable. In the twilight of his glittering career he returned to play for Mogi Mirim in Sao Paulo, the club where it had all begun for him.

In February 2014 he played alongside his son Rivaldhinho, one of his last acts before announcing his retirement a month later. The former Barcelona and AC Milan striker then came out of retirement 15 months later. At the age of 43 he returned to the side in June 2015 and scored in the same match as his 20-year-old son to seal a 3-1 victory over Macae in a Serie B match. Rivaldo had crossed the ball to set up his son's headed goal in the third minute of the game, scored a penalty and also assisted the other goal.

"I have only God to thank," he said, "because after stopping for 15 months I still returned, having the good fortune to start a game alongside my son and score a goal – and he did too. I think we made history. I had heard of father and son playing together, but never of father and son both scoring in a competitive match."

In English football, European Cup winner Ian Bowyer was player-manager of English Fourth Division side Hereford United. He signed up his son Gary who played with him in the team during the 1989/90 season.

"The first time we played together my dad was a sub and we were losing at Scunthorpe," Gary remembered. "He brought himself on and we came back to draw 3-3. I scored the equaliser and, looking back, I think he was the only one who didn't come and congratulate me, because it was my fault for the first goal."

Former Manchester City striker Alec Herd played alongside his son David for Stockport County on the final day of the 1950/51 Third Division North season. David would go on to play for Manchester United, where he would win League and FA Cup medals.

George Eastham's 1966 FIFA World Cup medal will be something he always treasures, despite being a non-playing member of England's squad. A medal he won in 1954 may well hold more emotional significance. Playing for Ards in Northern Ireland's Gold Cup he lifted silverware alongside his father. Aged 18 he lined up alongside George Eastham senior, his 39-year-old father scoring the winning goal in the final.

"My memories are still very strong of the Gold Cup final," he has said. "Surely we are the only father and son to have winners' medals from the same game?"

Russian midfielder Alexei Eremenko senior enjoyed two seasons in the twilight of his career where he shared a dressing room with his son, Alexei Eremenko junior. They played for HJK Helsinki in Finland and won back-to-back Veikkausliiga titles and the 2003 Finnish Cup. Eremenko senior then moved to FF Jaro and played with his second son Roman Eremenko.

"It looks like I can't teach my own sons any other playing role!" Eremenko senior had joked, with both boys continuing their careers in the same position he had played in.

In Sweden, striker Henrik Larsson had played 106 times for his country, but had spent the majority of his successful career at Feyenoord, Celtic and Barcelona. In 2013, in his early 40s, he returned home to play for Hogaborgs BK in his native nation's fourth tier. He played one match alongside his 15-year-old son, Jordan, who scored in the game.

"We didn't combine a whole lot but obviously I'm proud," said Larsson afterwards. "It is of course a rare luxury to get to play with your son."

If football had these examples I wondered whether cricket, the game I had already decided had more than its fair share of family ties, did too.

I began to investigate further.

CHAPTER FIVE

DARREN and JAKE LEHMANN
DAVID and GRAHAM LLOYD
MICKY and ALEC STEWART

"Other things may change us but we start and end with family"
Anthony Brandt

It was mid-November 2016 and the Darren Lehmann-coached Australian side had lost the second Test against South Africa by an innings. They'd been a paltry 85 all out on day one. The home nation's press described them as the 'Worst XI Ever' as they furiously sharpened their knives. Heads were going to roll.

As the media speculated on the potential for fresh faces, Lehmann's son Jake was mentioned. He'd begun the Sheffield Shield campaign well with South Australia and it was a legitimate question – 'would Jake Lehmann be considered for the dead rubber third Test?'

"I don't sit in on anything when they talk about Jake," Lehmann responded. "I don't sit on the panel and I don't know what they're saying about Jake."

And if Jake were to be selected? "I'm not involved and I'd be that nervous anyway I probably wouldn't be coach. I'd actually just go to the bar."

That final line was delivered with a mischievous grin. Lehmann senior had a reputation for liking a beer and a cigarette. But he could hit a cricket ball, as his 27 Tests and 117 ODIs for Australia testify. His 25,628 career first-class runs at 57.59, mostly for South Australia and Yorkshire, established him as one of the all-time greats. He remains the record run-scorer in the Sheffield Shield.

Those final lines to the media were seen as funny. 'Aussie coach to watch son from bar,' 'Son to drive coach to drink' ran the headlines.

So what surprised me, when I spoke to Jake Lehmann two months later, was his Dad had not been joking. The line may have been delivered with a twinkle in the eye but, if Jake were ever to play for Australia, there actually was every chance that Darren would step down as national coach.

"That's one thing that we have spoken about," Jake told me when I asked whether it would be strange to play for Australia with his father as coach. "I think a lot of people get perceptions, but sometimes it's harder to have the old man in a role like that.

"He doesn't want to be the one that makes the call on me. He wants other people to do it. Once again I think that's just a dad being a dad. He's always been like that – *make your own way and if you're good enough, you're good enough.*

"If it came to that, I don't think we'd be in the same side as each other," Jake continued. "It would be very strange. I think it would be a very hard concept to figure out dad versus player. I don't think either of us would like to be in that situation.

"We're just trying to make it clear that I'm playing cricket because I love cricket and I'm making my own way. It's not about doing it by yourself, but earning your own stripes and he's very supportive that way."

When I had finished the interview with Jake I grabbed a coffee. I'd spoken to him early evening Adelaide time so it was still the crack of dawn in the UK. I sat down, played my recording and began to transcribe his quotes. When I got to the paragraphs you've just read I rewound the audio and listened again.

Was Jake saying his dad would resign as Australia's head coach if he were ever selected to play for the national team? That could be next week, month, year, or never, but even so, that was quite some admission.

Was it a father prepared to sacrifice his country's top job to give his son a fair crack or was it a father unable to separate family from work? I also wondered whether Darren's departure could have the reverse effect and increase the media spotlight on his boy. From whichever way I looked at it, this was huge.

During my chat with Jake I'd not taken it all in. Instead I'd told him of my interview I'd carried out with Alec Stewart the previous day and suggested a father and son sharing an international dressing room had worked before.

"I guess if it works and everything goes well then it's fine," Jake said unconvinced. "I don't know if you asked Alec Stewart if he could go back and have the opportunity for his dad not to have been the coach, then I don't know if he would have liked that or not. But that's the way we look at it."

I didn't tell Jake that Alec Stewart appeared to be the only person I'd spoken to so far completely immune to suggestions that a father as a coach presented challenges. I didn't need to ask Jake's question as I had a good idea what Alec's answer would have been.

While I appreciate Michael Parkinson never reappeared on your television set an hour after the credits had rolled to submit his guests to questions that had entered his head after the show, I messaged Jake asking for confirmation. 'Were you saying your dad would step down as coach if you ever got picked?'

Jake responded: "Yeah I think he would think about it! But who really knows until something actually happens."

There was a decent chance Jake would follow Darren into Australian colours, every likelihood the family name would become the fourth added to a small list of multi-generational families that have represented Australia at international level.

Before I went back to the Lehmanns I turned back to my Alec Stewart interview to remind myself how black and white he had seen this father and son subject.

* * * * *

I'd never met Alec, but had seen him play on many occasions. It would have been difficult to miss him as he played a record 133 Tests for England, until passed in 2016 by Alastair Cook. His influence on England's international fortunes had been enormous. It was impossible not to respect the man and player.

My perception was that he knew his own mind, was hard working, diligent, determined and regimented in his approach to the game. Renowned for being tidy, his gear neatly sorted into OCD boutique store piles, exaggerated next to the jumble sale approach that was Mike Atherton. Was Alec's life like that? So often the reverse can be true. Outward appearances of order can hide mayhem and confusion elsewhere.

But I found the man, dubbed 'Peter Perfect' by his England team-mates after a 26-hour flight to New Zealand saw him disembark with nothing out of place while the rest of the squad were tired and dishevelled, to have had a very black and white approach to his life.

"I signed pro forms here at Surrey at The Oval when Dad was the manager and when I made my England debut he was the manager," Alec began. "It's not a pub side or club side where you might pick your son, brother or a relative. You are picked on ability. Whatever the outside world may interpret, in the hard professional game you are picked because you are good enough, or not picked because you are not good enough.

"No player I ever played with ever said 'you are only playing because of'. It was very clear," Alec added. "Professional sport is not about doing people favours, it's hard work. If you get selected you have earned that right and if you get dropped you've got to go away, work hard and get back in the team. So, from my point-of-view, it never affected me or bothered me at all.

"I didn't have a father at work, which people find strange," he stated. "I don't know what others have said, but I never felt I had a dad in that dressing room. He was the coach. I think Dad would say that he treated me the same as everyone else, but he may have been a little bit tougher on decisions about me. I'd rather have had it that way than been gifted things too easily."

Alec's father, Micky, was a Surrey stalwart. A one-club man, he played 530 first-class matches scoring 26,491 runs at 32.90 in a 19-year career as an opening batsman. His, and Alec's life could have been very different had he accepted a contract offered by Kent upon completion of his national service. Instead he signed for Surrey and the Stewarts have been synonymous with the South London county ever since.

Micky made his first-class debut in 1954 scoring 109 against the Pakistan tourists in his second game. He never looked back. He brought tremendous fielding into a Surrey side dominating county cricket at the time and took a world record seven catches against Northamptonshire in his debut season.

He was aged almost 30 when he finally got to play Test cricket against Pakistan in 1962, playing eight Tests before illness forced his early return from the winter tour of India in 1963/4. He was never recalled despite having scored 385 runs at a respectable 35 with a highest score of 87.

He was appointed Surrey captain in 1963 and continued in the role until his retirement in 1972, winning the County Championship in 1971. In 1979 he became Surrey's cricket manager, just as Alec was coming through into the professional ranks, and in 1986 he became England manager for the tour of Australia and continued in the position until 1992. He then worked for the ECB until his retirement in 1997. Alec's Surrey debut came in 1981, two years after his father had taken charge. Three years after Micky had taken over at England, Alec made his international bow.

"There were five or six other counties interested in signing me, but I only ever wanted to play county cricket for Surrey," Alec answered when I wondered if he'd ever considered taking the pressure off by playing elsewhere. "We spoke about it and both agreed that when we were at work I am the player and he's the manager and when I'm at home I'll have a Dad. At work he was the boss, coach, whatever you want to call him. He picked the side. He picked me fairly and dropped me unfairly (laughs) and that was just how it was."

Did he ever feel any added internal pressure to perform because of the surname? Wouldn't it have been simpler and easier to seek a different profession?

"No, because from a young age I wanted to play professional sport. I'll be honest, I'd have rather played professional football up to the age of 14, but then cricket took over."

Micky had played inside-left for Charlton Athletic, Wimbledon and Corinthian Casuals. No surprise then that Alec, a lifelong Chelsea supporter, had his sights as much on a football as a cricket ball. You get the feeling that whatever Alec set his mind to he could achieve. He's intensely driven. I wondered whether the pressure he exerted on himself to be the very best version of himself possible could have seen him respond badly to the odd and inevitable failures all sportsmen experience.

"I'm pretty single-minded and I set my sights on trying to achieve," he agreed. "The extra pressure? I believe pressure is what you put on yourself. I set myself high standards and always did and am probably renowned as someone that worked hard, trained hard and prepared well.

"Was that inbred or drilled into me at home? It was probably a combination of both," he determined. "There wasn't a pressure of *I'm Micky Stewart's son*. I say to him now, he's *Alec Stewart's Dad!*

"That's just how it was," he said. "I just had big personal pride in trying to be the best I could be, while trying to ensure that I made strong contributions to the teams I played for."

Most journalists will tell you that their best interviews are the ones where your subject tells you something over and above, adds extra colour or is a little unguarded, thereby providing extra ingredients to stir into the final piece. Alec played my interview like I was a medium paced trundler in a local park, with a straight bat, occasionally knocking me to the fence. He'd dealt with it all before and it had never bothered him. And I'd no problem with that at all. He was saying it as he saw it.

I thought back to my chat with sports psychologist Simon Hartley. *Some will see it as an issue and some will just see it as part of their life and get on with it.* Alec was most definitely the latter and he'd got on with it rather well.

8,463 runs in 133 Tests. He'd worked hard to make himself into a world-class all-rounder with bat and gloves. He'd taken 263 Test catches, made 14 Test stumpings, played 170 ODIs, scored 26,165 first-class runs, added 14,771 more in one-day games and been awarded an OBE. He was made England captain in 1998 before losing the job after a disappointing 1999 World Cup.

The son passed the father in most statistics, but the eagle-eyed will have spotted that Micky's first-class run tally exceeded his son's by 325. Whereas some of the people I would talk to would have made comment on that, I'd wager neither Micky nor Alec had even noticed.

The only semblance of any competitiveness between the two

Stewart generations came in a quote Alec gave after picking up his OBE in 2003.

"The great thing is that I've now managed to catch up with my dad because he was awarded the OBE a good few years ago," he had said.

Honours were even. It simply appears that Alec loved, admired and respected his father and it was reciprocated. Alec had followed his father's path every step of the way, knew what he had to do, had the mentality to cope, and the wherewithal to become one of the best cricketers England has ever produced.

* * * * *

Jake had already followed his father into the South Australia and Yorkshire sides, but in December 2016 Darren would have to find another reason to go to the bar. Jake wasn't selected by Australia and would have to wait a bit longer for his Baggy Green. Lehmanns are used to waiting.

It was 11-years-and-three-months after Darren's first-class debut as a 17-year-old that he finally got the Test nod when he played in the third Test against India in Bangalore in March 1998.

At the time of his selection, he set a record for playing the most first-class games before playing Test cricket, since beaten by Michael Hussey. He still has the distinction of scoring the most runs in Sheffield Shield cricket before Australia finally came calling.

He had to wait for his maiden hundred too. It came against West Indies at Port-of-Spain in his tenth Test, and then two came against Bangladesh and two more against Sri Lanka in the next 12 months.

Although more than useful in Test cricket, he was viewed as a more integral part of Australia's one-day unit, hitting the winning runs in the 1999 World Cup Final at Lord's and being part of the side that defended the title in 2003.

He'd had to wait a year after his December 1987 debut to play his second match and a season more before he hit his first century, going big for 228 against New South Wales. He made a hundred against the touring New Zealanders and then hit centuries in three consecutive Shield games. He was up and running, although his call-ups to the national side saw him not getting past 12th man duties.

He moved to Victoria to further his international aspirations, won his first Shield with them in 1990/91, before returning home to South Australia. His other Shield success came in 1995/96 and he was key to Yorkshire's success in the 2001 County

Championship. He finished his first-class career as the highest run scorer in Sheffield Shield and Pura Cup history, with 13,635 runs at 54.97.

Lehmann senior was a throwback to a bygone era before fitness coaches and dieticians, hill runs and bleep tests. The modern game's emphasis on strength, conditioning and speed in the field are as important to some as weight of runs. The Australian coach between 1986 and 1996 was Bobby Simpson, an advocate of building a team of athletes. Lehmann needed a bigger mould, but in previous eras would certainly have accrued many more Test caps.

Despite his rotund appearance his prowess with the bat was a joy to behold. When people talk about the elite batsmen having more time to play the ball, Lehmann immediately comes to my mind. I remember sitting on the point boundary at Headingley, watching this combative man with the daintiest of feet dance back on his toes and choose gaps at will to power, punch and finesse away any calibre of bowler.

He was a magician and I loved watching him as much as his team-mates enjoyed playing with him. A quick and easy filler in my match programmes when working at Yorkshire was to write a page of 'quick questions' I'd ask to members of the current team. I could fill in the 'best player played with' answers in advance. It was always Darren Lehmann. He was able to be many things to his team-mates – their mate, mentor, father figure and friend. He gained others' respect and provided the perfect grounding for the human side of coaching.

When Chris Lynn had sustained an injury, Lehmann's advice helped him through a tough period. Lynn told the *Sydney Morning Herald* how Lehmann had "really brought home to me that cricket's not the end of the world, that at the end of the day it is just a game. So when you're lucky enough to be out there, you should enjoy it. He said that if life is good, it will be good out on the field. After all, you start playing the game because you love it, and he really reminded me of that."

Speak to Jake and it becomes obvious this is Lehmann senior's mantra. That cricket, indeed life, is to be enjoyed. "Never forget why you first started playing this game," he'd always told his son.

That message had been reinforced when Darren's mentor, former Australian left-hander David Hookes died aged only 48 in 2004. As his great friend left him he squeezed his hand and "realised cricket was a game and life was more important. It changed my attitude," he recalled.

Lehmann had already had a good grounding. After leaving school he'd worked in a car manufacturing plant where temperatures regularly rose to 50 degrees Celsius. It was a constant reminder that he was in a fortunate position as an aspiring professional cricketer. He told *Adelaide Now* that his AUD 250 per week job "was a great experience though, a young kid working with men and how they had totally different lives. To grow up, learn about their lives and how I should act in the modern world. I really enjoyed my time there and loved those people. If you made a duck they would really give you a ribbing. If you made a hundred they said nothing. It was only if you failed that they said something."

It was his enjoyment of factory life he gave as a reason for turning down a place of the first intake to the newly formed Australian Cricket Academy after his mother had completed the application forms. In 2013 he became Australian coach, at the start of an Ashes tour with the team in disarray. He soon galvanised his team and, despite losing the Test series 3-0, the side quickly got back to winning ways.

* * * * *

Lehmann senior has prior form for being a genuinely unselfish team man. After Michael Clarke made his debut hundred in Bangalore, Lehmann offered to step aside, before injury forced him out later in the series. A poor return against Pakistan and his Test career was complete.

Known for being uncomplicated, he took no prisoners, made friends quickly and didn't stand on ceremony. A cynic would argue that he saw the writing on the wall and only offered the youngster his place before it was taken from him. An admirer would see Lehmann as uncomplicated and not in Test cricket for an ego boost.

In the same way he was happy to be sidelined for emerging talent, he also seems prepared to step down as head coach of his country to allow his son room to blossom in an international dressing room.

If people are expecting son Jake to be a chip off the old block, he has a lot to live up to. He's made a good start, also turning his maiden first-class hundred into a double century. He hit the first ball he received in the Big Bash for six when Adelaide Strikers needed four from the final delivery to beat Hobart Hurricanes and he'd followed his old man halfway around the world to play for Yorkshire. An average in the mid-forties in first-class cricket so far suggests he has what it takes to step up to the international arena.

Talk to Jake and it's as if he's been groomed and prepared for the life of a professional cricketer from the cradle.

"I've grown up with cricket my whole life," Jake told me. "There are young photos of myself holding a cricket bat and swinging golf clubs. In Australia, the first thing you play is MILO in2cricket [the junior game] with plastic bats and from there I've always loved the game."

That love was further fuelled by having a father who inspired him to play. Imagine being a youngster where the doors to the dressing rooms housing your heroes were often open.

"The cool things that you do, like going into the changing rooms, when they play home games and that kind of thing – that probably sticks in my memory the most," Jake said. "The South Australia changing room was awesome with the likes of Jason Gillespie, Graham Manou and all these blokes rolling around and playing cricket out the back with a tennis ball at the Adelaide Oval was always good fun.

"And the Aussie changing rooms, probably the biggest memory was the Boxing Day Test with the old man at the MCG," he remembered. "There was a rain delay in the Test Match and I'd just got a brand new bat from Father Christmas, I thought it was him at the time anyway," he laughed before continuing, "Michael Clarke, Brett Lee and Shane Warne were all bowling to me down in the changing rooms at the MCG and I thought I was the king of the world. That was special."

"I guess cricket's such a stats based game that everyone looks at them and you can't hide anywhere," he suggested. "27 Test matches, 400-plus first-class games with an average of 56 – those numbers are unbelievable. Include 100-plus one-dayers for Australia. There's a long way to go for me," he added in a wry tone, "but stats are stats and it's good fun.

"I think there's a couple of stats that come up and in Australia he's such a big icon and leading run scorer for South Australia and everyone speaks about him so you get to hear them a lot. I quite like my stats – both our first-class hundreds were double hundreds and if I get half as good stats as him I'm probably going to have a decent career."

Like his father, Jake converted his maiden first-class century into a double ton – further fuel to those suggesting he was shaping up to play at the highest level.

"After I made the double Dad text me and was kind of proud."

The Yorkshire Post cricket correspondent, Chris Waters, when he first saw Jake playing at Headingley in 2016 remarked that he felt a little strange watching him as it was like watching Darren. The body language, to him, seemed exactly the same. A number of people have suggested they are similar with bat in hand too.

"Being left-handed I like to cut the ball, play through the off-side, but that's a natural thing for most left-handers with the ball going across you most of the time. People say they see a resemblance in the cut shot or the cover drive and the way we play. But I think that's just typical left-handers.

"I think we've got some similar traits. I think we both are pretty relaxed and go with the flow. We take each moment as it is and are pretty straightforward so you could say we are similar.

"I've watched some highlights of Dad and when I was a bit younger I'd go and watch him play, but I don't think you take too much from that really. I don't think any two players are the same. You take a little bit from here and there and do that without even recognising it.

"The old man to me is just the old man. We speak about a lot of other stuff. He still sends me messages sledging me about me getting out to him or whatever, but he was more of a mentor and a father figure role than anything. We're just a dad and a son and we're just mates."

Just because your father has achieved success there is no God-given right handed down to the son. I asked Jake when he realised that playing cricket for a living was a genuine option as a profession.

"I was playing in under age representative sides and I went away from the game for a couple of years as I didn't play so well. Then, all of a sudden, I started banging them again and thought I had a chance again. So it's been a bit up and down and I think I always wanted to play cricket professionally and you always think you can, but you don't really know when you are going to get your chance."

Jake's chance came to debut for South Australia in March 2016 against Victoria. His father, in the middle of coaching Australia in their successful World Cup campaign, immediately hopped on a plane.

"I didn't know that he was coming and the flight was delayed so he had to get another flight and go to Melbourne and then back to Adelaide, so it was quite a journey for him and he rang me and said that he'd do his best to get there and he'd really love to do it and stuff like that," Jake recalled.

Darren flew 3,000 kilometres after a flight had been delayed and he missed a connection.

Jake resumed the tale: "Eventually he rocked up about half-an-hour before the cap presentation. If he gave a cap to anyone I think it would be a great honour for them, but to get your cap from someone you love and idolise and is in the family is awesome. I've never seen him speechless, but it was one time when he didn't have much to say and he was just a proud dad. Cricket didn't really come into it, nor did the match outcome or how well I did. He was just a dad being proud."

Darren remained in Adelaide for the first day's play, but had to return to his day job before Jake scored a half-century in his debut innings on day two.

"He was on the road with the Aussies so he literally flew in for one day and was with me the whole day," Jake stated. "Every time I'm playing I'm sure he's watching on the live stream, watching on TV and on the videos and he's always got a close eye on how I'm doing."

Despite Darren's career taking him away a lot, the two have remained incredibly close. The weight of expectation that inevitably falls on the son is something Jake seems comfortable with too.

"Some people are going to be really supportive and others might be a bit more on the other side, but I think going back to stats, they don't lie," Jake remarked. "So you can listen to who you want to listen to but I think overall in first-class cricket it's been quite positive towards myself. When you are getting runs no one can really sledge you too much.

"You have to remember and realise that the old man was one of the very best in first-class cricket and he's played for Australia. If I keep doing what I'm doing and be half as good as him hopefully I can have a good career.

"He was away a lot when I was young, but when we were at home we were always mucking around and having fun. And that's what cricket is to us. I think he'd say the same thing. It's all about enjoyment. You start playing the game because you enjoy it. There are always hints and tips as you play together and I think that's like any dad and any player, but the be-all-and-end-all is that we love the game. That's the biggest thing he says to me, 'Don't ever forget why you started playing the game'."

Jake remembered his time at Yorkshire fondly and if the schedules and stars align is hopeful he can return to Headingley again in the future. Who knows, it may be beneath a Baggy Green cap that he next walks out to play there. For a youngster, starting out in a game where the Twenty20 format is increasingly spoken about in the same hushed tones as Test match cricket, it would be easy to pursue the riches on offer in the game's shortest format. Refreshingly, Jake has a traditional outlook on his future ambitions.

"I reckon if you ask any young cricketer in the world, whether here, India, England or anywhere, you want to play Test cricket for your country and if the opportunity came up to play for Australia it would just be a childhood dream.

"You grow up loving the game and the goal is always to play for Australia and a lot of people don't get to do it. I think there have been only 450 that have so far played for Australia, so that's a very small percentage of the nation and it would be a great honour.

"I'd still say Test cricket is the pinnacle for the majority of players playing first-class cricket right now. Everyone wants that Baggy Green. It doesn't mean you don't want to play one-dayers or T20 cricket because that is a great honour too and it's very enjoyable cricket, but I guess the Baggy Green means that you've played and dominated first-class cricket in Australia and that's the strongest competition."

* * * * *

The possibility that Darren Lehmann might step down as head coach with Australia if Jake were selected for his country is in stark contrast to the attitude of Alec Stewart and also David and Graham Lloyd.

There have been 13 fathers and sons who have both played Test cricket for England. The Lloyds are a pairing often left off the list, with David, now a hugely popular television pundit, playing nine Tests and 8 ODIs for his country in the 1970s, followed by son Graham, who played six ODIs between 1996 and 1998. When Graham played for England his father was the head coach.

David, aka Bumble because his hyperactive character always saw him buzzing around cricket grounds, doesn't switch off. I telephoned him as he was arriving back at his house with his dogs after a session at his local gym – more of that in a few paragraphs time!

"I was Graham's coach at Lancashire and with England," David replied. "With England I worked with Micky Stewart and learned from how he was with Alec and got a good idea of how to tackle it. So we never had any problems."

When I phoned Graham, a man with his father's humour, but expressed in a wrier and laidback way, I asked him whether it had been different or strange to enter an England dressing room for the first time when his dad had been the boss?

"No, not really," Graham responded. "He's always been a big influence in the game. He's been going 50-odd years in cricket and he's got to the top at everything he's done, whether it's playing, coaching, TV or umpiring, although he never umpired a Test match.

"It didn't phase me at all that he was there, he was coach with England when I got selected to play and I just saw him in that dressing room environment as coach at that time and nothing else. Of course it's different when you're at home or away from the game and he comes back to being your dad."

I soon found with Bumble that a question was merely a cue for an anecdote. He had me in fits of laughter at times during the call. He has three sons and proceeded to tell me how they either took to cricket or they didn't.

"One of them was ok, he was pretty good, but he couldn't hack, for want of a better word, sledging on the field. As a 14-year-old they were talking about his dad and his brother and he just packed in playing. He didn't want to know.

"My third son never showed any interest in the game," Bumble continued. "And I was totally fine with that. I never put any pressure on any of them to play. He's a gardener these days. He likes sport but not necessarily playing. He likes to go out mountain biking, gets all the gear and that's his fun.

"And my lad that packed in, he's now World Heavyweight Amateur Bodybuilding champion."

For a brief moment I wondered if Bumble was joking. Whether he was throwing me a curve ball, but absolutely not. His son Ben, a 32-year-old personal trainer, had gone along to support some friends in a bodybuilding competition in March 2016 and thought he could beat them.

"He's very driven," Bumble told me. "There's a season for bodybuilding and Ben will have some time off and eat what he likes. During that period you'd walk past him in the street and not think twice, but when he gets in training he is completely focussed. He puts himself through the mill and is really disciplined. In the off-season he puts on a couple of stone and is happy as Larry, but when he's trained every muscle is there really clearly on him.

"So focussed that when he entered the North West final in Manchester in August he won. That took him to the British novice event in Perth, Scotland a few weeks later where he won again. So, in October 2016 he was on a plane to Miami and became the Drug-Free Athletics Coalition (DFAC) world champion.

"You get a lot of bodybuilders taking steroids and things, but they compete in different events," Bumble explained. "Ben competes in the DFAC events and it's all drug free. You don't just turn up and say you don't take anything. They do lie detector tests and urine tests all the way through."

Ben now has the 69-year-old Bumble on a strict diet and has suggested he train for an over 70s event. The former cricketer, umpire and coach has never been one to duck a challenge.

"I'm training hard now, but not in the best shape, so I probably won't enter this time, but will in the future," Bumble said. "I'm eating porridge, white fish and sweet potatoes and changed my diet. I've cut down on the beer and feel much fitter."

I went online and entered 'David Lloyd bodybuilding' into

Google and found some photographs of him not looking out of place alongside his incredibly muscular son. Bumble describes Ben as a "bit of a loner" who "likes his own company and loves being in the gym where it's just him."

Ben told the *Daily Mail*, "For me it's almost a fear of failure that's driven me. I've come from a family of high achievers. I always thought I needed to do well at something."

When I read that I immediately thought of Eric Douglas. Ben spoke about playing cricket: "You'd get a little bit of negativity on the cricket pitch, like 'You're not as good as your dad' and I just let it get to me. I should've been a bit stronger. I wasn't ever much good in a team environment in sports, but in the gym it's more you against you."

Bumble recalls how Ben never liked his family watching him play cricket and bans him from watching him in bodybuilding competitions even now. But Ben appears to have followed a piece of advice his father gave him a few years ago. He told him: "There's a lot of people in the world who are 'gunnas' – I'm gunna do this or I'm gunna do that, but they never do anything. Don't be a gunna, be a doer instead."

As Ben fulfils a need to achieve and a place he can sit comfortably within the Lloyd family the conversation returns to Graham. Whereas Ben struggled to deal with the sledgers as a youth cricketer, it was water off a duck's back to his brother. It was easy for me to see why Bumble describes Graham as "so laidback".

"It's just a game isn't it at the end of the day," Graham stated. "Grown men thinking they can find an edge and get a reaction. But it never bothered me and it soon went away because they knew it wasn't getting through. I wasn't interested at all.

"It didn't affect me. I think it probably did happen as I continued into the county stuff, but it never bothered me. It was very rare but it was no issue."

I asked Bumble whether he thought that cricket was in the genes. Had he handed Graham something special in his blood that made him become an international too? Or was it, that like Jake Lehmann, he'd been exposed to the game from such an early age?

"He was very natural," Bumble replied. "It just came to him, he watched, he copied and I couldn't teach him anything. He just got on with it.

"For Graham, you just said the word 'exposure,' and that was it with him," Bumble assessed. "He got dragged around cricket because of me from a young age and was immersed in the game. As a player my business was from home and there'd be bats and pads lying around and he'd pick them up and copy what he'd been watching. He'd come in the dressing rooms and spend time watching the elite players, being around them and watching them play."

Graham added: "I used to go and watch him from the age of six or seven at Old Trafford, saw him playing in the nets, and just sat there and soaked it all in. I think it's one of the best ways of learning, to copy others. He did coach me a little bit as well as other coaches along the way through junior stuff. I was coached all the way through the county age groups and he did do a bit too, mainly practice really. As I was growing up he had plenty to say.

"As a youngster I probably had a chat with Dad and he probably would have given me advice," Graham continued. "It would have been along the lines of *you need to work hard and practise hard* and *don't take your eye off the ball as you are growing up*. And *if you get in make it count*. Because he was a pro and that was what was being told to him by the coaches and professionals. It was good advice coming down to a young lad."

While everyone seems to see comparisons in the games of Darren and Jake Lehmann, Bumble is quick to highlight the differences between him and Graham. As Ben was quiet and introverted, Graham is relaxed and laconic, while their father is a more manic, social dynamo. But on the cricket field the roles David and Graham played were somewhat reversed.

"I was a careful player, but Graham was carefree," Bumble conceded. "He won the Walter Lawrence Trophy for hitting the fastest hundred in a season twice. He was a real dasher, a modern player and really quick between the wickets.

"It's funny," he added. "Michael Atherton's lad is completely different to him. You know what Athers played like, he would bat and bat and refuse to give anything away. His lad reverse sweeps, reverse hooks, dances down the track, plays every shot and Athers just watches and laughs. His lad Josh is outstanding in his age group, probably the best in the country, but he plays so differently to his dad."

Graham remembers being like brother Ben when it came to his dad watching him play. And when he did take a peek, Bumble was a bag of nerves.

"It makes me chuckle," Bumble stated. "You get pushy parents who are desperate for their sons to succeed, but what I always say is that if they are good enough to play at the highest level they will come through. If he goes out and scores a double hundred it's him that got it, not you.

"Graham played a game for Lancashire Boys and I've never been so nervous in my life," Bumble laughed. "At Under-15 level you want them all to do well, young kids coming to play their first game at Old Trafford. You don't want to see any of them get out for nought. But when Graham went into bat I was pacing around, hiding behind the curtains in the pavilion and asked the barman for a double brandy."

Graham responded: "I didn't really want him watching for some reason, although we did play for Accrington together from me being 14 or 15. He's a bad watcher and I think I'm the same now with my boys. It's agony watching. You want them to do so well."

As Graham grew up in a household where dad regularly took him around cricket grounds that exposure that Bumble had spoken about was intense and massively important to his son's development.

"I realise now how important that was and how lucky I was to have that leg-up, to be in that environment," Graham reflected. "It was what I wanted to do from the age of nine and I feel very lucky and privileged to have had that kick-start."

How much of an incentive was it having a father who played professionally? Was he the hero and inspiration to a young Graham?

"Yes, certainly," Graham shot back without hesitation, before adding another "certainly" by means of underlining his answer. "I was proud of watching him and I'd sit and watch him when he scored runs for Lancashire and I used to get upset when he used to get out. So I thought he was a proud role model and a great dad."

If Bumble was fraught watching his young son playing those early matches, how did he cope when his boy was selected for England and walked into the dressing room to play his first ODI?

"I'd lost the nerves by then," he replied matter-of-factly. "When they are kids you are willing them on and wanting them to do well. There comes a time when they are on their own and have to stand on their own two feet."

Graham agreed: "If I wasn't married or having a family I wasn't far off that stage. He was the coach and I was another player. I was certainly conscious of that because you'd hate it to be any other way. You have to keep it professional."

Could it work too much the other way? Could there be a temptation for the coach to make his son work harder in front of the rest of the squad to prove there was no favouritism?

"I can see the merit in that," Graham replied. "It's a natural reaction. If he did, I don't know. It wasn't an issue for me, we kept it professional in the Lancashire dressing room and the same during my brief spell with England."

Graham clearly had talent from an early age and something about him that belied his youth. His father was shocked when he decided to go and play a winter overseas.

"He was only 16," Bumble crowed. "At 16 he cleared off to Australia and played Grade cricket. Rod Tucker the umpire said 'Bumble I like the look of your lad I'm going to take him to Australia for the winter.' We just thought *blimey, he's only 16.* I hadn't been out of the country when I went away with England for the first time.

"But Graham was so natural," Bumble reiterated. "He went on an England A trip and Norman Gifford the manager rang me and said, 'He doesn't do enough. He's the fittest and fastest but in any work we do he's always at the back'. I asked Norman what he wanted me to do about it from miles away. In the end Norman told Graham that he needed him to set an example for the others and lead from the front. Graham took a moment to think before replying, "Look Norm, I know I may not get to do this again, come out here and so I want to stand at the back, soak it all up and take it all in."

Was Graham too laidback? I asked him about that England A trip.

"I suppose I might have been in those early days," Graham conceded. "It was amazing really, to be playing cricket as a job. I think I needed to grow up a bit from those early days.

"Then a bit later there was a risk of cricket not being a job much longer and getting sacked became a possibility. I really knuckled down and they were probably my best years."

Playing club matches together for Accrington the Lloyds shared partnerships as Graham was learning his trade. Bumble referred back to his son's ability to ignore the wisecracks and concentrate on his game.

"They could see he was good," Bumble said proudly. "They couldn't make a difference to him. Graham wouldn't get any shit on the pitch when he was playing for Accrington because he was too busy scoring runs and they'd be fetching the ball.

"There was one day when I was batting with him that he got smacked in the face by a ball and was down and absolutely out of it. He spent the night in hospital and was back playing the next day. Just got on with it and took it in his stride."

Graham remembered. Hard to forget I imagined.

"I've still got the scar from it," Graham agreed. "The advice he gave me then was as good as he ever gave me – *don't dwell on being struck by the ball, just get back out there as soon as possible, with a helmet on!*

"You could easily get a bit gun-shy or scared. So, I was back playing the next day."

But even as his son lay prone waiting for an ambulance, Bumble was conscious of their father and son relationship in a man's environment where weakness could be exploited. He remained rooted at the non-striker's end, hoping his lad would be okay, but determined not to rush down the pitch like a worried dad.

Graham chuckled: "Yes, I can see him doing that. I didn't know much about it as I was in a bit of a heap on the floor. I should have had a helmet on. I wore one after that."

I relayed the facts on fathers and sons in English cricket to Graham. The 13 pairings in Tests and just the Lloyds as Test and ODI father and sons - it's a proud boast surely?

"It is," Graham admitted. "I'm certainly very proud to have played for Lancashire and England, as I'm sure my Dad is. It is a rare thing, but if your father plays, even if he plays league cricket, you probably follow on. My boys play for Accrington. It's just an introduction and I was lucky enough to go quite a long way in cricket and make it a living for a while."

Having Bumble as a father hasn't come without its pitfalls though. Bumble told me a story. Graham had said to him that he was getting fed up with people coming up to him and, rather than ask about him, they'd always start by asking how his dad was. One day he decided to respond differently.

Man:	How's your Dad?
Graham:	Haven't you heard?
Man:	Heard what?
Graham:	He fell in the freezer at home.
Man:	What? He fell in the freezer?
Graham:	Yes. He was leaning in to get some peas out for tea.
Man:	Peas?
Graham:	Yes, for tea. And he over-balanced and fell in.
Man:	He fell in?
Graham:	The freezer door shut behind him and he couldn't get out.
Man:	He couldn't get out?
Graham:	No. Over-stretched and fell in. The door shut. He got trapped.
Man:	He got trapped?
Graham:	Yes, he reached for the peas and the door shut and he's dead.
Man:	Dead?
Graham:	Yes, he's dead.
Man:	My God. That's terrible. What did you do?
Graham:	We had to make do with carrots for tea!

Bumble added: "He's as laidback as they come is Graham, but he's a very funny lad."

Graham laughed when I mentioned the peas story.

"It's true," Graham giggled. "It was a starter of conversations I suppose. People's ice-breaker was always 'how's your dad?' and if I'd heard it once I must have heard it ten thousand times, so I tried different approaches back and that might have been one of them."

Perhaps I should have given Jake Lehmann Bumble's telephone number for when the international call-up comes. It might not help the Lehmanns conquer their fears about making the coach/son dynamic work in Australian cricket, but he'd have fun hearing the advice.

CHAPTER SIX

EVERYONE HAS A FATHER AND A STORY

"First your parents, they give you life, but then they try to give you their life"
Chuck Palahniuk

After delving around amongst cricket's fathers and sons I began to think of my relationship with my own father. Where had my passion for sport, cricket in particular, come from?

I know a lot of people would say the same, but my Dad actually is the best. Like most of us, I've not told him that enough. He's not a loud man, he doesn't walk into a room and command attention, he is warm and caring and he likes a smile. If you can find anyone to say a bad word about him I'd imagine you would have had a very long search and I'd question the person's sanity. I'd like to think some of his good points rubbed off on me somehow.

My Dad wasn't particularly sporty. We enjoyed the odd round of golf together when I was young, tennis too on the school courts in the summer holidays, he'd take me to the cricket at Trent Bridge or Scarborough, and he can always hold his own in a conversation about the latest Test. But there are probably a lot of fathers that did as much, or more, and their offspring weren't as obsessed with sport as I became.

At school I was always quite good at cricket without ever being exceptional. The school playing fields were directly behind our home. When I was 14 we played a match on the school's second pitch, while the 1st XI did battle on the main square.

We bowled our opposition out for 16 that afternoon. My new ball opening partner, or rather old ball shined up and re-used opening partner Richard took 4-8 and I finished with 6-8. I remember fielding at fine leg having just taken my fifth wicket, outwardly urging Richard on to take his five-for, while inwardly hoping I'd get another chance to take my sixth. I did. When we batted I ended on eight not out as we completed the easiest of victories by 10 wickets.

Throughout I'd noticed a figure at a window on the upstairs

landing of our house. My Dad was watching the game through binoculars. I had always wanted my parents to stay away when I played. I don't think I wanted to disappoint them by playing badly when they knew how important it all was to me. I was chuffed to bits he'd seen me bowl well.

I was disappointed he wasn't there to see my 7-24 for Grimoldby and delighted he missed an utterly shocking, hangover-ridden, two-over spell for Louth Taverners on a cricket tour of Derbyshire.

That's as far as I could take my sporting experience of wanting to impress my Dad, but it was enough to make me appreciate the stories I was hearing from the players I interviewed. I could imagine what it had meant for the Cowdrey boys to know their father had been in the Canterbury ground, how Ryan Sidebottom must have revelled in the achievement of going past his father's wicket tally and how it must hurt Jonny Bairstow not to have his father there at all.

When I played for Louth Taverners in the East Lindsey Cricket League in Lincolnshire, we had a competitive side in which I was by no means a star. But I enjoyed the matches we played, it was a team of varied ages, backgrounds, united in a common desire to enjoy our cricket and sup a few beers in some very good public houses, win or lose.

One of our players, a reliable medium pace bowler and lower order bat, was Rob Collinson. I don't need to tell you he was a good bloke because we didn't have bad eggs in our team. One of Rob's biggest fans was his son, a dot of a boy with white blond hair called Jason. He'd play mini-games on the edge of the boundary with us, gave a cheeky smile and at the end of play would disappear home with his Dad.

Many years later, long after I'd moved away, Jason, now a tall strapping 30-year-old, told me a tale. Rob was captain and inclined to bat himself down the order to give everyone else a go. But on 19 August 2006 he arrived for an away game against Skegness and decided that he was going to open the batting. Jason, the usual opener, dropped down to No 3. It gave Rob his only chance to share centre stage with his boy before submitting to his advancing years and calling it a day.

It could have backfired if Rob had been out early, but instead he would face the first and last ball of the innings, carrying his bat for an unbeaten 70 while Jason hit 128. They had shared a second wicket partnership of 219, set a club record stand and created an afternoon of memories they would both treasure forever. Rob retired soon afterwards.

Jason plays for Louth Cricket Club nowadays, moved onwards and upwards from his days with the Taverners, but he told me:

"My dedication and love for cricket has definitely come from growing up and watching my dad and Taverners every week, getting the throw downs from players that were waiting to bat or had already got out.

"Then to my first game as soon as the rules allowed me to play at 13," he continued. "I remember Dad telling me 'get out of the way if the ball comes too quick'. Love for it all stemmed from Taverners. It was a Sunday family event with my dad playing and mum being tea lady. I've got many fond memories of cricket, but the best are from those days watching and then playing with Dad."

Anyone who has ever played cricket, at whatever level, knows how that team environment can become an important and positive part of life. I'd been bouncing a few ideas for this book off the brain of a fellow cricket journalist called Graham. He told me that his father, Mike, had been an opening batsman who had progressed as far as the Lancashire 2nd XI. When Graham followed his father to Bradshaw Cricket Club in the Bolton League the players at the club were hoping he'd score the runs Mike had before him. Graham was a bowler.

"I never played a first team game there, but did okay in the juniors and seconds. It would be over-egging it to suggest that they expected me to be great, but maybe a more prominent figure than I was, but then I expected that too."

Whether people had gone on to play international cricket, or whether they'd been a moderate club hanger on, everyone had a tale to tell. For the ones that had sewn cricket through their lives, they'd firstly had the opportunity to play and encouragement to continue. They were taken to games, they played alongside their Dad's matches, maybe picked up a few pointers and that exposure at an early age led to many hours of playing the game as a young child, the age when it's easier to learn and develop skills. Equally, none of the parents had appeared at all pushy.

When a father had succeeded and played the game to a high standard they were confident enough in their own skin to allow their son's career to breathe and take shape. Also, in some cases, comfortable enough to allow their sons to pursue other angles as long as they were happy. As my quest for answers continued I'd speak to Brett D'Oliveira and find a lovely example of that.

It's a generalisation, but the more pushy the parent the less satisfied they'd been with their own achievements. They often have emotional issues and low self-esteem. They push because they want their child to succeed, but it's as much for them. And the pushing does not always produce positive results. They see their children as a second chance yet risk pushing them too far. Something, if done, risks making all parties disappointed. The motivation to have a successful sports player in the family and see them as a potential cash cow is, to me, the most sinister aspect of it all.

Wanting your child to succeed and along the way show the value of hard work is admirable. An aspirational parent who is able to see the strengths and weaknesses of their child and provide support and assistance at appropriate junctures stands a chance of getting it right. To extend that drive into something more abusive, masquerading as someone 'doing it for their kid,' becomes about experiencing vicarious glory where the child's role is not about their own destiny, but becomes one of fulfilling their parent's dreams.

It might be a mother micro-managing her child's group of friends ensuring they are 'suitable,' or enters them in beauty pageants as a toddler, or a parent desperate to see their child succeed in education or sport to the detriment of their natural path in life.

The Marylebone Cricket Club (MCC) and Chance to Shine charity conducted research in 2014, which revealed that almost 90% of eight to 16-year-olds felt that winning was more important to their parents than it was for them. Almost half said that instances of bad behaviour displayed by parents made them feel that they didn't enjoy playing sport.

The report is not happy reading. One child had witnessed a father telling a member of the opposition that he was "rubbish", while a mother was seen "shouting abuse at a referee". Children admitted to crying in front of team-mates as a result of parental abuse. Kids were called "losers" and "cheaters" by parents from the opposite team. A father had called his son "stupid" every time he played. Two parents from opposing sides had a fight that disrupted a game for over 30 minutes.

The parents agreed with their children, recognising the negative impact their conduct could have with 61% saying it was stressful for a child when their parents shouted during matches. 58% admitted that the situation had worsened since they were at school.

Who performs at their best in a hostile environment? Researcher Dr Clifton Evers discovered that children were often "appalled" and "frightened" when their parents behaved with aggression.

Sport, particularly when young, is supposed to be fun and a chance to throw oneself into a team environment and enjoy the results. Studies have shown that by the age of 15 between 80% and 90% of youngsters had dropped out of organised sport as the pressure to win and perform outweighed the fun.

In research conducted for her book, *Taming the Tiger Parent: How to Put Your Child's Well-being First In A Competitive World*, Tanith Carey had spoken to a 10-year-old tennis player who had been so intimidated by the behaviour of the parents of her opponent, questioning every line call and vociferously commenting on every points, that she had thrown the match to quickly get off the court.

Carey used the term 'eagle dads' for men desperate for their sons to succeed in their favoured sport regardless of talent. These parents believed that pushing their children increased their toughness, built character and led to better results. They'd refer to Serena and Venus Williams whose father Richard had trained them hard from an early age. David Beckham's father Ted was also known to have encouraged his boy's early dedication to football.

And Tiger Woods is known to have held a golf club before his first birthday. His father Earl had been a Green Beret and baseball player and was adamant that a child could be made great by practice. He put a golf club into Tiger's hands before he could even walk. Earl said "early practice is essential so that performances became totally ingrained and flows from the subconscious."

Earl would place the infant Tiger in his highchair and hit golf balls in front of him so his son could observe. Tiger would hit the course at 18-months-old. Before the age of three he had fully developed his pre-shot routine, had spent many hours with his father on driving ranges and putting greens and entered his first pitch and putt tournament in California. He was able to hit his driver 80 yards and get the ball close to the flag from half that distance. Earl brought in a professional coach for his son when he was four and at 13 Tiger won his first national major tournament. Earl would end his son's practice sessions with competitions, Tiger sinking putt after putt from three feet as his father kept count.

Was Earl a pushy parent or someone providing their son with an amazing opportunity?

Richard Williams had remarried to Oracene in 1979. Richard had three sons and three daughters from his previous marriage and Oracene three daughters by her late husband.

Serena and Venus were not born when their father Richard happened upon a tennis match on the television and watched Virginia Ruzici being presented with a winner's cheque for $40,000. He spoke to Oracene and began to write a 78-page plan, which would lead to one of the most amazing rags to riches stories.

Venus was born two years later and Serena followed a year after that. Richard had spent the intervening period studying tennis, watching tournaments and speaking to tennis coaches and psychiatrists. He and his wife had tennis lessons from a man called 'Old Whiskey' as Richard worked in security and Oracene as a nurse.

Venus and Serena grew up in the deprived area of Compton in southern Los Angeles County. Venus began to train properly when four-and-a-half, whereas Serena was three. Richard had accumulated 550 balls he'd keep in a shopping cart, feed them to his daughters, who would then be tasked with retrieving them all before they'd go hit again. Richard would get his daughters to hit with baseball bats, they'd serve at traffic cones to improve accuracy and they'd play for hour after hour. The backdrop was Compton, the venue a shabby municipal tennis courts, but the vision was clear and the aim high.

Oracene recounted how the girls would dash to the courts and be there before their parents.

"My Dad worked hard to improve our technique," Venus said. "He's really a great coach. He's very innovative. He always has a new technique, new ideas, new strategies to put in place."

Serena played her first competitive match when she was four-and-a-half. When the girls were 11 and 10 Richard invited a well-known professional tennis coach, Rick Macci, to come and take a look at them play. The family would relocate when Macci invited them to enlist in his Florida Academy.

Macci said: "Even though some of what he [Richard] said was left field, he treated his daughters like kids, allowed them to be little girls".

Venus said in 2007: "We were just young and playing hours of tennis, having fun, reaching for the dream."

What their father had given them was an absolute belief that they would succeed.

"We were brainwashed," Serena would say. "We just practiced, practiced, practiced because we believed we could reach the top."

Again, was Richard a pushy parent or just a shrewd strategist who gave his girls the best chance he could think of to succeed? He was certainly hands-on and very opinionated. Media interest in two black girls making their way in a middle-class predominantly white sport was huge, even before they had played a professional match. Richard was aware of racist remarks made by other parents during tournaments leading him to remove his girls from junior events for a period of three years. He would ultimately take them back from Macci and coach them himself again.

The real test of Richard's credentials would have come if either, or both of his daughters, had gone against him and expressed a wish to go down a different career path. Many children of pushy parents feign injury to avoid practice. Whenever Serena complained of soreness Richard is said to have called a day off and taken them all to the beach to recuperate. Neither girl has ever expressed a negative opinion on their father's motives. They genuinely seem to have always loved the sport he gave them.

At the time of writing Serena has 23 singles, 14 doubles (all alongside Venus) and two mixed doubles titles in Grand Slams to her name. Add to that four Olympic Gold medals and she is undoubtedly the most successful female tennis player of all time. There can be no one else like Venus who, despite winning seven Grand Slam singles titles and those 14 doubles crowns, has a smaller trophy cabinet than her sibling.

Serena's is estimated to be worth in the region of $145million and Venus is worth around $75million. Not bad for two kids from Compton. Richard, who divorced Oracene in 2002 and remarried a woman just a year older than Venus, is said to be worth around $20million. There's no doubt that he was incredibly protective and supportive of his daughters and was instrumental in making them worldwide legends of the sport. If part of his plan was to make them all rich, that too worked.

David Beckham practised like crazy in a park in East London, kicking a ball from the same spot for hours, honing the skills that would see him earn 115 England caps and an illustrious career with Manchester United, who picked him up when he was 14, before big money moves to Real Madrid, AC Milan and LA Galaxy.

"His dedication was breath-taking," said his father. "It sometimes seemed that he lived on the local field."

David would add: "My secret is practice. I've always believed that if you want to achieve anything special in life, you have to work, work, and then work some more."

Again no hint that Beckham junior felt pushed in any way to achieve someone else's dream.

But fathers attempting to emulate Williams, Beckham and Woods must concentrate on the short-term and not long-term riches. Venus, Serena, Tiger and David truly loved what they were being asked to do, enjoyed the training and bought into the vision, even if it had been foisted upon them. The fact that they were good, getting the results and reaping the rewards is unlikely to inhibit motivation.

In October 2014, Beddau Rugby Football Club in Wales posted a notice alongside the pitch, which read: "These are kids. This is a game. The coaches are volunteers. The referees are human. This is not the Six Nations." In other words, parents calm down! Sometimes expectations and frustrations need to be managed.

Former England footballer, Gary Lineker, writing in the *New Statesman* in 2013, described pushy football parents as "utterly depressing". He said: "The competitive nature of most mums and dads is astounding. The fear they instil in our promising but sensitive Johnny is utterly depressing. We need a parental cultural revolution. If we could just get them to shut the fuck up and let their children enjoy themselves, you would be staggered at the difference it would make."

Lineker, who has four sons, said that his own father sat back and allowed him to get on with his football. Lineker has said that his father watched his games, but never shouted at him to play better.

"I've stood on the side-lines of countless games over many years," Lineker said. "Oh the drivel I've heard, the abuse I've witnessed and the damage I have seen done. Promising young players are barked at by clueless dads. I've even seen a father pick his son up by the scruff of the neck and yell in his face, 'You'll never make it playing like that'. Who cares who wins an Under-8s game or if a youngster makes a mistake? It's how we learn."

The higher the expectations placed on a youngster the more of a failure they will feel should they fail to make the grade. Let's face it, only a very small percentage makes it to elite level. Even less earn legendary status and enormous bank balances. In turn only a very few parents get to travel the world and take a share of the spoils like Richard Williams has done.

Rod Jaques, the national medical director of the English Institute of Sport, highlighted the conflict in relationships where a parent also acts as a mentor and coach: "It's a very delicate balance between encouragement and support for that child, and its potential for being a mentor or a tormentor of the child I think is really quite real," he told a head teachers' conference in 2010. "It is often anecdotally said that behind every injured child is a parent athlete wanting to get out.

"Australians have gone a bit further and called this the ugly parent syndrome and we probably have witnessed this on the side of our rugby fields or football fields of the bawling parent, not just at the referee but at the child on the field of play. This love for their child should not be conditional on results and unfortunately it sometimes is."

When parents create a direct link between affection and sporting prowess it can lead to children succumbing to eating disorders and depression. It can be overwhelmingly confusing for a youngster who believes their parents' love is reliant on the sporting results they achieve.

Jaques added that those parents who had supported a child to elite level in sport had got the balance "absolutely right" and had created a relationship with their child where "caring and loving and the love is entirely unconditional".

My experience of talking to cricketers was in stark contrast to the formative years and experiences of Swiss tennis player Timea Bacsinszky. In 2015, world ranked 26, she had a tremendous French Open where she reached the semi-final. En route to her then best display in a Grand Slam event she spoke about her 'pushy parent' who had almost robbed her of a career in professional sport.

"He doesn't deserve to have kids," the 25-year-old said of her father Igor, who she described to the BBC as a "control freak" and told of the extreme measures she had taken to steer her mother away from a controlling marriage.

"I kind of forced my mum to divorce because I told her 'okay it's unliveable,'" she said. "You cannot live that way, it's not possible."

As a child in Switzerland, Timea had been placed under tremendous pressure from the age of three by her Romanian-born tennis coach father. She found her only freedom on the court and revelled in defying her father's instructions.

"I was living in Switzerland and seeing all those other kids around me who had nice families, and then me on the other side," she said. "I am my own boss. I own my own life. it was quite difficult for me earlier to understand that. When you are the kid of a parent, who is that kind of pushy parent, who wants to live his dream through your life, it's difficult.

"As a young girl, you can never go against the power of the dad. You have no money or nothing. Actually, you have no chance to get out of it. Or you tank your tennis career and you lose matches. I had to win matches because otherwise my parents would fight."

Bacsinszky took an apprenticeship as a hotel manager, and by 2015 had developed a more carefree approach to tennis. She'd seen colleagues at the hotel struggling to make ends meet and began to appreciate the opportunities that professional tennis offered.

A pushy parent urging better performance, more training and harder work can also have massively negative effects on their child's health suggested the Sports Medicine team at Children's Hospital, Colorado. A young athlete pushed too far, by their own desire or that of someone else's, is susceptible to overtraining syndrome which worsens performance and can also increase levels of physiologic or emotional stress, fatigue, problems with sleep, immune system failure, chronic muscle or joint pain, mood swings, decreased appetite and weight loss, infections and a lack of enthusiasm or ambition.

All of this can be avoided with better targeted training, good and proper coaching, gradual progression, appropriate rest and rehabilitation, sportsmanship, skill acquisition and more emphasis on fun. But highly pushy parents are unlikely to settle for anything less than what they deem to be a 100% commitment to success.

* * * * *

Andy Murray's rise to the top of world tennis has seen him become one of the most revered sportsmen in Britain. His older brother Jamie has also achieved great success as a doubles player, the siblings combining to win the Davis Cup in 2016.

Their mother Judy however, always in the viewing gallery providing her boys with support, hasn't always experienced the goodwill from the British media she has received more readily of late. The Scot was accused of being a pushy parent. She'd sacrificed a lot, certainly financially, to see her lads grow from a small tennis club in Dunblane, to receive the best coaching in Spain and France, before reaping the rewards of a professional career. And the media's criticism upset her.

"Yes it did," she said on *Desert Island Discs*. "That whole pushy Mum thing. I've never been a pushy Mum. I've encouraged my kids and I've supported my kids, but I've never pushed them to do anything and if you asked either of them that they would tell you exactly the same.

"I really do believe that as a mother of sons I came in for more criticism and more attention than if I'd been a father of sons, or even a mother of daughters," continued Judy "There's something about that sort of competitive sporty mum that particularly male sections of the media don't appear to like. But I never rose to any of it, I never spoke out about it or had a go about anything, I just thought *don't get distracted*. The people that write these things don't know you as a person and they don't know anything about our family or what our journey has been like."

Judy had given professional tennis a shot aged 17 in 1976, rose to eighth in British women's tennis, but after being robbed when playing in Barcelona she suffered from homesickness and called it a day. Her accusers would suggest that after being denied her dreams she pushed her sons into the sport. She qualified as a coach and oversaw the development of both her sons, but there is a difference between a blinkered pushing and the love, support and guidance both Andy and Jamie have said they received from her. When Andy went to train in Spain and a few years later Jamie went to France the fees involved were more than Judy's salary as a coach with the Scottish Tennis Association. There were sacrifices, grants from the Lawn Tennis Association, some funds provided by family members and a hefty loan was taken out to give her sons the best chance. Andy had been determined to go to Spain after seeing the facilities already at the disposal of his rival Rafael Nadal.

"Anyone who knows me can tell you I'm not pushy at all," she told *The Standard* in 2010. "I don't try to dominate the lives of my sons. I've always been a believer that if you make a decision yourself and it's a mistake, you're going to learn much more."

Andy's response was to say: "I can't remember the last time I was in an argument with her. Genuinely can't remember. I never slammed a door. Never said 'I hate you'. I think my mum's the only person who gets me, who understands me really well."

As time passed and Andy in particular achieved enormous success, becoming the first British player to win Wimbledon in 77 years and a Gold medal at the 2012 London Olympics the mood changed. In addition to the success of her sons, Judy attributed the tide turning to people recognising her credentials as a coach rather than a frustrated tennis player.

"I think getting the Federation Cup captaincy job showed a lot of people, who thought I was just Andy and Jamie's Mum, that I am a coach and that I know what I'm doing," she said, "and I have a lot of fun while I'm doing it. And that's given me a lot of confidence."

Andy, when a teenager, wrote in a Christmas card to his mother that he thanked her for "always believing in me, always supporting me, always letting me make my own decisions, but most of all being the best Mum in the world."

Doesn't sound like a resentful son does it? It's easy to see the joy that a son's success ultimately brings a parent and attribute that to self-fulfilment, forgetting the hours of soul searching that have gone before.

If you have children, would you describe yourself as a helicopter parent? Dr Madeline Levine in 2006 coined the terms for parents who hover over all aspects of their children's lives. Often middle-class and high earning, a parent's keenness to meddle, pressurise and shape a child's existence can leave the youngster stressed and depressed. The bar is raised too high and when the child inevitably falls short it leads to feelings of hopelessness and failure. When expectations are unrealistic there is usually only one outcome.

For every high achiever there are countless under achievers. For every Judy Murray, Richard Williams and Earl Woods there are countless parents who have seen their example and want the rewards of emulating it, at all costs.

Levine found that children from affluent households were three times more likely to suffer depression and anxiety than an average teenager. As a result, instances of children resorting to drug abuse, self-harming and, in the most extreme cases, suicide, were more common.

Levine contended that there was a big difference between being pushy and providing the discipline and moral framework everyone requires to develop self-control. But parents should avoid damaging a child's self-esteem by criticising their efforts too often.

"The most dangerous feelings a child can have are of self-hatred, yet middle-class parents are unwittingly instilling those feelings by expecting so much," Levine said. "Kids aren't having the experiences that are mandatory for healthy child development - a period of time to be left alone, to figure out who you are, to experiment with different things, to fail, and to develop a repertoire of responses to challenge. It's all about performance and performance is not real learning."

And there's the rub. Growing up, finding one's place in the world and making the best of what you have to offer is all about trial and error, making mistakes and trying not to do them again. That's easier said than done, as most of us know. When a parent sits on your shoulder and places their stamp on everything you are confronted by, it becomes their life and not yours.

Back to cricket. More than most sports, performance can be measured in all formats, across all disciplines by robust measurements, averages and statistics. There's no escape from being judged and compared. And that's assuming you are playing well enough to be selected for the team in the first place.

One aspect of this book has been the consistency of approach of the fathers. Most have said that they stood back and allowed their sons to develop and enjoy the game, while the sons have talked about the support being there only if they needed it. But then I'm talking to fathers that have enjoyed a good career and are comfortable in their own existence. That's a solid place to inspire from.

I haven't found myself speaking to the children whose parents were pushy and opted for other careers instead because those families haven't made the book for obvious reasons.

It was at this point in the process that I began to think instead about young aspiring cricketers with a seriously famous and successful father. The Cowdreys had already provided a glimpse of how that might be, but Chris had mentioned Liam Botham and I decided to give him a call.

In the same way a pushy parent, or the helicopter mum or dad, infiltrates all aspects of a youngster's life, when your father is a true all-time great of the stature of Ian Botham, Viv Richards or Don Bradman there is absolutely no escape from their presence in your life.

Brett D'Oliveira, embarking on a career two generations on from Basil D'Oliveira who transcended sport into the world of politics and the anti-apartheid movement in South Africa, cannot even hide behind a common name like Smith or Brown. I've only ever heard of his family of D'Oliveiras, as have I'm sure millions of cricket watchers around the world.

How tough is it to find your own light when Dad's deeds have been so appreciated, lauded and remembered? The pressures of expectation have to be intense.

It's easy to understand why the sons of the very famous want to follow their fathers into the game. We all have had our heroes and wanted to be them. For these children their hero ate breakfast with them and tucked them in at night.

But as Eric Douglas had proved, having an iconic father does not guarantee happiness or self-fulfilment.

I would soon be dialling Liam Botham's number, but first I wanted to know more about an Australian called John Bradsen I'd been reading about.

CHAPTER SEVEN

DON, JOHN and GRETA BRADMAN

"I've been through the desert on a horse with no name
It felt good to be out of the rain
In the desert you can remember your name
'Cause there ain't no one for to give you no pain"
'A Horse With No Name' by America

The soaring soprano voice of Greta Bradman mesmerised onlookers with a stunning vocal rendition of Andrew Lloyd Webber's *Pie Jesu*. It would always be remembered by those cramming into St Peter's Cathedral, the thousands watching on from the Adelaide Oval or the millions around the globe. The date was 25 March 2001 and the world was mourning the loss of its greatest ever cricketer.

Greta had lost her Grandpa. Remarkably hers seemed to be the only dry eyes in the house. Don's son John, asked her later, "Sweetie, how on earth did you do that?" Greta answered, "I went and sat in front of that portrait of Grandpa and kept singing that song until I could sing it without crying."

If you love the game of cricket you know the name Don Bradman, or 'The Don'. He played 52 Tests for Australia, had scored 6,996 runs and hit 29 centuries. His highest score of 334 was then a world record for the highest individual Test innings. In 1948 he captained the Australian team, which became known as 'The Invincibles' during their unbeaten tour of England.

Needing just four runs in his final Test innings at The Oval in 1948 to ensure he retired with a batting average of over 100, he was bowled by Eric Hollies for a second ball duck. That infamous failure and a final Test average of 99.94, if anything, made his legend greater and appeal stronger.

His country needed a hero and a reason to smile amidst a serious economic depression. Bradman was that man.

Cricket writer Geoff Armstrong explained to ESPN: "Bradman's importance to the people of Australia during the depression was enormous and I think one of the factors behind that was that he gave to them a sense of certainty at a time when there was absolutely no certainty in their lives."

Dean Jones, a cricketer of 52 Tests and 164 One Day Internationals for Australia in the 1980s and 1990s said: "Sir Donald Bradman is the most famous Australian ever, not just happened to be the greatest cricketer of all-time, but the most famous Australian ever. He was the closest thing to perfection... he had all the answers."

Nelson Mandela, former South Africa President and a hero to many around the world said this when Bradman died: "He became a real hero far beyond the borders of Australia. He was a hero."

"Don Bradman was the greatest cricketer I ever saw," Bill O'Reilly told ESPN. "And I would say he had the greatest repertoire of aggressive, damaging strokes that ever a batsman carried. In fact, I am quite certain that he was the best cricketer to ever walk on to a cricket ground in any part of the whole wide world."

I could fill this book with quotes from all over the world to illustrate Bradman's triumphs, career and legacy. This book is primarily about sons that have become cricketers after their fathers, but John Bradman's story interested me because there are some men whose footsteps are so big the path they leave behind is more a precipice.

John was the son of Australia's greatest. You note I didn't add 'player' or 'cricketer' at the end of the previous sentence. Don Bradman, even after his death in 2001 aged 92, is, to Australians, the greatest full stop. To understand the footsteps John walked in is to recognise genius.

In 1972 a 32-year-old John told a newspaper that he had changed his surname to Bradsen in order to step out of the shadow of his legendary father. His new surname was a pun on the 'son of Bradman' and had been inspired by visits to Norway when a young man.

"I'm tired of people 'discovering' who I am. I'm me," John said. "And I am no longer prepared to accept being seriously introduced as simply someone's son. I'm an individual, not a social souvenir. I was popped into a metaphorical glass cage to be peered at and discussed like the other exhibits."

He told the ABC News programme *The Australian Story*, in 2015, 14 years after his father's death, "[It wasn't] to pretend I was someone other than who I was but simply to say 'people please give me a break'."

In response his father had said: "Only those who have had to live with the incessant strain of publicity can have any idea of its impact. I understand and appreciate what John has had to endure and hope this action will enable him to enjoy the privacy he seeks and which is right."

Privately however, Don found his son's name change hard to take. John had initially raised the possibility of a move away from the Bradman surname when he was only 18 and the mere fact it took another 14 years for that thought to become reality illustrates that it was not an easy decision to take.

Throughout his childhood he had felt his own life, wishes and achievements had been secondary to those seeking to get close to his father. People felt they could get hold of a bit of Bradman and vicariously prosper.

"Some people are fascinated by fame," John said. "It just draws people to be part of it. There is absolutely nobody who ever lived who could enjoy that process less than my Dad."

And like his Dad, John had no wish to be pored over and stared at because he was the son of someone that had once been rather good at something.

Judith Bradsen, John's former wife, added: "John felt he was not his own person, that people saw him as Don Bradman's son, and it was crushing him. I knew he'd gone through some very difficult times before I met him. We'd go to Government House to a ball and people would treat him as if he were just an object and would point at us."

Judith also appreciated the more anonymous existence. "We were married soon afterwards and people did not know," she said. "I did not ever, ever get a Bradman question all through the time I was teaching as Bradsen."

John's daughter Greta added: "When people would come up to him [John] as a child quite often the first question would be, 'And are you going to be a sportsman like your Dad when you grow up?'"

"Greta and I grew up as Tom and Greta Bradsen," John's son Tom told *ABC News*. "We had anonymity. That was a great thing. I wasn't under particular pressure to be a certain way or to achieve certain things. I was simply me."

'Being simply me' was the gift that John had given his children and the thing he had always yearned for himself.

Genevieve Levinson, friend to both Greta and Tom, remarked: "John had just wanted his kids to grow up without that sort of weighted expectation on them...rather than having most people expect them to be the most amazing cricket players of all time."

John knew his father would be upset. "My father wrote some letters to a friend in which he expressed his anguish over my changing my name which reflected the fact that it must have been difficult for him."

The letters had been sent by Don to his close friend Rohan Rivett between 1953 and 1977 and gave glimpses of the strain between himself and John.

"I think that Grandpa did understand, or at least he certainly came to understand Dad's reason for changing his name," Greta suggested. "I don't think Grandpa felt shunned. Grandpa was, on the one hand, in the moment, quite black and white, but also quite complex in terms of how he'd think about things and he was quite emotional."

* * * * *

If John had struggled to have a man of Sir Don's stature as his father, Greta would also be confronted with deciding whether or not to forge a public life with Bradman as her surname. She had proved her talent as a soprano at her Grandfather's funeral, but that was entirely different to making singing a professional career.

"Having a name like Bradman as a classical singer is actually a little bit of an impediment because you run the risk of being seen to be a gimmick," Greta admitted.

But even her mighty performance in St Peter's Cathedral had garnered a mixed reaction because of who she was. A professional career in music might not be plain sailing.

"I remember listening to the radio and having someone call up and saying, 'Oh, you know, it was clearly dubbed'. Like, 'She couldn't have sung like that'. I was adamant I wasn't going to sing as a career. And I would be asked, you know, 'Oh, what are you going do? Where are you going to go next?' And 'Oh, no, no, no. I'm not going to sing. You know, this is just a hobby'."

Music was a hobby that had been largely stemmed from her Grandparents ever since she'd been a small child.

"I associate my Grandparents' house with family and music," Greta recalled in 2015 as her professional career saw her on the verge of global success. "My Grandmother whistled every moment of the day and as I went in the front door I would hear my Grandpa playing the piano.

"My Grandpa was hugely into music. He composed music and also had a very large record collection. He was really interested in certain sopranos and conductors. He and I would sit and listen to his record collection and talk about it. My music connects me to my Grandparents and to my extended family. I think that's why it is that I want to sing as well as I possibly can."

Greta's mother Judith confirmed: "Don was very fond of the female voice. I think that would have inspired Greta."

Despite her parents splitting when she had been a teenager, Greta was well aware of her father's struggle for his own identity and her Grandpa's view on fame. As a married woman with two young sons she was also conscious that she did not want the international travel that would accompany any singing success to effect her own family.

"I can't imagine that my Grandfather's travel and so forth wouldn't have had an impact in the sense of my Dad missing him and noticing his absence," Greta remarked.

It was easy to understand why John had removed himself entirely from playing cricket and carrying the burden of the Bradman surname. Instead he had become a lecturer in constitutional and environmental law in Adelaide. But now Greta was publicly following 'The Don' and was on the threshold of international recognition in her own right.

Greta had won the Australian International Opera Award and consequently spent time in Wales at the International Academy of Voice. During her visit to the UK she had the opportunity to sing in front of Richard Bonynge, an internationally renowned operatic conductor. She had made her mark.

"I heard her and I was astonished," Bonynge stated. "I don't get astonished by singers very often any more. I've heard too many of the great ones over the years. She should be in Covent Garden. Because I've heard many singers there who are not as good as she is."

* * * * *

From a Grandpa that had struggled with the international fame his unparalleled success had attracted, to a father that had sidestepped any attention the family name had brought him, to a Granddaughter receiving public adulation for her talent. The Bradmans had almost gone full circle.

Don had found the Australian public's adoration of him too much to bear. He spent his post-cricket years ducking the public eye, uncomfortable with adulation and revelling in a 'normal' family existence. Deemed by some in the media as reclusive because he invariably refused invitations to be interviewed, he also turned down an invitation to attend a 90th birthday party held in his honour by Cricket Australia. He rarely made public appearances and if the world demanded a Bradman comment they were usually made via the South Australia Cricket Association.

Greta remembered: "Privacy was absolutely important to my Grandpa and to my Dad and to all of us really as privacy equated to just being like everybody else."

"He was a very private person," said Jack Egan, the producer of The Bradman Era. "He didn't like the intrusion on his private life that the fame brought. That's not to say that he was a recluse. When you met him he was open, quite light-hearted, entertaining and he had a great sense of humour. He had a great shout of a laugh and he liked telling stories and hearing stories."

In the modern age where so many youngsters seek fame for its own sake, almost regardless of what they have to do to attain it, Don struggled to understand why an unprecedented weight of runs impacted so much on his simple desire to be a private family man.

In that regard, John's stance on his own private life seems at first glance to have mirrored his father's, but then the two situations were vastly different.

As a youngster Don had probably dreamed of runs, the Test match baggy green cap and international success as he knocked a golf ball with a cricket stump against a water tank in the backyard of his childhood home. The scale of his triumphs would have exceeded any of those young dreams. The attention and unrelenting nature of the public life that followed would have been a far cry from that carefree existence in rural New South Wales. But at least he was courted for his own deeds, the fame was his and the public chanted his name.

For John the circus was inherited. He was always the 'son of' and the battle to exert his own personal identity led him to change the one thing he publicly shared with his father – the Bradman surname.

It was of little surprise to me that my attempts to gain access to John's thought process via an interview received no replies. He would undoubtedly view me as part of the media he'd spent much of his life endeavouring to keep at arm's length. I could empathise and respected his wish to remain private.

Father and son appear to have experienced a rollercoaster relationship. Reports suggest they spent long periods estranged from each other. When his father died, John described him as "a human being and foibles and contradictions like the rest of us".

I've seen that comment used to suggest a serious rift between the Bradman men, but I didn't read it as such. John is an intelligent man and he saw cracks in his father's perfect public persona. His relationship with his father was not perfect, but then none of us can pretend to be free of flaw.

There are claims that father and son had become estranged, but according to Alan Eason, in his book *The A-Z of Bradman: A Comprehensive Companion to the Life and Career of a Legendary Australian*, they were "a pair inhabiting different worlds."

Don wasn't an extrovert and on the rare occasions when he attended large gatherings he found the spotlight uncomfortable and relied on his wife Jessie who was more adept than him at small talk.

"She was so good at conversing with people and keeping the conversations sort of light and keeping Grandpa feeling really comfortable because he, socially, I don't think he was quite as fluid in his conversation as she was," Greta said. "Grandpa wouldn't come to school concerts and things like that because he just wasn't comfortable with people staring at him and he didn't want it to be different for me.

"After school each day I would bolt up the stairs and run into his den and launch myself at his lap as hard as I possibly could. And then I'd give him a head massage, maybe make his hair into funny horns or do funny hairstyles with him. I would tease him mercilessly and I think most of the time he was okay with it."

Judith told of how John had enjoyed watching his children forge a strong bond with his father: "He had this half smile on his face which was a mixture of awe and wonder. I've never seen such delight on his face. I think that touched John. He certainly didn't have that relationship with Don himself. Don was away playing cricket for much of John's very early years."

Family was of huge importance to Don. He and his wife Jessie had experienced health problems with all three of their children. Their first son Ross had died in early childhood in 1936 and Shirley, two years John's junior, had cerebral palsy from birth. John had contracted polio at the age of 12.

"I remember my father being terribly distraught," John said. "He gave up virtually everything and resigned from everything for the period that I was in my polio frame. It was like a bed on wheels and my mother used to take me all over the district in this thing."

Again, it had been Don's childhood sweetheart Jessie Bradman who had glued the family together through adversity. When Jessie died in 1997 it ended a 65-year marriage Don had described as the greatest partnership of his life.

"It was very clear my dear old Dad was really struggling and so I started seeing him and kept on seeing him literally every day for three-and-a-half years," John recalled. "There is this discussion about us having a big falling out and then a rapprochement. You know, that's absolute nonsense. There was never any such thing."

Tom added: "If it wasn't for my Dad being so close to my Grandpa and spending every day with him over those few years, I'm not sure how he would have coped."

John continued: "My Dad remained fairly well until he had a stroke when he was 87. That was an event which was illustrative of his life. People came from everywhere, including medical people, with scraps of paper for him to sign, because they wanted an autograph. And the stroke affected his right hand and he couldn't sign, but they were still trying to get him to sign his autograph, the dear old boy. And he recovered reasonably well from that."

For John the conscious metamorphosis into being a Bradsen had served its purpose. By distancing himself from the most famous surname in Australia he'd gone under the radar. The questions, media attention and pressure had eased. Two altered letters had seemingly made all the difference. He's had a chance to be himself and as the new millennium approached and his father's health deteriorating the time was right to become a Bradman again.

"The period of its effectiveness had somehow drawn to a close," Tom said. "We were ready to, I guess, resume our family name. The thing I remember most was taking my name-change forms into the bank to change my name on my bank account. And I handed over all these forms to the teller. She looked at me and said, 'You must be a really big fan'."

John told Don of his intentions. "When I told him, he just smiled and said, 'Don't do it for me'."

John was introduced as a Bradman when representing his father at a dinner in Melbourne in November 1999 to celebrate the naming of Don as Australia's Male Athlete of the Century. And John increasingly embraced his role at the head of the Bradman family after his father's death.

"My Grandpa was truly tickled pink," Greta said. "People would actually treat me differently. Instead of calling me Greta in restaurants, people would call me Miss Bradman. There was far more interest from guys, all of a sudden, in me. And that was bizarre."

A family friend, Genevieve Levinson, recalled how the dynamics of Greta's dating life changed with her name. "She went on a date with a guy and she turned up at his house. He opened the door and said, 'Oh, I just have to let you know before you come in that I'm a bit of a fan of your grandfather'. And then she walked into the house and it was wall-to-wall Bradman memorabilia and pictures of her grandfather on walls. And I don't think that one lasted very long."

Greta was struck by the difference the surname had made. "I wrote Grandpa a letter. I said, 'I get it now. I get what it is to have people looking at you differently. I can understand how for you that would be a really difficult thing'."

A lot had changed in the years since Don had conquered bowling attacks around the globe. Greta had enjoyed the relative anonymity of growing up as a Bradsen, was pursuing a career far removed from sport, but her move into the public eye still presented pressures. Her husband Didier said: "People think, 'Well, she can't be a singer because her grandfather was a cricketer,' which is ridiculous."

The Bradman name must have had its advantages for Greta though who kept the surname despite being married to Didier, whose surname was Elzinga.

After her performance at the memorial service for her Grandfather, Greta had been inundated with requests to perform. "The conservatorium office fielded so many calls, asking me to sing at things, and I just said no to everything," she said. "I'm never going to get past being Grandpa's granddaughter. I just had this sense of: I don't want to just be good at singing; I want to be like everybody else. I was still, in terms of university, really unsure as to what I was capable of and I would give myself a hard time over every assignment, thinking I was going to fail.

"I wouldn't have any idea of what I was doing," Greta continued. "I was so angry with myself for missing the school that I did [because of teenage depression], I needed to prove to myself that I could do something else and as long as my voice was there, that would never happen. And so I would drink salt water on an empty stomach so I was sick to try and actually burn my vocal folds."

Greta's mother Judith stated: "I knew that she was unhappy and that she had fallen down this slippery slope and couldn't get up. I tried to just give her lots of support and kept reminding her of our values here and life here."

"Obviously she is aware of her name and she's aware that what she does will be connected to that name," Didier said. "She said, 'Actually, you know, I can sing. I can sing professionally. I can do this and I'm going to explore it and see how far I can take it'."

At a dinner held in Sydney in 2008 to celebrate what would have been Don's 100th birthday John was in attendance and Greta sang in tribute to her grandfather.

"It may very well be she is the second famous Bradman coming out of Australia," Judith suggested. "I don't think that people will ever dissociate the Don from the Greta, but they'll appreciate them in their own right."

Greta remains grateful for the influence her Grandparents had on her life: "I wish I could share this with my grandparents," she said. "I wish that they were here to witness this, because each one of them contributed so much musically in my childhood to my passion for music and also, I guess, my love for singing. I think we are ready to perhaps come out of the shadows a little bit more."

I wondered if it was easier to celebrate your legendary grandfather, or father, if he was no longer around. Had Don's passing created more space for John and Greta to finally be themselves?

Cynics had suggested that John's reconciliation with his father had more to do with dollar signs than family harmony. Money is important to everyone, but I didn't entirely subscribe to that notion. John was either a very good actor or was expressing genuine affection in the few interviews I'd seen him give after his father's death.

I did wonder why Greta, who spoke a lot about the pressure of the Bradman surname and the attention it brought, had kept it after marriage. Had she simply followed her father's lead, been a woman that didn't like the idea of taking her husband's name, or had it helped her singing career?

Greta has two young sons. I wanted to ask her how she'd feel if they ever asked for a cricket bat for Christmas and wanted to pursue a sporting career. Would she advise against it knowing how much attention they would receive?

I attempted to ask Greta these questions, but got no response to my requests for a chat.

Greta released her third album in 2015 and joined ABC Classic FM in 2017 to present *Sunday Morning with Greta Bradman*.

* * * * *

While Don Bradman's shadow was colossal, none of his descendants had ventured into the sport he had dominated.

I thought back to the conversation I'd had with Simon Hartley, the sport psychologist, at the start of this project. He'd mentioned Liam Botham as a potential interviewee.

While there will only ever be one Don Bradman, for a certain generation of England cricket fans no one could touch the charismatic feats of Ian Terence Botham.

For a young man desperate to follow his father into the sport he loved, Guy the Gorilla's shoes would prove impossible to fill.

CHAPTER EIGHT

IAN and LIAM BOTHAM

"To be yourself in a world that is constantly trying to make you someone else is the greatest accomplishment"
Ralph Waldo Emerson

When I picked up the phone to call Liam Botham I remembered the chat I'd previously had with Chris Cowdrey. Both Liam and Chris had followed fathers where the term legendary was not misplaced.

For many people of my generation Ian Botham was nothing short of a cricketing God. He had played in an era blessed with many world-class all-rounders. Imran Khan was the Pakistan hero, Kapil Dev ruled the roost in India, Richard Hadlee led the way for New Zealand and the South African Clive Rice would have certainly been an international star had the apartheid sanctions not restricted his Test career. But Ian Terence Botham was cricket's version of football's George Best or snooker's Alex Higgins. He seemed to write his own scripts, batted opposition attacks into oblivion, always took vital wickets and grabbed hold of absolutely anything at slip. No one wandered into the bar, went for a smoke or fell asleep in the stands when 'Beefy' Botham was anywhere near the action.

The statistics tell the tale: 102 Test caps, 383 wickets, 5,200 runs, 14 Test centuries and 120 catches. If anything, certainly with the bat, they underestimate a man who often fell in the quest to entertain or add quick runs for the team. I remember an Ashes Test where, in a bid to boost an already imposing total, he walloped his first three balls for six, six and four, before smashing the fourth Craig McDermott delivery into the hands of Jeff Thomson on the square leg boundary. He breezed off as quickly as he'd batted, completely oblivious to his average being reduced by a few decimal points. The crowd had loved it.

Add to his Test credentials a further 116 One-Day Internationals and you've got one of the greatest all-round cricketers that ever played the game. One wonders what his market value would have been in the current Twenty20 leagues played around the globe.

He always seemed to save his best for a tight situation and was one of the few Englishmen of his generation who could stand toe-to-toe with the Australians and give back more than they threw at him.

His feats in the 1981 Ashes series wrote his name into folklore. He had lost the England captaincy before bouncing back, reborn as a superhero, with centuries and 5-fers to wipe the smile from Aussie faces and reclaim the Ashes almost single-handedly. Not many Test series become eponymous. 'Botham's Ashes' thrilled a nation in times where terrestrial television meant the country could not escape the achievements of a new national favourite.

More than that he was the cricketer we all wanted to be. He appeared to love playing and, off the field, he enjoyed life too. While Best and Higgins may have succumbed to addictions through their excesses, Botham just seemed to have an enormous appetite for life.

He was almost perfection. He could pummel the Australians, drink you under the table, rub shoulders with rock stars, yet seemed normal enough to be invited around to Mum's for tea and not let you down. That he was 'almost' perfection was vital too – when you are looking for a hero you need a few flaws.

A self-confessed rebel, he'd had more than a few run-ins with authority and the media.

While Don Bradman had the stats to beat any batsmen he was a very private individual. If Botham wanted to remain private his lifestyle courted attention. He was as big a personality as English cricket has ever served up. His friends were tycoons, rock stars and movie actors. It was the celebrities who sought him out and he belonged in their company. So, in many ways, Botham's legacy was as big, or even bigger, than Bradman's, certainly in terms of notoriety.

I said as much to Liam as I suggested that while Alec Stewart and Mark Butcher had followed cricketers, both he and Chris Cowdrey had followed genuine legends.

"I agree with that," Liam responded. "And no disrespect to Micky and Butch, they weren't in the same league. But again, they had something to do and they were always going to have a bit of pressure. But certainly not the sort of pressure that myself and Cow were under as kids, and I suppose trying to make our own way in professional sport as well."

As a toddler Liam had been photographed with his Dad, bat in hand. "He's a cheeky bugger who reckons he is going to be better than his old man," Ian had told reporters.

I recalled turning on the 6 o'clock news and watching as the mass media covered Liam's Hampshire debut. I'd never seen anyone else making as many column inches on first-class debut.

"I remember my first Under-11s cricket match and three press guys turned up and I was 10," Liam said in agreement. "It was like water off a duck's back. As a kid you just get on with it. I think the realisation that something was really different for me was when I made my debut for Hampshire against Middlesex and I got my 5-for. It was such a big thing. It was all 'son of this,' 'son of that,' 'Beefy's chip off the old block,' blah, blah, blah.

"I'd always had that all the way through, but I realised that day, you know what, for me to do anything, I'm going to have to better my old man to make my own name and get recognition for who I am instead of being 'the son of'.

"Dad's record speaks for itself. I'd have to have taken at least 383 wickets and beaten what Dad did," he added. "I'd have had to have been the quickest guy to score 1,000 runs and take 100 wickets, then to 2,000 runs and 200 wickets. And I'd have also had to be able to smash it out of the park and do this and do that, because, at the end of the day, the guy was an entertainer. I'd have always one hundred per cent been compared.

"I'd have had to have been the best all-rounder ever basically to be able to turn around and be satisfied enough to say 'that's my own thing'. He was also a big character. Everyone would have expected me to smash a quick hundred and then go and drink 10 pints.

"I was very lucky that I could try something else and do something else," Liam admitted. "I'd played cricket, rugby and hockey as a schoolboy to a very high level, so the rugby was always there. It had never been an option because for me it was always cricket, cricket, and cricket. It was always the first love.

"If I hadn't have had the option of going into rugby I would have carried on with cricket and who knows. But I had that opportunity to try something else.

"Rugby had just turned professional, whereas cricket at that stage was at a bit of a standstill," he explained. "I also knew that if I failed at the rugby I was young enough to be able to come back and the door was always open for myself to go back to Hampshire.

"When I'd rung Tim Tremlett up at Hampshire to say 'I'm going to give the rugby a go' and told him West Hartlepool had offered me a contract, he was really understanding. I had the opportunity to play the rugby and I took it. At the time I thought that if the rugby didn't work out I could always go back to the cricket.

"I just felt that early on you are going to get 'the son of' and whatever, but my decision was vindicated when I scored my first try for Hartlepool, we won the game and for the first time I had my own headlines.

"That was such a huge relief and I think it justified my decision.

And then things happened very quickly with the rugby and that's why I stuck with it instead of going back to cricket."

I'd read an interview Ian had given to the Daily Mirror in July 2015. "I couldn't spend much time with my children because I was away playing all the time," he had said. "It's not just you who suffers, it's the people around you too. You have to be quite selfish. I wasn't there to be a father, but the chance to spend time with my grandchildren makes up for that. I still travel a lot, but I spend as much time as I can with my grandchildren. I have a great relationship with them and it's wonderful I've had that second chance. We are a much more tightly knit family now."

The newspaper had suggested that for a young Liam and his sister Sarah, their 'easiest way to see their dad was usually to turn on the television'.

"Dad has always supported me," Liam began. "Our relationship is a bit of a strange one because even when Dad was playing for Somerset and Worcestershire our family home was in Yorkshire. So I didn't really know my Dad that well.

"Yes, I spent the summer holidays with him, but the winters – the England tours were different then to what they are like now and you certainly didn't have what the cricketers have now. The modern day cricketer has babysitters all paid for, crèches and all this sort of stuff, and the wives are really looked after. On the 1986/87 tour to Australia it actually cost Dad money to bring the family out with him. It was a totally different environment.

"It was only when I was 16 or 17, when Dad moved up to play for Durham toward the end of his career, when he was then based back at home and we spent some time together. So, although we are father and son we are more like brothers in the relationship.

"In later life Dad has always been supportive," Liam reaffirmed. "He's always been there in the background and said 'if you need help come and see me'. He'll give his advice, but certainly I was never under any pressure to go down any particular route.

"I think the only decision he thinks I really cocked up was when I decided to play for England instead of Wales in the rugby. It's the only one where he looks at me and smirks when it's talked about. I should never have left Cardiff anyway, but there you go."

With a cricketing colossus as a father I guessed it could go one of two ways, to be turned on or off by the thought of playing the game. I asked Liam if cricket had always been the ambition?

"Absolutely, totally, one hundred per cent," he rattled back emphatically. "I think I was inspired as a kid by being in and around the dressing room. All my life I lived and breathed cricket. I used to watch 'Botham's Ashes' as a kid.

"During the summer I'd spend a good part, if not all, of my summer holidays with Dad. I say 'with Dad'. Dad was there, but

Andy Williams, his minder, was the person I basically spent most of my time with. He was a great guy.

"When you live and breathe it," I could sense Liam was going back in time as he spoke. "It would probably never happen now, but I spent all of my time in the England dressing room when Dad was there," he continued. "It was a pretty amazing upbringing. When you are getting looked after and babysat by Elton John. You're with Eric Clapton. You're with the Bee Gees. We all know Dad's lifestyle was more rock'n'roll than it was cricket.

"For me it was just an amazing way to spend the summers. And it's not just a case of me dropping names. That was literally it. That was the lifestyle. There were plusses and minuses of it. We had the lifestyle but then we had the press on the other hand, so it was a balancing act."

I'd sensed Liam's mistrust of the media. He had told me during an initial and brief chat a few days before that he didn't really do interviews these days. I got the impression it was a case of once bitten twice shy. The Botham family hadn't been so much bitten as devoured by the press. Some of it was asked for. Ian had courted controversy at times, but that bad boy image allied to his greatness had made him, and his family, newsworthy. Wife Kath and the two children hadn't wanted the attention, but it came anyway.

Without being disloyal to my writer brethren, the Botham family were a media target. Regular interviews would be twisted to sensationalise their impact. Once a sportsman migrates from the back pages, where most journalists are happy to cover what happens on the field of play, to front-page headlines, life changes and everything is seen as fair game under the guise of selling newspapers.

From what Liam had said initially when I asked to interview him I assumed he felt journalists had previously hoodwinked him. Whether true or not negative headlines hurt and the Botham family had endured more than its fair share of pain. It's testament to the strength of Kath and the kids that Ian is now able to say: "We are a much more tightly knit family now." I guess love and loyalty conquer anything if strong enough.

"Again, I'm not being negative to any of the other guys, but they didn't have the press coverage or have to live with a story about your Dad in the paper every weekend. Myself and Mum joke that the reason I'm very good at pouring a gin & tonic was because of the shit we had to go through as a family. We know Dad's no angel and everything. But to have that and people going through your bins and experience all that sort of stuff as a family – it could have ruined a lot of people but we are a very close family."

I asked my stock question. What would have happened if Liam Botham had been called Liam Smith?

"I think one hundred per cent I would be a cricketer and I'd have been a very good one," Liam answered without hesitation. "If you ask Freddie Flintoff and those guys, I was, at one stage, right up there with anybody who has gone on and made it in cricket.

"On the sport front there was the added pressure. But if you asked me if I would change anything I've done the answer would be no. I had the most amazing life as a kid and all the way through.

"I once did an interview where I said 'I sometimes wish my name was Joe Bloggs' and I ended up getting a contract with Joe Bloggs modelling for them! It just shows you how things can happen so differently.

"I do believe that if I wasn't a Botham it would have been a different story and I would have been a cricketer all the way through.

"I'm not saying I went in my shell, but mentally I realised and it became very, very clear to me that you were always going to be under the microscope and that there were always going to be stories and it was always going to be about the old man," he said. "I remember as a 13-year-old kid people always saying 'he's only here because of his name Botham'. If I'd been Joe Smith, they'd never have made a comment and the sun would have shone out of my arse if it hadn't have been for the surname.

"Again, I know it probably sounds pretty arrogant, and no disrespect to anybody you've been speaking to, I don't think any of them would have understood or been quite as big as what my old man was."

Indeed, Botham was different. By virtue of the fact he'd gone from back-page match reports to front-page news he carried an aura of celebrity and hung out with many of them. I was on the cusp of becoming a teenager when the 1981 summer made Botham a megastar. I've seen people at Test Matches approach Ian between Sky Sports commentary stints, shake his hand warmly and say 'you are the reason I am here – what you did got me hooked on the game'.

"He was the George Best of cricket," Liam agreed. "You're talking about a guy that changed the sport. What a lot of people forget about 1981 was the riots and everything else going on. England needed something to happen, not just in cricketing terms, but England as a whole. That series stopped the Stock Exchange, which had never been done before."

"I've always been hugely proud of all our family, especially the old man, very proud of Mum for putting up with him and going through what she went through. I'd never swap any of that and what I've learnt has been from Dad's mistakes.

"I keep myself very private and I don't do any social media because I suppose I've learned from years and years of being in the limelight in respect of it being through my family or myself."

Fresh from examining John Bradman's struggle to find his identity in the shadow of the great Don Bradman, I wondered how easy it would have been for a young Botham to establish a strong personal persona.

"I've always been Liam Botham and done my own thing," Liam countered. "But in terms of my public identity I really only got that when I went to rugby.

"There was so much press about my debut for Hampshire that people started knowing me wherever I would go. I was walking through London and people came up to me to say 'well done Liam' and that was a buzz, but for my own personal name and recognising what I needed to do, making my own way, yes it was when I went to rugby and making my own headlines there.

"There was always interest if Dad would turn up and watch the rugby games, but there was nothing for them to justify a story or to compare me with."

Botham senior had made his name with Somerset before moving on to Worcestershire and ending his career with Durham. As I was shaping my question Liam jumped in.

"Again, because I didn't want to go anywhere my old man had played," he explained anticipating my 'why Hampshire?' "I wanted to be away from the family home in Yorkshire and make my own tracks. I'd been with Hampshire since I was 15, playing 2nd team and making my debut in 1996. It was one full year in first-class cricket after I'd left school before the rugby came along when I was 19."

Liam played three first-class matches for Hampshire with the 5-67 on debut being the highlight.

"Hampshire had been up playing Durham and it was difficult because Geoff Cook was a very strange character," Liam told me. "He didn't want anything to do with me, while other counties were chasing me. I don't know why that was. He was just a very odd ball.

"I can remember a first team cricket session at Durham," Liam continued. "Dad had got me down and I went in the nets and got a few wickets and smashed a few. I was 15 or so. Geoff Cook disappeared for a long run. He was a very strange guy and as a result I never wanted anything to do with Durham because of his attitude.

"We had a barbecue when Hampshire were up playing Durham

and Robin Smith and David Gower asked me where I was wanting to play. They said 'come down' and that was it. They got me down there and I really enjoyed it and that was the end of it."

As Liam told me, it's hard for anyone outside the Botham bubble to fully appreciate what it was like to be him. A young man blessed with prolific sporting talent whose young life had been anything but mundane. But like other people in this book, it's the only life he had known. On that basis the pros of being called Botham surely outweighed the cons?

"Oh massively," he shot back. I liked the way he answered my questions. The ball hit the long-on fence before the bowler had completed his follow through. His manner was confident, but easy. And he knew all the answers with a certainty, which I wondered was born from a fair degree of contemplation.

"Like I've always said, I would never change my life for anything. To have lived the life I had was just fantastic. I'd do it all exactly the same again. I've had a fantastic life.

"We can all look back and say I wish I'd done this and I wish I'd done that but I've had an amazing time.

"I'm very proud of my father, I'm very proud of my heritage and I feel I learned a huge amount about life, how to treat people, which on the business side will help me no end. I'm an entrepreneur, got a few different ventures, but the biggest things now are a couple of businesses up in Yorkshire to do with the waste industry."

You've probably gathered already that I'm a cricket badger, cricket tragic, obsessed with the game kind of a person. Consequently, to hear Liam describe the best batsman I'd ever seen as Uncle Viv made me smile. I'd known that Viv Richards was Ian's great friend from his Somerset days and Liam's godfather.

We were talking about Liam's current relationship with his father and whether there were similarities between the two men as people.

"We're very similar I think," he confessed. "I'm very outgoing, I love life, I'm a country person and I have my views. I think the way to describe me is very similar to the old man, but slightly softer.

"Uncle Viv couldn't play in a Rest of the World XI against Dad's XI and I went down and played at Hove," Liam explained. "The only disappointing thing was that Dad was coming on next over to bowl at me and the rain came down. That was disappointing because you go back to that father/son rivalry and that would have been fantastic.

"But now our rivalry is who can shoot the best, who catches the first salmon and who wins on the golf course. The competitive edge is very high within us and also my sons have the same thing."

And that brings us to the next generation of Bothams as the name continues in professional sport. Does that make Liam over protective?

"James is going down the rugby route himself," said Liam. "He's with Cardiff. He's not going to have the same thing as me.

"I was a good rugby player but I certainly was not an Ian Botham on the rugby pitch. I got respect in it, but Jimbo will be able to go out and enjoy himself. The guy is seriously talented, more so than what I was on a rugby field, but he has the opportunity and we'll all be able to support him and give him the best possible start."

Liam's initial transition to rugby union saw him represent England Under-21s in 2000. He had left West Hartlepool in 1997 and spent three seasons with Cardiff, played for Newcastle for a further three before swapping codes for the colours of Bradford Bulls in rugby league. In 2003 he signed for Leeds to play both codes with Leeds Rhinos (league) and Leeds Tykes (union) before his career was cut short by a serious neck injury in 2005 after playing five games for Wigan Warriors.

It was easy to gauge the pleasure Liam took in watching his son James' fledgling rugby career take shape. James made his Wales Under-19s debut in March 2016, scoring a try in a 31-30 win over Scotland in Swansea.

And we'd gone full circle. Back to Ian's six grandchildren. Liam has provided four apples for his Dad's eyes. Regan, James and Imani-Jayne with his first wife Sarah-Jayne and another son Benji arrived in 2015 from his second marriage to Lisa Harrison.

"It's funny for me as I didn't really know Dad like that – him messing around with the kids and stuff is something he never really did with me," Liam said. "I understand that now. You do have to make sacrifices as a parent. You realise now that's what grandparents are for."

At that point I realised I was being guilty of utter hypocrisy. If not, I was validating everything Liam had told me. My voice recorder was taking down his words, which as you've just read were fine ones, but my mind was still on the man he'd called Uncle Viv.

I remembered watching that mighty Somerset team as a youngster. Viv Richards the muscular Caribbean height of cool who chewed gum as ferociously as he blasted bowling attacks into next year. I pictured him moving across to off stump and clipping a good ball off his toes over deep square and swaggering away as if it was the easiest thing in the world. I thought of Ian Botham, who as we've discussed had done it all and gone back for seconds.

Not forgetting the 6 foot 8 inch fast bowler Joel Garner who I reached up to pass my autograph book and got neck ache as I waited for him to hand it back down from the heavens.

Although it was hard for someone who would have given his right arm to have Liam's cricket talent, I could see why he'd made his choices. He'd have to have been some cricketer to have rivalled the records of any of those guys. With Ian as father and Uncle Viv you couldn't have two bigger figures as patriarchal role models in your life?

"No, you couldn't," Liam responded. I was back in the room.

"I grew up with them both at Somerset, but that was the environment I was around. It taught me a lot about life.

"When I was in the England dressing room, you'd learn about winning and learn about losing and how to deal with different situations and that was the biggest thing for me. It was a huge privilege to see all that.

"You see someone like Dad, or Uncle Viv or how any sportsman behaved," he added. "Or meeting people like Eric Clapton, Elton John or any of those sorts of people – how they behaved and how they did things in life. It was fantastic as a kid growing up.

"When you are in an environment like Uncle Viv and Dad were it's very hard to explain actually what it was quite like.

"It was an amazing, crazy time and there are plusses, there are minuses but I'd never swap it for the world."

* * * * *

Towards the end of my conversation with Liam I asked him if he still spoke much to Mali Richards.

"Uncle Viv is Uncle Viv," he'd answered. "When you see him you see him. He's certainly his own man. I've spoken to Mali a couple of times.

"He obviously went down the tennis route and I should imagine he probably had similar things going. God help him in West Indies," Liam snorted. "He'd have the same situation as I had here."

So I was heading for the Caribbean, or at least in spirit.

CHAPTER NINE

VIV and MALI RICHARDS

"But take your time, think a lot
Think of everything you've got
For you will still be here tomorrow
But your dreams may not"
'Father and Son' by Cat Stevens

"At times it can be extremely difficult but it can also be a joy," Mali Richards said in 2007. "I haven't always dealt with it the best but as I have got older I have learnt to live with it. It is the path I have chosen after all.

"I used to get frustrated with the comparisons. They would see me and say, 'Your Dad would have hit that for four'. I'm never going to play like him. He was one of the greatest. I want to be judged for being me."

That was Mali Richards talking in 2007. By then he was fast approaching his 24th birthday and was refusing to give up on his dream.

I made an approach to Mali for an interview. He turned me down. He was very polite, courteous, but very definite in his denial. I got the impression he was fed up to the back teeth of discussing that he was the son of Viv. He'd had people like me talking about it all of his life.

An interview he'd given to BBC Sport in June 2007 gave a glimpse into the pressure he was under at the time. It was apparent that Mali was acutely aware of people's expectations, that he'd be a chip off the old block and blessed with the ability to annihilate oppositions as his father had, often.

"It's something I've had to live with for as long as I have been around," he confessed. "I used to be a tennis player before I played cricket and I was expected to be good at that even though my father had nothing to do with tennis.

"Coming over here [to England] has been a bit of a spotlight - going to different grounds, every person you meet it's something to do with your father," he continued. "I am proud he's my father but at the same time in the past I haven't handled it as well as I could have. But in the past year I have set about doing it in my own way, not distancing myself from it, but I have to be my own person and carve out that space for myself really."

Viv had been very supportive of his son's aspirations to play tennis, conscious of the attention his son would face if he took the cricket route.

"He loved it when I was a tennis player because he felt the pressure wouldn't be the same," Mali recalled. "Then, when I made the decision to play cricket, he was fully supportive as well. We talk about cricket all the time.

"He doesn't tell me to go out and play shots like he does because he knows I can't do it, but the basics of the game are to hit the ball and do it your way and if you have confidence doing it your way that's half the battle."

If you are getting comments along the lines of 'you're not as good as your Dad' when you are playing a different sport, it's a brave, possibly foolhardy, decision to decide to give your father's sport a go. But when Mali devoted his efforts to cricket he was initially very successful. In a way that only made his task harder.

Regular centuries, most made with the confidence and command usually associated with his father, only raised interest in him further.

"I scored one or two in India, but never in Goa," Viv had told viewers when news was relayed to his TV commentary box that Mali had scored a century on a Cheltenham College tour. Said with immense pride and no little self-depreciation, the comment was nevertheless another reason to believe the lad may even have something his Dad hadn't.

As a 14-year-old Mali had scored 106 for Antigua Under-15s, a knock he described as "special". As a 17-year-old he underlined his progress with 958 runs at 56.35 for Cheltenham College, including a tremendous unbeaten 144 against Repton and an 86-ball 116 against Dean Close.

Middlesex took a punt on his potential after winning the race for his signature, but in his two seasons at the county he didn't deliver the runs or the wickets either party was seeking. In 12 second team matches he scored 286 runs at 16.82 with a best of 57. A 1st XI place had been out of reach and his departure not unexpected.

He told BBC Sport a few years later that he would "rather forget" his time at the county and expressed criticism of his treatment while at Lord's. He said: "In two summer contracts I had one net session there where some coaching was available. I just seemed to be someone who was there, who had a name, and nothing really happened to me.

"I don't think I was particularly helped by the club," he added. "It was something I would rather forget because I didn't take much away from it other than meeting some really good guys, like Owais Shah and Paul Weekes.

"Apart from that it wasn't particularly enjoyable. I was very young and immature and I take some blame for what happened there."

Middlesex chief executive, Vinny Codrington, responded to Mali's comments, saying: "Communication at the club was poor."

As I read the articles about Mali I could understand why he no longer wanted to talk about the father son thing, or at least publicly. Some of the pieces written in the noughties painted him as the second coming. I didn't get the chance to tell him that my motive was not to add to the list of writers that deemed him a failure for not threatening his father's iconic career. I simply wanted to know what it had been like – but that probably wouldn't have loosened his lips.

In July 2002 the Observer Sport Monthly had run a piece entitled *King Richards the Second*. At the time Mali was 18. No pressure there then!

When I was preparing to sit my A-levels, I had no idea what I wanted to do or be. Any hope I'd had of replacing Chris Cowdrey in the Kent team and getting back into that Canterbury dressing room had long been condemned to memory through an inconvenient lack of talent. If Mali was anything like me, or I'd imagine most of us, his view of himself and where he fitted in to the world would have been sketchy at best, with or without Viv Richards as his Dad.

"The schoolboy prodigy is making his own way in the sport his father has dominated," proclaimed the piece, before adding, "he is already an exceptional sportsman. In only his second year at Cheltenham College, he is the school's best tennis player (although he seldom has the chance to go on the courts) and hurtles down the wing, head down and energies boundless, for the first XV. But it is on the cricket field that his heart really lies; cricket, indeed, is his present and will be his future preoccupation … For Mali Richards is the son of Sir Vivian Richards, and was born to play cricket."

When playing for Cheltenham in the previous summer, Mali had been the second highest scoring batsman in public school games with 958 runs at an average of 56.35. In his second year he'd been made captain. Previously he'd skippered his school team at St Joseph's and also the Leeward islands under-15s and Antigua Under-19s. He was batting in his Dad's No 3 berth and also opened the bowling.

If Mali was to fulfil his destiny it could have been for West Indies or England. Born in Taunton while his father was playing for Somerset in 1983, he had grown up in Antigua and educated at St Joseph's Academy next to the famous Recreation Ground. Viv had taken him into the dressing rooms where he'd hang on every word Brian Lara, his hero, would utter.

Mali, like Lara a left-handed bat, had said about his future Test aspirations: "Dad hasn't said too much to me on the subject although he's gone on record to say it's all really up to me. I know what he is thinking and where he'd like my future to lie. I'm aware of that, knowing him and his feelings as I do, though I must say he hasn't tried to influence me.

"I'm in spirit a West Indian cricketer and I suppose that in my heart I have always wanted to play for West Indies. I'd feel disloyal to my community and friends at home if I opted for England and suggested I had an ambition to play for them. But wait a moment, I have first to prove that I'm ever going to be good enough to be considered for that level of cricket."

And in that last sentence there's the crux, for many score runs as schoolboys. Very few progress to be first-class players, let alone get interviewed as teenagers and asked to state which Test team they'd like to play for. Those others are able to remain relatively anonymous and would only have to bat away such queries after scoring many more runs at a much higher standard.

Mali was on the radar for a number of English counties, each eager to have a left-handed Viv Richards in their XI. He's already played a game for Gloucestershire 2nd XI, he'd returned in the winter for nets and also practised with the Somerset Academy, with Worcestershire and Middlesex known to have followed his embryonic career with serious interest.

His mother Miriam would take Mali to the County Ground in Taunton in his pushchair and when Viv moved to Glamorgan between 1990 and 1993, Mali would sit in the Sophia Gardens ground and watch his father play. He saw much of his father's last West Indies tour to England in 1991 as a fascinated 17-year-old.

As role models go, his father was one of the very best. Who amongst us hasn't dreamt of taking a step across to off-stump and flicking some of the best bowlers off your heels into the Mound Stand at Lord's – effortless genius.

Viv Richards had invented swagger. Not just normal swagger, but a cool, nonchalant, intimidating swagger. He was the man you'd want in your corner regardless of situation. A huge chest hid a large heart. If Lee Majors had been the *Six Million Dollar Man*, the technology didn't exist to have built Viv Richards. The guy's muscles seemed to have muscles of their own and he did more to sell chewing gum than any advertising campaign. He was the height of cool. His head, protected only by his maroon West Indies cap, he would hook to the fence off his nose and stroll down the pitch as if walking to a bar to chat up the best looking girl in the place. She'd probably have already bought the drinks.

Viv had an arrogant air, well backed up by his ability to deliver the goods. He'd shown glimpses of feistiness, almost petulance too, when as a youngster he refused to walk when playing for Antigua against St Kitts. It was his first zone match and a two-hour delay ensued as the incensed crowd ultimately got their wish with their batsman reinstated at the crease. He was suspended for two years in the fallout.

On his school tour to Goa, Mali at a similar age was censured for an on-pitch tantrum and as captain of Cheltenham would often go a little too far when demonstrating his disappointment at rejected appeals or when dismissed. His wasn't a big enough name to avoid fines for lateness either.

A friend had suggested Viv enrol Mali at Cheltenham, but the pair remained close with dad providing advice and visits to watch him play rugby, cricket and attend speech days.

"We continue to talk all the time," he said. "He gives me advice. Tells me how to cope with pressure, something no doubt I'll have to handle. At home we have a big concrete garage where we practise together. It used to be all tennis for me. That was my major sport. I was a junior champion back in West Indies and I seriously wondered whether I might make it at the highest level. Now I've made my choice."

So cricket it was going to be. Described by a coach at Cheltenham College as "one of the most promising and exciting players I've seen", Mali had developed a second string to his bow with some handy right-arm pace bowling and was ready to take on the world as an all-rounder.

He played club cricket in Australia in 2002/3 and then in 2003 his reputation was further enhanced when he made 319 for Antigua and Barbuda, the highest individual score in the 90-year history of the Leeward Islands tournament. His 420-ball knock against the Combined Virgin Islands at the Recreation Ground came on day two of the three-day non-first-class match and contained 22 fours and six sixes.

"It is a lot of hard work being rewarded," he said at the end of his innings. "I'm really pleased it could be done in front (of my supporters). I'm just really, really overjoyed."

Mali Richards added that his father telephoned to congratulate him: "I spoke with him and he seemed really pleased, I guess we have a lot to talk about afterwards."

That innings announced him to the world. The new Viv Richards was on his way.

The questions being asked back then were how many runs will he score, when will he break into the West Indies side, or can he be as good as his Dad? The weight of expectation had never been heavier. In truth, the answers to those questions were not many, never and a resounding no. The contrast between the two careers could not be vaster.

In 2007 Mali was playing for Oxford UCCE and his club cricket for Stourbridge in the Birmingham League. It was alleged that his commitment to the UCCE team cause was questioned when he went AWOL from 12th man duties during a game at the Parks.

He seemed to be planning for a career outside of the game, three years into a four-year tourism degree at Oxford Brookes University. His performances on the pitch hadn't suggested that a return to county cricket was imminent, although he was planning to play for Antigua that winter.

English had been his favourite subject as a student and a career in sports journalism was also a viable option. At 23, however, the lure of the cricket field still burned brightly.

"I think I could possibly make a go of it," he told the BBC. "It's something I love and if I keep working hard I could definitely make a career of it. You cannot give up on your dream."

Mali played for the MCC against West Indies in Durham in early June 2007, an experience he described as "quite weird" as he played against a lot of his Caribbean friends. And then in June 2007 he got a surprise call from the West Indies selectors after an injury crisis had hit their squad while on tour in England. Only five fit players were left standing in a one-day squad of 14.

"It was a massive surprise, but very welcome," Mali confessed. "They were struggling with injuries and with replacements coming over so I was just glad for the opportunity when the team manager Michael Findlay called me."

The one-day fixture was against an England Lions side at Worcester and reduced to 24 overs due to rain. Mali took the field alongside Chris Gayle, Denesh Ramdin, Darren Powell, Marlon Samuels and Runako Morton of the original touring party. The rest of the team being made up of hastily drafted qualified players like him. The Lions made 174 for six and West Indies won by eight wickets with five balls to spare with Ramdin and Morton sharing a match-winning second wicket stand of 130.

Mali hadn't batted, bowled or taken a catch, but he had played for his country. By the time the squad played Derbyshire three days later some of the walking wounded were back on their feet, replacements had arrived and Mali was not required again.

Viv had been born and raised in Antigua, the son of Malcolm, an assistant governor to the island's prison, "So there were times when he would bring some of that discipline home. He was the enforcer, whereas my mother [Gretchen], who was a stay-at-home mum, was always the pacifier.

Viv was the youngest of three brothers. Mervyn and Donald played for Antigua as amateurs.

"You can imagine the little fights and scraps we had," he told

The Guardian in 2017. "I had a wonderful childhood in Antigua. Sport was a huge part of family life. Seeing my dad play so much inspired me. He represented Antigua and the Leeward Islands. I started playing as soon as I started walking. I'd take the pads from Dad and put them on and pick up the bat, which was sometimes much taller than me.

"Where we lived there was a cricket club, where we played every day except for Sundays, which our parents felt was a sacred day," he added. "The other kids would pass by and make fun of us, saying our parents were too strict, but when you look at some of those kids who perhaps didn't hold dear the same values, they ended up on the wrong side of the law."

Young Viv would play cricket with his brothers, his father and Pat Evanson, a family friend who had been captain of Antigua. He left the Antigua Grammar School aged 18 and worked for D'arcy's Bar and Restaurant in St John's. His boss, D'Arcy Williams effectively sponsored his early cricket career, providing him with whites, gloves, pads and a bat.

He played his club cricket for St. John's CC and then Rising Sun Cricket Club until he started to play for Somerset in 1974.

Viv goes down in cricket's history books as one of the best batsmen ever, corroborated by his inclusion as one of the five Cricketers of the Century in 2000, alongside Sir Donald Bradman, Sir Garfield Sobers, Sir Jack Hobbs and Shane Warne. The *Wisden Cricketers' Almanack* named him in 2002 as the Greatest ODI batsman of all-time and he was third in their Test list behind Bradman and Sachin Tendulkar. That is exalted company.

He scored 8,540 runs in 121 Test matches at an average of 50.23, including 24 centuries. He also scored nearly 7,000 runs in One Day Internationals and more than 36,000 in first-class cricket. A very successful West Indies captain he was knighted for his contributions to cricket in 1999.

Mali played only 18 first-class matches in a career that saw him debut for Oxford UCCE in April 2004 and played his final match for Leeward Islands in March 2014. He made 376 runs at an average of 13.92 with a highest score of 50 and took 15 wickets at 57.00. Add six List A and one Twenty20 match where he contributed little and that's the story of a career that never took off. It simply wasn't to be. It hadn't been his destiny.

In Mali's defence his emergence in West Indies cricket coincided with a chaotic period of administration and a decline in appetite for the Caribbean's national sport. During Viv's international career that began in 1974 and ended in 1991 the West Indies had ruled the world. So often you hear this period of domination put down to the side having four fearsome quick bowlers that decimated batting attacks worldwide. But their batting line-up was to be envied too and Viv the most successful.

But in the era after the teams led by Clive Lloyd and Richards there were good players, but the team subsided. Interest waned from Tests with crowds declining, unheard of in the years before when spectators would literally hang from the rafters for a vantage point.

If Mali's career had been managed better who knows what he could have achieved? He undoubtedly had talent.

I was tasked with painting my Grandma's hallway in May 1984. I laid down some sheets, arranged my equipment and settled in for a long haul with only Test Match Special on my radio for company. England were playing West Indies in a One-Day International at Old Trafford.

In 1984 England could barely lay a finger on their visitors. The tourists, led by Clive Lloyd, would 'blackwash' their hosts 5-0 in the Test series later in the summer. But as I painted English hopes of beating the best team in the world remained high as the 1st One-Day International got underway.

With West Indies at 102 for seven England were in a dominant position, but one man had just past fifty and was about to spoil their day with a brutal assault. When you cast your eye down the scorecard on that first innings only Eldine Baptise (26) and last man Michael Holding with an unbeaten 11 joined Richards in making double figures. His innings of 189 not out from 170 balls contained 21 fours and five sixes, 86 of his runs coming from the final 58 balls he faced, enabling his team to wriggle from 166 for nine to a final total of 272 for nine and ultimately a victory by 104 runs.

It was then the highest ODI innings of all time and only the fourth in excess of 150, he himself claiming one of the other three.

My Grandma had apparently been concerned that I was concentrating too much on the commentary and not enough on painting. The end result was the best paint job I could muster as Richards had firmly concentrated my mind.

I could list many other occasions where the Antiguan Master Blaster took centre stage and not only racked up the runs but also royally entertained in the process. Even in the current era of Twenty20 cricket and increased run-rates throughout all formats of the game, very few players have got close to matching the lethal mastery of IVA Richards.

So how could Mali ever compete? He would never fulfil his cricket dreams. He played his last first-class game for Leeward Islands in March 2014. He may not have achieved the heights of his father's career, but he'd given it a damned good go.

Viv had three children. Matara, two years older than Mali from his first marriage, lives in Canada and works for the Antigua and Barbuda consulate in Toronto. "I'm very proud of her and what's she's achieving," Viv said.

His third child is Masaba, from his second marriage to Neena Gupta, an Indian actress. "I'm very proud of her too. She designs clothes for the Bollywood film industry."

And Mali is now part-owner of an art gallery in Antigua.

"I'm very happy for him as well," Viv said. "He tried to partake in cricket, but I guess that was always going to be tough for him, following in my footsteps.

"I did have a chat with him about what he was trying to pursue and how hard it was going to be for him and how much pressure would be placed on him. I guess he didn't quite take my advice."

* * * * *

When I thought about West Indies as a cricket nation, full of communities and families where cricket had been central to their social existence it amazed me that there were so few examples of fathers and sons that had progressed to play for West Indies.

You'll see at the back of this book there are only three Caribbean families who have passed on the international baton.

There may be a fourth soon though. A young man called Tagenarine Chanderpaul was making his way into first-class cricket with Guyana. Shivnarine, his father, is statistically the second best batsman West Indies have ever produced. A limpet at the crease with a crab-like stance, Shiv had been one of the toughest wickets to take in an international career that began in 1994 and ended, some would say prematurely, in 2015. During that period he played 164 Tests and another 290 one-day games for his country finishing just a whisker, if a whisker is 86 runs behind Brian Lara on 11,867 runs, and seventh in the all-time run-stakes in Test cricket, until overtaken by Alastair Cook anyway.

He didn't have the array of shots of a Richards or Lara, but he could churn out the runs all the same. Still playing domestic first-class cricket aged 42 as his 2017 English county season begins with Lancashire the dogged left-hander appears to be allergic to giving his wicket away.

Tagenarine shares many of the same qualities. 16 games into a first-class career with Guyana he has hit three fifties at a mid-twenties average, but he's only on the cusp of his 21st birthday and a lot is expected, not just because of his surname.

The Chanderpauls have shared two remarkable partnerships as one of only a very select group of fathers and sons to have played together in the same match.

Tagenarine, also a left-hander who marked his guard by banging a bail into the ground with the bat handle, was aged only 16 when he played alongside his father for the Gandhi Youth Organisation against Transport Sports Club in September 2012. They added an unbeaten partnership of 258 as Shiv clattered 10 sixes in his 143 not out and his son added six more to also remain not out and walk off with his father with 112 to his name. They took the total to 313 for two in 40 overs before their opponents were dismissed for 187 in reply.

Tagenarine had previously been named the 2011 Under-15 Cricketer of the Year by the Guyana Cricket Board and would progress to debut in first-class cricket for the island in February 2013. But it was in March 2017 that the Chanderpauls hit the headlines again as they became the first father-son duo to play in the same first-class game in West Indies since 1922. Playing for Guyana in the WICB Cricket League Regional 4-day first-class tournament against Jamaica they both posted half-centuries as Tagenarine opened the innings and Shiv batted at No5. They shared a fourth wicket stand of 38 before Tagenarine was out for 58 in 135 balls. His father was the eighth man out for 57.

The record books don't have comprehensive records of fathers and sons playing in the same game, but it is believed that the Chanderpauls were the 19th instance. Prior to them the most recent pair were Denis and Heath Streak in Zimbabwe. They played together for Matabeleland in a Lonrho Logan Cup match in April 1996.

"Having my father play with me in the same match was special as he was my mentor and inspiration," Heath Streak told journalist Bipin Dani for my website cricketbadger.com.

When asked whether it was him or his father that was under the most pressure, Heath responded: "Probably my father as his age was the challenge. However, the experience carried him through. I on the other hand didn't want to be outclassed."

So the competitive juices were flowing, although Streak quickly added that they had no issues if both had failed, or if one failed and the other had succeeded.

"Failure was not an issue," Heath continued. "It is a part of the game. Luckily when we played we had more success than failure. Parents are more understanding though."

Denis Streak, 24 years Heath's senior, played 14 first-class matches as a right-arm paceman. Heath, in the same playing style, played 65 Tests and 189 ODIs for Zimbabwe.

CHAPTER TEN

The BAADER-MEINHOF PHENOMENON

"Success and failure are greatly overrated,
but failure gives you a whole lot more to talk about"
George Bernard Shaw

Have you ever discovered a new word, phrase or fact and then, after never knowing it had existed, stumbled across the same thing again, often repeatedly, over the following few days? It was happening to me as I wrote this book. Suddenly I became aware that a lot of people were talking about famous people and their offspring. Perhaps I was paying more attention.

It struck me to such a degree that I typed some salient phrases into Google and discovered there was a name for such an occurrence. It's known as the Baader-Meinhof Phenomenon and was something else I'd never heard of before. A day after my Google search I heard someone mention Baader-Meinhof on BBC Radio 4.

Whether suddenly becoming more aware of your own book's subject matter is truly a Baader-Meinhof experience I'm unsure. It certainly came in handy as I realised there was a world away from cricket that required a second glance.

During a few months in 2016, if I needed telling, it became abundantly clear that parents and children existed in other sports and areas of life.

* * * * *

Like most Brits during the 2016 Rio Olympics I found myself in awe of the soon to be married Jason Kenny and Laura Trott. Team GB's cyclists had taken 11 Olympic gold medals, were the talk of an ecstatic nation and the golden couple had been the stars. Kenny had won three more golds in Rio to take his Olympic tally to six and equal Sir Chris Hoy with the most gold medals by a British athlete. Trott had two to her name in Rio and her four career gold medals put her ahead of any British woman Olympian.

Their final triumphs had come within minutes of each other on 16 August. Trott had breezed to the top of the podium in the omnium event and waited as her fiancé made two false starts in the keirin, escaped disqualification before winning again.

With their medals in the bag the watching public and media wanted more. A tearful Trott gave her man a hug and a kiss before expectant photographers and then the most famous tweet of the 2016 Olympics landed on social media.

An excitable Trott exclaimed to the world: "Arghhh!!!!! I love him to bits. Our kids have to get some of these genes right?"

As the message was retweeted, commented on and interpreted by the media Trott attempted to calm the baby talk down, saying: "I only put it out there because everyone kept going on about it. So I was just like, 'It could be the best omnium rider in the world, couldn't it? Bit of sprint, bit of endurance. You never know'. Twenty-something years down the line, you never know."

A myriad of newspaper and magazine articles followed. It was good-natured speculation about a nation's golden couple. The pair married in September 2016 and said since that babies may have to wait until after they've added to their medal tally at the 2020 games in Tokyo.

The chances are the innocent comment will be forgotten. But, I couldn't help wonder what would happen if Trott's prophecy were to come true. Can you imagine the expectation if their child decides to pursue a cycling career?

* * * * *

Of course it can turn out swimmingly. Roll on a few months to 27 November 2016 and the Formula One Yas Marina track in Abu Dhabi. Nico Rosberg clinched the F1 World Drivers Championship for the first time and, in doing so, emulated his father Keke's victory in 1982. The Rosbergs became only the second father and son champions after Graham (1962 and 1968) and Damon Hill (1996).

I have to admit to being guilty of wondering whether the name Rosberg had enabled Nico to secure an F1 drive. It may have helped, but after being runner-up to team-mate Lewis Hamilton in 2014 and 2015 his ability had shone through.

Keke had kept a low profile to allow his son to take the limelight in his own right. "My role is one of private support," Keke said after his son's win. "I haven't made one interview since January 2010. This is the first time, and it was hard to avoid today."

Rosberg senior had maintained his distance during the season finale, choosing to watch the race in a Dubai hotel and then a friend's house before arriving in Abu Dhabi after the finish.

"The time had come to take a step back," he said. "There was no choice but to come here, because if I was to come here for three days doing nothing, there would not have been a peaceful minute for me. So we discussed with Nico and I said, 'look, I can't come, it doesn't work'. So that's why I didn't come here. I don't think he knew exactly where I was, but he knew I was in Dubai."

It was a selfless decision. Opting to miss a proud paternal moment for fear his presence may somehow detract from it. It's a decision that only a father that had trodden that path before his son could have made, or would have needed to make.

He was also at pains to avoid any comparison between his success and that of his son.

"It is remarkable and I admire him for his mental strength and commitment," Keke added. "We have to remember that the commitment of someone like Nico is 110% and it has nothing to do with how I went about being a Formula One driver.

"My wins don't count anymore. They are such a long time ago. It's all about Nico and his performance and success now. You cannot really compare the eggs – the eggs look the same but they were quite different in those days. It is not easier, or more difficult, it is just a completely different game. It is a family sport and he knows what it means to me and what it means to him."

Nico was quick to say 'Danke Mama und Papa' and if ever Twitter were required to validate its existence the four minute and 53 seconds of video footage released on Nico's feed shortly after the Abu Dhabi Grand prix would make for a great start.

Footage recorded when Rosberg was a mere pup starting out on karting shows his father patiently recording his son's lap times, refilling his fuel tank and ensuring his helmet is properly secured. The enduring image is the blue eyes of Nico, staring up at his father as he watches his every move and absorbs his advice. There's a son's love, but also massive respect on show.

A little later in the day Sky Sports aired a musical montage of the season. It ended with Rosberg held aloft by his team and then cut to a young Nico alongside his father. Nico must have been asked why he hangs on his father's every word. His answer was particularly poignant: "Because he's a world champion. He can teach me go-karting and later I can drive Formula One. Then I can try to become World Champion."

It really brought it home to me. We all have sporting heroes, but when that role model is your own father, what greater incentive can there be?

Nico had been exposed to motor racing from being a youngster. Every detail had been ingrained in him and become the essence of everything he wanted to be. There's only one winner when placing the nature versus nurture debate into the same sentence as Nico Rosberg. He'd been learning to become a champion from the moment he'd been born.

* * * * *

In July 2014 the news of Rik Mayall's death affected me. I'd grown up with *The Young Ones*, *Comic Strip* and *Bottom* in the new alternative landscape of humour. Mayall had made me chuckle more than most and his cameo appearances in *Blackadder* were legendary.

As I read the tributes I also devoured information about Mayall's great mate and comic partner Adrian Edmondson. It was not news to me that he was married to Jennifer Saunders, of French and Saunders and *Absolutely Fabulous* fame, but my Internet surfing led me to their daughter Beattie Edmondson. The daughter of two of the standout comic talents of the last 30 years was following their footsteps.

"I'd love to have wacky stories about them but they were fairly normal parents," Beattie had told the Daily Mail in April 2013. "Dad was embarrassing and Mum was annoying. They're still very involved with our lives.

"Once when I was at school, a boy got told off for breaking wind," she remembered. "When I told Dad he said, 'don't let anyone ever, ever tell you that farting isn't funny'."

It seemed to me to be sound advice. Beattie had grown up in a household where Dawn French, Joanna Lumley and Ben Elton were frequent visitors, so there was no shortage of comedic inspiration, although she recalled them as "the grown ups".

At the time of the interview she had taken a part in an Elton comedy and admitted, "It took me a while to be an adult around Ben."

It raised an issue I'd not dwelt on before. Would a cricketer have similar thoughts? Would the transition between being a child visiting a dressing room and, a few years later, being a man in the same environment be a tough one as the dynamics of your relationship with older players altered?

"I had to stop being so embarrassed," continued Beattie. "It didn't help that almost everything he said had some kind of rude joke attached".

Three years later and Beattie's career had taken off. She was starring in Josh Widdicombe's BBC comedy 'Josh' as flatmate Kate. When Kate's mother featured in a second series episode, the actress who played her was Jennifer Saunders.

She was also performing with her comedy trio Birthday Girls, alongside two university friends. The Evening Standard caught up with her and her Dad at the Soho Theatre in October 2016.

The Birthday Girls were appearing in the cabaret space downstairs and Adrian was starring on a one-man tragicomedy 'Bits of Me are Falling Apart' in the main auditorium.

"I'm a bit embarrassed for her, having her old Dad around," Adrian commented on the booking quirk that had seen the two generations performing under the same roof. "I feel like I'm impinging on her space".

One of the joys of parenting is getting the balance right between being pushy and proud yet distant enough to allow growth and space. In return the child establishes their role in the family unit. To do that they must understand what their parents do.

Beattie confessed to not knowing what her parents did as she was growing up. Once she'd established some degree of understanding and assessed her own ambitions she believed her surname was a hindrance.

"I remember asking my Mum if she was Jennifer Saunders, because kids at school were asking me," she said.

I found it difficult to accept that the surname was of no help. Surely having famous and influential contacts could do little harm.

Beattie did however elaborate in a November 2015 interview with the Daily Mail: "I think it evens itself out in the end. I guess the pros are that people are interested in you initially so you can get them into a room, but the cons are you are immediately compared to your parents, which isn't always easy."

Note too, that in every interview I've found and taken quotes from the main thrust of the piece has been about parents. It's the easy way in, the chance to secure promotion, but as Beattie suggests, she is then expected to perform – to be as funny and engaging as her Mum and Dad.

It would also appear she's had many years to prepare herself for the possibility of keeping it in the family.

"I've always said this is what I wanted to do, even when I was very little," she said. "I remember me and one of my friends deciding we were going to be a double act when we were about six. We had a book of jokes."

On the nature versus nurture spectrum, I'd put Beattie somewhere in the middle. Born into a creative and arty family she has been steeped in that culture, but then don't people say that comedians have funny bones? By all accounts the anarchic alternative comedian parents have formed a very tight-knit and traditional style family. Fun, japes and taking the mickey out of each other seems to have created a happy home and laughed Beattie into show business.

With the genes Beattie has laughs must be in the DNA. Beattie's older sister Ella is a musician and the youngster in the family, Freya, is a costume designer. The Edmondson offspring, whether they knew it or not, appear to have soaked in their parents' creative psyches.

Adrian recalled how he and Jennifer had been "terrified when Beattie first said she was doing comedy and invited us up to a show. We thought *how are we going to react if it's shit?*" Fortunately for all, it wasn't.

* * * * *

On 2 May 1993 Peter Schmeichel was a 29-year-old. The Manchester United goalkeeper was waiting on another side's result. His team's rivals for the title didn't win. Manchester United were Premier League champions.

On 2 May 2016 Kasper Schmeichel was a 29-year-old. The Leicester City goalkeeper was waiting on another side's result. His team's rivals for the title didn't win. Leicester City were Premier League champions. The only difference was his father had been there before.

At odds of 5,000/1 Leicester City had defied all logic and won the biggest trophy in English football. Central to their success was one of the biggest surnames in Premier League history.

Peter Schmeichel had been a monster between the sticks for Manchester United in heady times for a club well used to success. He'd won Euro 1992 with Denmark, four Danish League titles and a Danish Cup with Brondby before joining Manchester United ahead of the 1991/92 season. The Red Devils won the Super Cup in 1991, added a League Cup in 1992 and then secured three FA Cups, five Premier League titles and the European Cup – an unprecedented treble coming in Schmeichel's final season at Old Trafford in 1999. He finished his career at Sporting Lisbon with a Portuguese League title in 2000.

Quite simply, Peter was as good as it gets as a keeper. In addition to the honours he'd won with clubs and country, he was named Premier League Player of the Year in 1996 and was UEFA's Goalkeeper of the Year in 1992, 1993, 1997 and 1998. For much of his career he was the best in the world and is undoubtedly one of the best goalkeepers ever to play the game.

Unlike Nico Rosberg, Kasper hadn't set out to directly emulate his father. He played as a striker until the age of 15, although he'd had brief forays in goal. It wasn't until he'd been accepted into a sports college in Denmark that he was required to state his position and "for some reason I just chose goalkeeper, so that's where it all started."

The physical traits between father and son are uncanny. The

Scandinavian blonde thatch of hair would lead you to believe you were watching the same man, the build is also very similar, and the only obvious difference is Kasper hasn't inherited his father's ruddy nose.

For many years he was no more than a journeyman player. He told Oliver Holt of the *Mail on Sunday* in December 2015, with Leicester City riding high in the Premier League and still five months from their ultimate glory, that the Schmeichel surname had been a real burden.

"It's been no help whatsoever in my career," Schmeichel stated firmly. "It's been quite the opposite, I feel. I think I would have played longer in the Premier League if that wasn't the case. The issue is that I am 29, I am married, I have two kids, but people still see me as someone's son. They still see me as a child."

By now I'd heard a lot of the younger generations state that their famous surname had been an issue, but Schmeichel took it a step further. Being the 'son of' the legendary Peter, a Manchester United legend, was a tough act to follow.

Kasper's journey to the top of English football had taken him on a circuitous journey. He began his career on the other side of Manchester with City, but was farmed out on loan to Darlington, Bury and Falkirk before making seven starts for Manchester City in the 2007/08 season before being ousted by future England keeper Joe Hart. He was then loaned out to Cardiff City. When surplus to requirements he'd prefer to move on and play games.

"I hated not playing," he said. "I hated getting to a Saturday and not having a game. I had missed playing and I had been starved of football for so long that I didn't care where I played."

He spent the 2009/10 season at Notts County before moving to Leeds United in May 2010 before he was finally able to lay down stronger roots at Leicester City ahead of the 2011/12 season.

With Leicester, Kasper won Championship promotion in 2014 and after a Houdiniesque escape from relegation at the end of the 2014/15 season, the Holy Grail of Premier League glory shocked and delighted the world in 2016.

Peter spoke to the Daily Mirror after Leicester City had secured their route back into the Premier League. "It has been a very long road for him, longer than it should have been," he said. "But this is just the nature of being someone else's son. It has its challenges, being the son of someone who has played in the Premier League at a big club Manchester United.

"I am pleased for him," he continued. "It was his choice and he is doing well. It has always been his choice. When your kid makes choices like that all you want to see them do is do well and succeed. He is having a good time.

"You don't see many sons in the Premier League. For whatever reason people compare them to their fathers, which is unfair to the sons. But I now think he is much better equipped by having had to take the long road by having had to sort of not get the same opportunities many others had."

Kasper played every second of Leicester's promotion season and was named the PFA Championship Goalkeeper of the Season for the second successive year. He'd made the Danish gloves his own too.

"My son has done fantastically well," Peter continued. "Kasper has worked really hard and I think he is more than good enough. He has invented his own style of play. He is very capable of what he is doing and he should be credited for that. I think now that he is a Premier League goalkeeper with Leicester he is much better equipped than players who might have got opportunities earlier.

"I am proud and think he has done really well, but I would have been proud of anything he did. Just because football is high profile and people follow it, it doesn't make it a better thing. Leicester are playing well, but I am not too sure I am going to talk too much about that. That is his department and he should speak for himself."

There is no doubt Peter has taken a lot of satisfaction in watching his son prove the doubters wrong. As soon as Leicester's 2015/16 title was assured he changed his Twitter bio to 'Father to a Premier League winner'. He tweeted that "proud does not cover it" and that he couldn't "find the right words" to describe his delight.

The Schmeichels became only the second father and son duo to both win the Premier League title after Ian Wright (Arsenal 1998) and Shaun Wright-Phillips (Chelsea 2006). And perhaps the Leicester fairytale has finally changed the dynamic and people will now be more inclined to say 'that's Kasper Schmeichel's dad' rather than view the shot-stopping son as the footnote. In Kasper's view that would be the perfect legacy of Leicester's success, and it's been a long time coming.

Every step, save and success of Kasper's journey have received critical comparisons with his father. Despite being pivotal to Leicester's success, Kasper believes people's inclination to compare his every move with his father's career has only got stronger.

"It's getting worse and worse every month," he complained. "I thought it would get better. I don't know why. For some reason, people are more interested in it than ever.

"I have never seen the interest in it," he admitted. "It's probably because I'm in it. I can't see what the hype is, what the interest is. For me, it's completely boring. It's irrelevant. People will talk and will compare. That's their prerogative but to me it's irrelevant.

"People are surprised when I say I am 29," he continued. "They're like, 'Really?' One day, maybe when I am 40 and hopefully still playing, then I might be considered a mature enough person."

Being inside the bubble perhaps Kasper is unable to see that the increased comparisons and attention he has received is actually a compliment. More people are noticing him, but it doesn't alter the fact that he is bored by people's obsession.

Kasper, like all children, has striven to create his own identity and wants to be recognised for his own achievements. One of the most futile, yet enjoyable, elements of following any sport is to try and compare eras. The game changes and so do the players.

For the young Schmeichel, like any of us, the aim in life is to be happy with his own performance and who he is. The look in the mirror and be proud of who we are scenario. For Kasper this is now, this is his movie and when the credits role he wants to read his name as leading man, not 'son of Peter'.

"I have had intrusions from the outside since the day I was born because of my dad. I had it from my first memories. For me, it's a thing that has made me very guarded around people.

"I might not be very approachable because through my whole life, from when I was eight, I had people camping behind my goal and hearing whispers, 'It's Peter Schmeichel's son'. They think it's fun, but with me it's just not fun any more."

In early December 2016 Kasper recounted a fan approaching him for an autograph at the team hotel in Swansea. He'd kept three clean sheets in six games and the team were flying high.

After getting his autograph the fan said: "You're doing well, you'll never be as good as your dad, though."

When Kasper sarcastically responded with, "Thank you mate, cheers," the fan complained, "Oh. Come on, I'm only having a laugh."

Kasper went to leave, but the fan continued to protest his innocence and defend his attempt at humour.

"Mate, you don't think I've heard that before?" Kasper proffered. "I've heard that for the last 15 years. Well, you've had your laugh, so can I leave please?"

Kasper suggested this was a frequent occurrence. Things like, 'Great save the other day, but I think your dad would have caught it', may be seen as a joke by someone eager to make a quick impression during their solitary meeting with the Dane. From Kasper's viewpoint it had become increasingly tiresome.

Kasper bites back more often these days, but his father is far less tolerant. Father and son had been out for dinner together when a man approached their table, shook Peter's hand and told him he was a legend, before adding: "Your son's doing well but he'll never be as good as you". Peter responded with: "Just go. You're going to come here and insult my son and think you're going to get away with it?"

Kasper added: "It's got to a point now where if you're going to talk to me, talk to me. Don't come and try and have a laugh and try and half-insult me. I'm happy to talk to anybody but do it in the right manner. I'm not going to buy into it any more.

"My dad was always guarded with that type of thing – he tried to shield me and my sister as much as possible," Kasper explained. "My wife hates that life. She doesn't live that life. I don't want my kids exposed to that kind of thing either".

* * * * *

As I was writing this chapter Real Madrid scored a goal in their Copa del Rey match against third tier Cultural Leonesa. Just 18 minutes into his senior debut at the Bernabéu Stadium a 21-year-old named Enzo Zidane had grabbed his first goal as his head coach and father, Zinedine Zidane, watched on from the touchline.

I soon realised that all four of Zizou's sons are on Real Madrid's books. Enzo, the eldest, wears his mother's maiden name Fernandez on the back of his shirt, perhaps there's slightly less pressure that way. He is a Spain Under-19 international but, and like his brothers, has the choice of playing for three countries – Spain through birth, France through their father or Algeria via his grandfather's heritage.

Enzo plays in the same position as his father, an attacking midfielder. Next in line is Luca, a goalkeeper tipped by many to be the best of the bunch and he most likely to go all the way. Then Theo, in his early teens, and the youngest, Elyaz, yet to become a teenager, are both midfielders playing in Real Madrid's boys' teams.

Enzo already playing under the management of his father is a remarkable story. If any, or all, of the other three were to progress, the Zidane dynasty is potentially the biggest father and son story in world sport.

They have big shoes to fill. Zidane senior played 227 matches for Real Madrid, won six domestic trophies and scored the winning goal in the 2002 Champions League final. He was the prized asset of a France side that won the 1998 World Cup and the European Championship two years later.

Football is a harsh environment at the best of times and if they do pursue a professional career the Zidane boys' every move will be scrutinised.

Nigel Clough played under father Brian and Jordi Cruyff under legendary Dutchman Johan and both enjoyed respectable careers.

Pele's son, Edinho, played as a goalkeeper for Santos but could never be expected to match his father's achievements and ultimately served time in prison for drugs and money-laundering offences.

Diego Maradona's son, Diego Sinagra, gave football a go too as a youth player with Napoli. An Italian journalist was asked whether the young Maradona could emulate his father as a player. He said: 'If you threw Maradona an orange he'd catch it on his foot, juggle it and balance it on his head. If you threw his son an orange he'd catch it in his hands, peel it and eat it'.

Sport can provide emotional rewards and riches like no other area of life. It could also be an unforgiving and frustrating world where there is no place to hide.

Baader-Meinhof just couldn't stop giving.

The Zidanes had made me think that sporting prowess had to be in the genes somewhere. Four children excelling at the same sport as their father could not be a coincidence.

I picked up the phone to give Mark Butcher a call. Perhaps he could shed further light for me.

CHAPTER ELEVEN

ALAN and MARK BUTCHER

*"When everything goes to hell, the people who stand by
you without flinching – they are your family"*
George Bernard Shaw

I was dodging beer snakes on a very boisterous Western Terrace
at Headingley on 20 August 2001 on what became a career-
defining day for England batsman Mark Butcher.

The Surrey left-hander played in an era where England
regularly came up short in tussles for the Ashes urn. That 2001
summer had been no different with England three-nil down in the
five-match series when they arrived in Leeds. They would lose the
final Test at The Oval, but for that one day in Yorkshire the
flashing blade of Mark Butcher proved the Aussies were beatable
after all.

I remember a straight drive to the Rugby Stand boundary off
Glenn McGrath shortly after Butcher had reached fifty. It was the
moment I started to believe. A flurry of cuts and off-side drives
took him to a century and then cavalierly on to an unbeaten 173.
There are many people with better records who never experience
the high he must have felt as he walked off in triumph with
England victorious by six wickets.

It was an innings that now sits in Ashes folklore, even more
poignant in an era of drought, and a knock that could easily never
have been.

Mark's father Alan had played one Test match for England
against India at The Oval in 1979. A solitary One-Day
International followed a summer later. In the days before central
contracts gave newcomers a little more time, his 34 runs in three
innings hadn't been enough. It seems scant reward for a man
whose first-class career spanned 17 seasons for Surrey and
Glamorgan.

Mark had seemed destined to stall on 27 Test appearances. Five
Tests on the 1999/2000 South Africa tour had failed to produce a
fifty and he lost his place to Marcus Trescothick. His poor form
continued into Surrey's season, which saw him dropped to The
Oval's second string. His marriage to Alec Stewart's sister Judy

had broken up and his love of cricket was going the same way. He was lost until a good friend gave him a much-needed pep talk. He thought it through and phoned his Dad.

"It was the closest we ever got with cricket, when he was trying to resurrect my career," Mark stated. "I asked him if he'd help me and we had two or three months when we were together nearly every day, just the two of us working one-on-one.

"The culmination of that was him in tears on Test Match Special after I'd made 173 against Australia. That period was our entire relationship as father and son in cricket really.

"It was desperation that led me to ask him," he recalled. "I didn't really want to play anymore, I'd stopped enjoying it, I couldn't play the way that I wanted to and other things in life were not going particularly well and I just thought *I've had enough of this*.

"A good mate of mine said 'come on, get yourself together' and then I began to think about what I was going to do to get back. I wasn't really thinking about playing for England again," he admitted. "I just wanted to play in a manner that was pleasing and if I did that then I had a good chance of scoring a few runs.

"So I called Dad up and said 'look, I need some help, is there any chance you can spend a bit of time' and he said 'oh great, I've been waiting for you to do this, I've been wanting to help and do something for six or seven months, but didn't quite know how to go about approaching you'."

When I spoke to Alan he remembered the time he'd spent getting Mark's game back on track with great fondness. He'd been watching his son's struggles in South Africa as he hosted England supporters while working for a travel company.

"I knew that he needed help and felt that I knew what he needed to do," Alan remembered. "While he was playing and had coaches working with him it was very difficult for me to do anything.

"I didn't want to confuse the issue," he confessed. "There is also an issue with coaching your son. It can be very difficult. Very often it's better letting someone else do it. It's sometimes very difficult to tell your son what he needs to do.

"But Mark lost his place in the England side after South Africa and he came to me, which was perfect then because I could say 'look this is what I think you should be doing' and we set about it for a couple of months. It took him a while to assimilate it into his game and then he had a bit of luck.

"He thought he was miles away from the England team, but I think three batters got injured in front of him and he found himself in the side and got 500-odd runs in that Ashes series".

Alan had separated from Mark's mother when his eldest son

was 13. Even prior to that the life of a professional cricketer hadn't been conducive to offering much family time, certainly not as coach and pupil.

Mark confirmed: "That had never been part of our relationship before. When my brother Gary was at Glamorgan, he and Dad had a bit of an odd relationship around that. Gary always felt like his Dad was interfering or picking on him when he was actually trying to help. I think as a consequence of that my Dad had thought *sod it, I'm not going to get back into that* and decided he was not going to say anything unless he was asked."

Alan appreciated the opportunity of helping his son out: "I certainly enjoyed that aspect of it and I think in a relationship sense it was very good. I'd like to think that he enjoyed it as well."

Mark enjoyed the time working with his father and benefited greatly from the process. The first session they spent together had begun very much from a standing start.

"I'd got to the point where I was willing for him to do whatever he wanted to do," Mark said. "We were never going to have a fight over this, that and the other. If he'd told me to hold the bat the other way up then that's what I'd have done. I had given up fighting it and that's why it worked.

"At the beginning it was incredibly difficult, but I was in a position where I was playing so badly that it kind of didn't matter," he chuckled. "I had to be useless in order for it to do me good. Otherwise I'd have walked away in a huff and said it wasn't working.

"You work with coaches and you work with other batsmen, but generally speaking a coach doesn't have that much time to devote to one player. They are the coach for the squad or team and you might get half-an-hour with someone in the net and then you are left to your own devices.

"We literally had two-and-a-half months in the Indoor School at The Oval for two or three hours a day, literally tearing everything apart. We went right back to the basics of how to hold a bat properly and the stance, to cutting, hooking and pulling 95mph tennis balls from a bowing machine, which is where we got to in the end."

The proof was in the pudding. Runs for Surrey encouraged England to turn to Mark's experience for the visit of their Ashes rivals. I'm sure Geoffrey Boycott would have grumbled into a microphone that Butcher had not capitalised on good starts after scoring 38, 41, 21, 83, 13 and 1 before being run out for 47 in the first innings at Headingley.

As Alan sat in the Leeds crowd he could have been forgiven for fearing the worst as England resumed on four for no loss, chasing 315 to win. Mark was soon in at No 3 with the score nine for one after Atherton edged Glenn McGrath behind. Nasser Hussain joined him 27 runs later when Marcus Trescothick edged Jason Gillespie to slip.

In the crowd Alan was not hopeful. "I can remember watching the first hour and thinking that the 315 we needed to get seemed a long way away. For the first 40 minutes I thought we'd be lucky to get 115 because the ball seemed to be going everywhere.

"Mark said it changed when Nasser hooked somebody for six and the ball landed in the car park," Alan revealed. "It mashed up the ball and it didn't do as much afterwards and suddenly the game changed and became a lot easier. He took them apart didn't he? He was excellent.

"The other thing was how he played Shane Warne on that day, and then spinners generally, because he hadn't been very good at playing spin. For a major part of those two months in the nets I was trying to give him a method to play spin comfortably. He then went on and got runs against Warne, Murali and the Indians.

"When I'd been watching him struggling I felt like he was trying to play shots because he wasn't confident that he could stay in," Alan added. "I told him that he might hit Warne for three fours in his first over, but it's not going to scare him and you're also going to need a hell of a lot of luck to get a hundred. You'd need luck for about three hours and that's not really going to happen."

No fortune was required as Mark powered to his century in 142 balls, passed his previous highest Test score of 116 and shared in a stand of 181 for the third wicket with Hussain. A stand of 75 with Mark Ramprakash ensured there were no wobbles, before Usman Afzaal joined him to secure a famous win.

What had started as improbable had become carefree and comfortable as Mark found the extra gear in his game that most players get to use a few times in their careers, if they are lucky.

Mark has often said that was his greatest day in cricket. "It wasn't emotional for me at the time, but afterwards it was because there's absolutely no chance whatsoever that it would have happened had Dad not helped me. Not a chance."

And Alan had enjoyed it too. "I get a lot of satisfaction from coaching all players, but it's certainly heightened when it's your own son. Any Dad is going to be proud that his son plays for England. It may be a bit heightened if you've been in the profession and done it yourself. It is quite special.

"Probably the best day of my cricketing career was watching him get that hundred against Australia at Headingley to win that Test match. That's one of the highlights of my life".

For a while Mark played shackle-free for his country, scoring 555 runs at 55 in 2002. He'd play 71 Tests for England, his final match played in South Africa at the end of 2004. A knee injury saw him quit the game during the 2009 season, instigating a move into the media.

That ended a professional career that had begun over 23 years earlier on 28 July 1991 when he'd debuted at The Oval for Surrey against a Glamorgan side captained by his father.

"It was extraordinary, my debut and my first 1st XI appearance too," Mark told me. "There were a lot of very special things happening that day".

Alan agreed: "It was an exciting day, I wasn't going to play in the game actually because I'd had a knee problem for a while, we'd been playing a lot and it needed a rest. But then Ian Greig told me in the pub after the Saturday's play that Mark was going to make his debut and my knee got better very quickly! I decided that I couldn't really miss that".

Mark continued: "I remember my competitive streak really came out when Dad came out to bat and I was fielding on the boundary. He came back for what should have been a very easy two and I belted around the boundary, picked it up, hurled it back in his general direction to make sure that he had to hustle to get in and gave him a glare. It was really weird ultra competitive stuff, trying to make a mark or whatever.

"I was in the side as a bowler really and I came out to bat at No 9 and we were losing horribly. I smashed 48 not out in 30 balls and very nearly won us the game. I needed to hit a six off the last ball of the match and didn't quite manage it.

"In the end it turned out to be a good day as I'd scored some runs. Dad said that it was the best of both worlds for him. As Glamorgan captain his side had won the game and his son had scored a few on debut."

Alan added: "It was obviously a great day and he played well in the end to get Surrey close. He had to hit the last ball for six. I asked him afterwards, because I interviewed him for *The Cricketer Magazine*, and he told me he had a plan as to what he was going to do. Steve Barwick was bowling and he had really good control and Mark knew he was going to try and slam it in the blockhole.

"So Mark said he was going to take a step down the pitch and then get right back, deep in the crease, to try and get underneath it. I'd positioned myself at long-on, so he was probably going to have to hit it over my head to win the game. In the end, Mark just stayed still and Barwick did get it in the blockhole. So I asked him what happened to his plan. He told me 'you took so long to set the field that I forgot what the plan was'."

* * * * *

I told Mark that the 'youngsters' I'd spoken to so far had used phrases like, 'I just wanted to be like my Dad,' and that they had always wanted to play the game.

"And that goes for me too," he responded without hesitation. "I always wanted to do it. There was no doubt it was something that I was going to do at all. I absolutely loved it. I was obsessed with the game when I was a kid and I don't know if it happens to everybody, but it happened to me slowly that you become a bit more of a cynic about your job. No different to anyone else I guess except that an awful lot of people would have wanted to be doing what I was doing.

"I think I was always quite driven to want to be better than anybody. It was a bit of a challenge, to not only follow in my Dad's footsteps but to go further, or as far as I could possibly go. I was quite driven in that way.

"It wasn't a spoken thing, we didn't banter each other in that awful modern common parlance, but I think it was an inner light I had. It was something to go after. I didn't find many things that drove me like that. I'd have competitions in my own head with team-mates of mine. I grew up playing for Surrey where Alec Stewart and Graham Thorpe were the legends and the guys I was gunning for. If they were playing for Surrey I wanted to score more runs than they do in the match.

"I always had that and that was probably a similar thing with my Dad. I'm not stats driven at all and never was, which is a bit of a problem for a batsman as they are the things that people tend to remember!

"But I was aware that my Dad was a fantastic player. Everyone that I speak to that was around in the 1970s and 80s tells me that he was very unlucky not to have played for England more. He was a fantastic player of fast bowling and it was an era when the West Indian quicks were terrorising everybody. I think he deserved to have had more than the one Test match he played.

"I was very aware of all that. I wanted to gain a similar respect that I saw people gave to him. It wasn't stats based or more Test caps or anything like that – nothing as numeric as that".

I wondered if Mark had experienced any negativity as he came through as a youngster because of his father. I asked Alan first if he'd been aware of any issues.

"I'd left Surrey at that stage and was with Glamorgan, so if there was any of that, I didn't notice it and Mark never mentioned it to me. I can't say that thought was ever forced upon me or came into my head," he said.

Mark added: "When I signed my first contract at The Oval in the winter of 1989, my Dad had been at Glamorgan for four or five years by then. Very few of the players that were left at the Club, with the exception of Monte Lynch, David Ward, Stewie (Alec Stewart) a little bit, hadn't grown up playing with him. It was never really a factor at all.

"When I was a kid coming through the age groups, and at school, people would maybe bring it up as a bit of schoolboy sledging, but it wasn't something I was particularly aware of, or bothered by.

"There are other dynamics involved in it, in that my Mum and Dad split up when I was 13, so my Dad wasn't around a great deal. Even when he was at home with us the life of a professional cricketer meant he was away a lot. The most time I spent with my Dad when I was growing up was when he was a teacher at the school that I went to, where he taught PE in the winter when he wasn't playing for Surrey. That was where our relationship was most of the time. I was close to my Dad, but in terms of my cricket it wasn't until I'd played for England and been a pro for ages and he came back to be coach at Surrey that we had any real working relationship.

"He never pushed me in the direction of cricket at all. That was all down to my circumstances in that I grew up around The Oval and stuff and the fact that he played. There was never any push or guide from him that that was where I was going to go - that all came later.

"Dad didn't have a massive amount of input in my game when I was a youngster. In fact I can barely remember anything at all, other than from toddling around and watching him play it was something that I desperately wanted to do and I wanted to follow in his footsteps, but I don't recall long sessions in the back garden and having been coached. That wasn't the way that it went."

The Butchers are an incredibly sports-focused family. Alan's two brothers played cricket. Martin was four years younger and played one season and just one first-class match for Surrey in 1982. His only contribution in the match was to bowl one over, but you've got to be pretty good to get that far. Ian was four years younger still and played 11 seasons for Gloucestershire and Leicestershire, scoring 5,480 first-class runs at 29.62.

Mark's brother Gary also played for Surrey and Glamorgan, playing 53 first-class and 69 one-day games in an eight-year career as an all-rounder. Alan's father had been an all-round sportsman of some repute.

Only 18 years separate Alan, his younger brothers and Mark. Sport was played regularly in the back garden and became the topic of many conversations. There was little chance of escaping it.

"It was huge and it wasn't just cricket," Mark explained. "We all played and enjoyed football at various levels. Anything to do with not having a proper job," he laughed. "My Dad's brothers were good fun and competitive when I was growing up but they didn't really coach me either. It was very much the whole *never letting you win when you're a kid* thing, pushing you around a little bit and hardening you up a little to the realities.

"Granddad was the same," Mark added. "I had this thing when I was about 12 when I decided that I wanted to be a goalkeeper. We went out in the back garden and Granddad used to be a really good football player when he was younger, but became a metal worker instead. But in the mud of the back garden he hit five scorching penalties at me and scored with four of them. I tipped the last one around the post. By then I'd nearly broken my wrist trying to stop the others.

"My uncles were exactly the same if they were bowling at you, or if you were bowling at them, they'd not take any prisoners and it was good," Mark insisted. "There are ways and means, you don't have to destroy somebody, but giving things away is not particularly helpful in the long run. You then go and play with your peers and you feel head and shoulders above them already. It filters down and it filters up I suppose."

I chose to have a quick chat with Mark's uncle Ian to get a viewpoint away from that of father and son.

Ian told me: "Dad was a very good footballer and had been offered professional terms with Leyton Orient, but we were not talking £200k a week back then and so a stable occupation and a steady income won over. So the sport genes were obviously there.

"We lived in Adelaide for five years and that gave us the outdoor lifestyle which would have allowed the cricket bug to flourish," Ian continued. "And it did, quickly! You learn a lot by simply watching and the fact that our older brother was playing cricket on a regular basis in the garden meant that Martin, and then me were drawn into the game.

"It was a play cricket, or play on your own, sort of situation. Although it would appear quite remarkable that so many of us played the game to a high level, the nurture part, albeit possibly subliminal at times, had a huge part to play."

Ian added: "When it became apparent that I had a chance of making it into the professional game, that was really where my ambitions lay. I just wanted to be a professional cricketer, full stop. We didn't have the financial rewards of the franchise

Twenty20 tournaments around the world, or indeed the central contracts that there are now. And so the very thing that now drives the modern player to want to become an international cricketer, so that they can reap the financial rewards wasn't as big an incentive then.

"My most productive seasons were in the mid 1980s when I was close to an England call-up. But then I looked around at the batters in that side. Gooch, Broad, Lamb, Smith, Gatting, Gower, Botham and I thought 'where do I fit in there?' So a degree of practicality was called for at that point."

Since retiring, like Alan, Ian has gone into coaching. A day on the golf course sowed the seeds of his future plans.

"The time when I was fully made aware of our family's little place in cricketing history, was in fact on the West course at Wentworth," Ian began. "I was partnering a golf pro from Sunningdale and we were talking about coaching when he asked what my surname was. I told him, and his response was very interesting. He said, 'As a golf pro and coach, what I would give to have a brand like that!'

"A *brand*? I had never heard that before about us," Ian remarked. "I brought that into my thinking when I was setting up my coaching business, Butch4Cricket five years ago. It helped me to develop my coaching philosophies and along with something that Alan said to me about the time when he was working with Mark stays with me even now and has a huge bearing on how I teach batting to my clients at whatever age.

"So on that day when you were dodging the beer snakes at Headingley, something that you saw in that straight drive of Mark's is still being taught now. Family legacy I suppose.

"I would like to think that in the not too distant future we can all get together and put some coaching on to pass on our experiences and knowledge - from on the field, oh, and off it!"

So, Ian had once again stressed the importance of those early year knockabouts. How they hone skills, competitiveness and the inspiration to take it further. When I moved my conversation with Alan on to the sporting prowess among the ranks of the Butcher family, he laughed and said, "There are quite a few of us.

"The unfortunate thing from Gary's point-of-view was that when Glamorgan signed him I was captain and he came down. I'd got a group of kids for a trial, as we didn't have much coming through. It was 1991 I think. Gary was coming down to stay with me for the weekend anyway so I said 'why don't you come along?'

"Alan Jones and Don Shepherd, who were the coaches at the time, said that he was the best and we should sign him. He was only 16 and I got injured and didn't play so I left him in Cardiff on his own at that age, which probably wasn't the best thing for his career. It was really unfortunate timing and so I didn't really have a lot to do with Gary either as I went off to coach Essex and wasn't there.

"Gary has had his moments. It's inevitable that people will talk about Mark, but until 2014 when Alfonso Thomas took four wickets in four balls Gary was the last to do it.

"They get on really well and I love them both the same."

And it doesn't end with Mark and Gary. Look up the scorecards of the Essex Women cricket team and you'll see the name Bryony Butcher, Alan's daughter from his second marriage. Bryony's twin sister also played to a high standard.

"There is an interest throughout the family," Alan concluded proudly. "Cricket has brought us a lot of joy as a family, and some employment too."

* * * * *

What is it that makes a child follow their father into cricket? I'd been thinking a lot about the mechanics, the factors and ingredients that would have to come together to forge someone into a young cricketer. If it was in the genes, that surely was not enough on its own. A cricket gene was just part of the recipe and would need other elements to see it blossom.

I found what the Butchers had to say on the subject fascinating. I began by asking Mark whether the existence of cricketing families was due to the nature of club cricket, even at a professional level. From the boundary, it seemed to allow families the opportunity to be part of the community and for children to become immersed in the game.

"Yes possibly, but I also think there aren't that many people who get to be quite good at it," Mark reasoned. "It's something that a lot of people enjoy and a lot of people play, but there is quite a big difference in ability between most amateurs at club level and those that make it playing ten years as first-class cricketers.

"Cricket is an extremely technical game and the coordination required just to get the movements right aren't things that a lot of people can do," Mark suggested. "If you grow up in an environment where you are exposed to those movements and get tiny pointers about the right way to hold a bat from a very young age, you've got a much better chance of grasping it rather than someone who picks it up a bit later on.

"It's quite a wild generalisation, but I do think that it's because the movements are so alien. Like the bowling action – the movements are ridiculous and it's not something you are ever going to do otherwise. You don't see people performing that sort of movement as they wait at bus stops.

"With batting – hitting the ball with a straight bat in a side-on manner isn't something that's natural at all," he continued. "Unless you've seen it, watched it and it's gone in.

"So yes, being in a cricketing family, without any doubt, that there are a lot of professional cricketer fathers and sons, is something that is entirely understandable."

Mark was suggesting that he, and others, had a head start because they were exposed to the frankly bizarre techniques required to play the sport.

I thought back to Tiger Woods at a few months old being placed in his high chair to watch his father swinging a golf club. The early acceptance, understanding and normalisation of what others may view as very peculiar movements allowed them to seep into the psyche of the child.

Alan agreed that a youngster's early exposure was a vital factor.

"The other side of Mark and the family thing is that you watch cricket and learn it," Alan said. "I always say it's done by osmosis. You absorb it, and obviously if your old man is playing first-class cricket and you are watching good players all the time you are picking up good habits, whether you realise it or not.

"From my own point-of-view it was my Mum who really liked cricket," Alan furthered. "I'm not saying my Dad didn't, but she was the one who really pushed cricket. In the school holidays I'd sit and watch the Test match and then go out and practice what I'd seen. That was my learning process.

"Mark and Gary watched me a lot. They also had a good coach when they were at primary school. I didn't really have a lot of time to help them. I think watching, copying and learning like that is a good way of doing it."

Alan was saying the same as David Lloyd had about Graham's aptitude for mimicking him and then putting what he had learned into practice. A son of a professional had the opportunity and the environment where it was okay to give it a go.

But equally, that process only works when there is an end product. We've all given new things a go only to become quickly disillusioned when we make no progress. A true champion might fight through those early setbacks if the desire and motivation burns brightly. But it's also understandable for a youngster to give up and look for something else they are instantly good at.

Mark remembered his early days at The Oval where he'd play small games with other sons, some who didn't buy into the joys of cricket like he did.

"I also played with Pat Pocock's son," Mark recalled. "He had no interest whatsoever in playing the game. It doesn't automatically follow that just because you are a member of a cricket family that you'll be excited by the game.

"It can work both ways," he added. "There's an aptitude thing in every sport, not just cricket. If you don't feel that you are good at the game then you might be turned off it even more."

I could see that happening. I'd been predominantly talking to the success stories. But when others watch and expect to see talent because of the father's pedigree, it must be soul destroying if you cannot deliver the goods.

I'd been reading about the Hadlee family in New Zealand. Walter, a New Zealand captain had five sons, three of which had followed him into the national side. But why had they been successful and what had happened to the other two? I sent a couple of emails to set up interviews with the Hadlee clan before deciding I wanted to know more about the theory behind what I'd discussed with Mark and Alan. They had whetted my appetite to discover more about the nature versus nurture debate in sport.

I'd got some reading to do, but at the time didn't know quite how much!

CHAPTER TWELVE

NATURE VERSUS NURTURE
IS THERE A CRICKET GENE?

"Although nature commences with reason and ends in experience it is necessary for us to do the opposite, that is to commence with experience and from this proceed to investigate the reason"
Leonardo Da Vinci

How does a batsman manage consistently to hit cricket balls projected in their direction at speeds approaching 100mph? If your father had fast eyes and hands does it mean you will be more capable of countering a fast bowler's hostility too? Is cricket skill handed down through the generations? A few of the players I'd spoken to had suggested they felt that was true.

It's not like a menacing quick bowler is trying to make things easy, far from it. A bowler's *raison d'être* is to intimidate, flummox and ultimately use everything in their armoury to prevent the batsman hitting the ball. Figuratively speaking, a quick bowler wants to inflict as much pain as possible.

If we ignore variables such as swing, bounce and movement off the pitch, a batsman has 40% of a second, or 400 milliseconds, from the ball leaving the bowler's hand until it reaches the stumps. A human being, and by the way there's nothing to suggest an elite sportsman has quicker reaction times than the average Joe, takes 20% of a second to see, process and send instructions to the body to respond appropriately. So once the reactions have been sparked there's only 20% of a second left to move and play a shot. The ball itself is only in reach of the bat for a five-millisecond window, or 0.5% of a second, as it jets by.

I've often heard coaches tell their pupils to "keep your eyes on the ball" or "watch the ball all the way on to the bat." I've never heard them add that this is physically impossible. Our simple human visual systems cannot process and track a ball all of the way through its flight at such speeds.

Professional cricket teams are moving away from the standard bowling machine because they don't train the batsmen to pick up on the clues they receive from a human bowler. When one examines the mathematics of batting against quick bowling it's a wonder any batsman ever scores runs!

So how do they do it?

Bruce Abernethy was an Australian cricket-loving academic. In the late 1970s, when an undergraduate at the University of Queensland, he filmed bowlers and used the footage to test a batsman's reactions. Batters were given contact lenses, which blurred at the bowler's point of delivery. Abernethy found that the more accomplished the player, the more they were able to read the bowler's action, predict the ball's path and respond successfully.

To hit the ball the batsman had to rapidly make a series of predictions based on what they saw. They would read the bowler's body language, action and shape. For elite athletes success is all about how they perceive the game.

Abernerthy had developed his cricket study as an extension of research performed by Janet Stokes in 1975. As a graduate student at the University of Waterloo she set out to find what separated the best athletes from the also-rans and began her sports 'occlusion' tests by showing a number of volleyball players assorted photographs of matches, some with the ball in shot and others where the ball had left the frame, often where the scene would be almost identical. If you've ever done 'spot the ball' you know that the ball can move a distance through a photograph while the players remain relatively static.

The snag was that the slides were displayed for only a fraction of a second, not long enough for the human eye properly to see and focus on the ball. Stokes would ask players whether the ball had been present in the shot they had been shown. The results proved a marked difference in understanding between the elite and less experienced players she had surveyed.

A Canadian international, known as one of the best volleyball players in the world, was correctly able to determine the presence, or not, of the ball in the photographs shown for only 16 milliseconds. As Stokes told David Epstein, in his book *The Sports Gene*, "That is a very difficult task. For people who don't know volleyball, in 16 milliseconds all they see is a flash of light." The Canadian player was able to correctly state whether the ball was in shot and also volunteered supplementary information on venue location, team colours and which team won the game.

In a later study of the Canadian hockey team Stokes established that the best players in team sports were able to recall the positions of players on the pitch from a quick flash of a slide.

Both Stokes and Abernethy had shown that elite athletes had learned to read their sport. Repeated exposure to match situations allowed participants to process information more rapidly. Their success was not down to faster reactions, but because they could see the game and the bigger picture better than their amateur counterparts.

The 1940s work of Adriaan de Groot, a Dutch chess master and psychologist, had previously examined the qualities that separated elite chess champions from average club players. He had quickly dismissed the misconception that better players thought numerous moves in advance. For three seconds he'd flash pictures of chessboards to grandmasters, masters, city champions and average club players who were then asked to reconstruct the board they'd been shown.

The grandmasters' and masters' success rate in correctly memorising the positions of the pieces across the study was over 90%, whereas the city champions managed around 70% and the club players only correctly repositioned half of the pieces they'd seen. De Groot found that the grandmasters understood more of a match context in five seconds than the club player did in 15 minutes.

In 1973 psychologists at Carnegie Mellon University extended de Groot's work, but also showed photographs where chess pieces were in alien positions they could not reach in normal play. In these instances the better players were no better than the club players. The better players had acquired the ability to read and understand the board, but only in the context of understood rules. When the rules changed their advantage disappeared.

This research gave birth to the 'chunk theory' that elite players grouped pieces of information together in understood templates that they'd effectively housed in their brain after many hours of play and experiencing many scenarios. They understood and recognised these templates, whereas less experienced amateurs are confused by what they see as new or random.

In simple terms, imagine a 300,000-piece jigsaw built on a photograph of the traditional child's drawing of a house. The elite athlete looks at the pieces and sees a roof, chimney with smoke, four windows and a path leading to the front door. They recognise the image and remember it. The amateur sees 300,000 disjointed jigsaw pieces.

Epstein wrote: "Perceiving order allows elite athletes to extract critical information from the arrangement of players or from subtle changes in an opponent's body movements in order to make unconscious predictions about what will happen next."

As a result the grandmaster sees the right move, the volleyball player can instinctively establish where the ball will go and the cricket batsman can read the delivery of the ball from the bowler's hand.

This was the reason that professional cricketers were moving away from batting against traditional bowling machines. They did not recreate the true sensation of seeing a bowler turn at the top of his run, steam in and go through his bowling action to bowl the ball. The clues were not there. Some machines now have an electronic image of a bowler running in and bowling. Other batsmen have gone for a coach manually feeding a ball, or facing net bowlers and more realistic recreations of game scenarios.

When Mark Butcher had told me that he thought his speed of eye when wielding the willow would have been a trait passed down by his father, according to the research I'd read so far, he was mistaken. It was all about hours of serious practice. Or was it?

* * * * *

It's still a widely held view in modern society that our genes, or natural abilities are the only limitations on what we can achieve. That people are born with the ability to be sporting champions and first-class cricketers.

The very best are heralded as special. Diego Maradona has said that he was born with "soccer skills in my feet". Some cricketers, David Gower or Andrew Flintoff, have been described as naturally gifted, whereas Geoffrey Boycott has always been viewed as someone who honed his formidable defence on hour-upon-hour of serious practice, with or without a stick of rhubarb.

In reality, the players we tend to describe as flair or natural players are likely to be just as hard-working as those that make the game look like harder work. The stories of Eric Cantona arriving at training early and being the last to leave are said to have inspired David Beckham to do the same so he could bend it as naturally as he did.

What we are seeing is that hours of playing the game and practising creates talent and an ability to assess situations and scenarios within a match. In the case of sons following professional fathers, everyone I'd spoken to had talked about being "dragged around" cricket grounds with their family, playing little games of cricket with friends and being bowled at and guided by elite players, who they'd copy and be inspired by.

I'd also started reading a lot about the 10,000 hours, or 10-year, principle that explained how important that early exposure and game time would have been to those cricketers' sons.

In 1991, Anders Erickson, a psychologist at Florida State University researched what it was that created and built outstanding performance. Violinists at the Music Academy of West Berlin were placed into three groups by their professors. The outstanding students, destined to flourish as international soloists, were placed in one group, the very good violinists, likely to become top orchestra members, placed in another group and the least good players, destined to be music teachers, in another.

All members of the three groups were incredibly similar in background. They had all begun playing the violin at around eight, they had all decided to make music their career at 15 and could play on average another 1.8 instruments in addition to their violin. Based purely on those findings the study would have led to nothing, but there was something else. It was a response that allowed Erickson to put a new perception on what made people world-class.

The overwhelming difference between the groups was the number of hours that the violinists had devoted to serious practice. By the age of 20 members of the elite group had practised for an average of 10,000 hours, whereas members of the middle group had practised over 2,000 hours less and those in the lower group, over 6,000 less.

There were no exceptions. Nobody that had practised like mad was in the lower group and no one in the elite group had got there without many hours of productive practice. Erickson had found that the violinists had not been born to succeed, or with a predisposition for greatness, they had earned their respective pedigree as musicians with sustained hours of practice.

This viewpoint was furthered by the '10,000-hour-rule' popularised in Malcolm Gladwell's 2008 book Outliers. Gladwell held that 10,000 hours of practice could make anyone an expert in a given field. But, the caveat is, that genes are important too. Gladwell used Major League Baseball players as an example. While they put in the required practice, they also had exceptional eyesight.

Epstein suggested that some people have the genetic potential to benefit from intense practice, while others wouldn't. Two people could follow identical training regimes and experience wholly different levels of success. Basically, practice is useless without the genes and the genes are never going to achieve anything on their own without the stimulus of practice.

"Most athletic traits," Epstein concluded, "are a braid of nature and nurture so intricately and thoroughly intertwined as to become a single vine."

Andre Agassi, in his autobiography Open, wrote: "My father says that if I hit 2,500 balls each day I'll hit 17,500 balls each week and at the end of each year I'll have hit nearly one million balls. He believes in math. 'Numbers,' he says, 'don't lie'. A child who hits one million balls each year will be unbeatable."

Think back to Serena and Venus Williams, to Tiger Woods and David Beckham. In their respective sports they were no different to the elite violinists. They had, from a very early age, put in the many hours of practice required to become world-class.

* * * * *

There are exceptions to every rule. Professor Tim Noakes, an emeritus professor in the Division of Exercise Science and Sports Medicine at the University of Cape Town, tells a story of a trip he took to Kenya to attend the Nairobi marathon.

In a rural village a woman had been woken each morning by excessive noise emanating from her chickens. Fed up and tired, she raced out one morning and discovered that her chickens were being frightened by a group of runners out at 6am each day training for the Nairobi Marathon where prize money was on offer. Three months later the woman won the marathon after joining the group's early morning training regime. It's possible some people are just naturally gifted.

The opposite can also be true. Some people are not built to be basketball players, others might be too bulky to be a gymnast and no matter how hard some people trained they would never be able to run 100 metres in less than 10 seconds.

While success doesn't come without hard work, training like a madman does not guarantee success.

A natural disposition to a sport is required. We often hear the phrases 'he has a VO2max of 85ml/kg/min,' 'his lung capacity is 5.7L,' 'the most slow-twitch fibres' or 'he only produces 2mM lactate at 80% of PPO' - we are hearing a winning athlete's performance dissected into numbers and being given a genetic determination of why they succeed. The reasons are biological and therefore that athlete has been born to perform. But then again the athlete that tops the scientific charts doesn't always end on the top of the podium.

The 100 metres sprint is the most likely to be affected by genetics. Usain Bolt has been described as 'the most naturally gifted athlete the world has ever seen'. He's seen to be built to sprint, yet I watched a documentary on his training schedule and it was obscenely tough. He works hard to make it look so easy.

Look also at the long distance events and it is no coincidence that the leading protagonists hail from the African nations. It's physiologically determined, although the exact science is blurred.

Winners are not one-dimensional. They are built from a combination of physiological, psychological and environmental factors that sports scientists have yet to quantify properly.

That said, whatever current theory you read, there is one constant. For all people with a natural base level of ability and opportunity, the defining factor on whether they achieved elite success was always how hard they had worked and practised. The 10,000 hours required seemed to be beyond debate.

* * * * *

That word 'opportunity' is important. I'd asked most of my interviewees the Fred Bloggs question, 'do you think you'd have become a professional cricketer had you been born into a different family?' One thing they all might have lacked if they'd been born to other parents was the cricket equipment that they had all found lying around their cricket father's house in abundance.

In his excellent book 'Bounce' Matthew Syed uses his own rise as a champion table tennis player to give an illustration of how small details can be the difference between success and failure.

Syed's parents, who were not table tennis players, bought a table tennis table and installed it in the garage. He subsequently accumulated many hours of competitive practice against his older brother. One of his teachers at primary school, Peter Charters, was a table tennis fanatic, a top coach in the sport and a senior figure in the English Table Tennis Association. He was also the key figure in a local table tennis club called Omega, where the Syed brothers were invited to become members. Omega would produce a disproportionately large number of England's leading table tennis players, all from that one school and neighbourhood.

"In particular all of the sporting talent was focussed ruthlessly on table tennis and all of the aspiring players were nurtured by an outstanding coach," Syed wrote. "I was the best of a very big bunch, only a tiny fraction of who had my opportunities. What's certain is that if a big enough group of youngsters had been given a table at eight, had a brilliant older brother to practise with, had been trained by one of the top coaches in the country, had joined the only 24-hour club in the county and had practised for thousands of hours by their early teens, I would not have been number one in England. I might not have even been number 1001 in England. Whenever I'm inclined to think that I'm unique and special I remind myself that had I lived one door farther down the road I would have been in a different school district, which would have meant that I would not have attended Aldrington, would never have met Peter Charters and would never have joined Omega."

What Syed had, and what millions of people don't get, was opportunity. For all the Syeds out there, consider the number of aspiring champions that are never exposed to their sport at all. The record books of every sport would change beyond recognition if every child was given a level playing field of opportunity, or an equal chance to shine.

It stands to reason that there are potential Wimbledon champions out there who die trophyless after never holding a tennis racket, Major winners who never set foot on a golf course or international cricket stars who never held a bat. The same applies to any sport, or indeed any skill-based activity.

When you are born into a family where sport is already very much on the agenda because your dad is a professional athlete, the opportunity to play, mimic and become inspired is there from day one.

In his book Outliers, Malcolm Gladwell, wrote: "The people that stand before kings may look like they did it all themselves, but in fact they are invariably the beneficiaries of hidden advantages and extraordinary opportunities and cultural legacies that allow them to learn and work hard and make sense of the world in ways others cannot."

Take The Beatles, meeting in Liverpool and joined together by the working-class background, friendship, music and a drive to achieve. What if they had never met? Gladwell suggests that the success of any pop star, actor or sportsman is circumstantial. That's pretty obvious and a slightly lazy way, in my humble opinion, of explaining events. It's more appropriate to use Gladwell's theories to explain underachievement, people not becoming successful because they did not experience the right environment or came in contact with the right people at the right time.

* * * * *

All I had read so far indicated that sporting prowess, the ability to react to a fast bowler, the mastering of complex technical movements required to bat and bowl, were learned behaviours. That countless hours of proper practice was the only way to become world-class and get to the very top of your chosen sport or discipline.

That would mean that the nature versus nurture debate is defunct, isn't it? If everything could be learned then nurture wins all the time? It's never been considered that simple.

So to what extent are our skills and character traits inherited from our parents and what propensity is there for our personalities to be shaped by the environments we inhabit?

Certain physical characteristics are unequivocally inherited. The colour of our eyes, whether we possess straight or curly hair and the pigmentation of our skin are biologically determined by the genes we inherit. Certain diseases are also handed down. Other traits, although not directly predetermined by our genes, are heavily influenced by them, such as our height, weight, hair loss, life expectancy and our vulnerability to certain illnesses.

The nature versus nurture debate is as old as the hills. Are our characters and abilities the product of nature or nurture? Are traits inherited or shaped by our experiences? Are people born to be sporting champions or are they made successful through years of endeavour and training?

I could quite comfortably write a book just on nature versus nurture, and many people have. Throughout history psychologists have lurched from one extreme to the other, often coming up with what today we'd deem to be politically incorrect assertions on issues around race, sexual orientation, class and intelligence.

Here's a potted history, and trust me, there's plenty of reading material if you want to delve further...

Victorian psychologist Francis Galton is credited with coining the nature versus nurture phrase in his 1885 book Hereditary Genius. He'd been influenced by the book *On the Origin of Species* by his half-cousin Charles Darwin and believed in natural talent, that intelligence was genetic and high achievers should marry each other and reproduce while the less intelligent amongst us should be discouraged from multiplying.

Galton wrote: "I propose to show that a man's natural abilities are derived by inheritance under exactly the same limitations as are the form and physical features of the whole organic world. I have no patience with the hypothesis that babies are born pretty much alike and the sole agencies in creating differences are steady application and moral effort."

Early philosophers like Plato and Descartes believed that certain character traits were inborn and occurred naturally regardless of environmental influence.

The predominant viewpoint of the 19th century, argued by William James, was that human instinct was key - that humans had more psychological instincts than animals that allowed greater freedom of action.

John Locke coined the term *tabula rasa*, a view widely held during much of the 20th century, that the mind begins as a completely blank slate and that everything we become is determined purely by our personal experiences.

John B. Watson suggested in 1930 that anyone could be trained to do anything, regardless of background. "Give me a dozen healthy infants, well-formed and my own specified world to bring them up in," he said, "and I'll guarantee to take any one at random and train him to become any type of specialist I might select – doctor, lawyer, artist, merchant-chief and, yes, even beggar-man and thief, regardless of his talents, penchants, tendencies, abilities, vocations, and race of his ancestors."

Throughout the middle of the 20th century Ashley Montagu was a pure behaviourist contending that, "Man is man because he has no instincts, because everything he is and has become he has learned, acquired, from his culture".

Bandura, via his 1961 Bobo Doll experiment, determined that children could learn aggressive behaviour by observing another person acting aggressively. In that case environmental factors were the dominant factor.

But by the 1960s Robert Ardrey turned the argument back towards human nature being the dominant factor and by the 1970s the mood had swung back to heritable factors holding sway. It was said that up to half of our characteristics are inherited and that therefore the argument between nature and nurture was not black and white. I think I could have told them that!

By the late 1990s the blank slate viewpoint had been completely discredited and Judith Rich Harris had published a heralded book that appeared to suggest that parents don't matter in the child-shaping process.

We seem now to have reached a point in modern psychology where all sides accept that both nature and nurture influence our development. The majority of scientists responding to a 2014 survey believed that the nature versus nurture debate was now obsolete. They believed that nature and nurture work together and influence each other.

If a person succeeds academically did they inherit intelligence or were they brought up in an environment that encouraged study? Was an abusive husband born with violent tendencies or did his parents display similar behaviour? The question now, in such instances and many others, they believed, was how much of each factor was in play. Is it nature or nurture that had the greater impact or was it an alliance of both aspects?

Kevin Davies found in 2001 that the ability to detect the perfect pitch of a musical tone without external aids ran in families and might be tied to a single gene. But possessing that gene alone was not enough to develop this ability. Instead, musical training during early childhood then allowed the inherited ability to manifest itself.

It is accepted that our height is influenced genetically, but put a child with tall parents into a poor environment where they lack a healthy diet then resulting growth may be limited.

Steven Pinker argued in 2002 that the blank slate theory had been accepted as desirable politically and socially because it meant that crime and aggression were cultural and could therefore be removed with the right actions by the state.

In 2007 Saul McLeod published *Nature vs Nurture in*

Psychology where he asserted that we are pre-wired and our psychological characteristics such as behavioural tendencies, personality attributes and mental abilities are "wired in" before we are even born.

However, in recent years there has been a growing realisation that the question of 'how much' behaviour is due to heredity or nature and 'how much' to the environment may be the wrong way of assessing situations. Rather than searching for numbers a more qualitative approach was required. It seemed to have been accepted that both nature and nurture played their respective parts and that it was impossible to separate them. It's how they interact we should be measuring. A psychopath would have a genetic disposition and environmental triggers for a mental disorder to manifest. So we should look at each person and ask whether their situation is 'mostly' down to nature or 'mostly' down to nurture.

The Human Genome Project has researched certain types of behaviour by looking at particular strands of DNA located on specific chromosomes. Newspaper reports announce that scientists are on the verge of discovering (or have already discovered) the gene for criminality, for alcoholism or the 'gay gene'. This can be where the controversy creeps in. People with preconceived ideas of what are the right and wrong ways to live our lives can abuse results.

As recently as 2005, American psychologist Arthur Jenson, upon finding that the average IQ scores of black Americans were significantly lower than whites he went on to argue that genetic factors were mainly responsible, suggesting that intelligence is 80% inherited. His conclusions caused huge controversy with opponents arguing that IQ differences stemmed from inbuilt biases in testing methods and that people brought up in deprived areas are denied the same life chances that more affluent people are afforded.

In studies on the psychology of sex and gender, where the question of how much of the supposed differences in male and female behaviour are due to biology and how much to culture has provoked similar controversy.

In the 1920s the American Eugenics Society campaigned for the sterilisation of men and women in psychiatric hospitals. The most chilling of all implications drawn from this view of the natural superiority of one race over another took place in the concentration camps of Nazi Germany. It's a dangerous area!

So, in a nutshell, and putting the controversial elements of the debate to one side, I'd read about theorists who thought everything we did, achieved and became was the product of our parents. And equally there were plenty of experts in their field who had thought we were the product of conditioning, environment and learning. And there were more middle-ground viewpoints.

But ultimately, the current message seemed to be that some things were inherited and others learned and depending on what, where and when the percentages involved could change. I have to admit to feeling a bit cheated. Forgive me for saying this, but quite frankly I could have told you that given a spare 20 minutes to think it through.

* * * * *

I'd had enough of books and websites that lurched me from one extreme to another before putting me back exactly where I'd begun.

I needed to talk to a human being who knew about these things and could answer the question of can sporting excellence be inherited?

I had come across the name Alun Williams, Reader in Sport and Exercise Genomics at Manchester Metropolitan University, as I'd been investigating. I asked him for a chat.

While I appreciate that the players I'd spoken to were not scientists, I was aware that many of them had been inclined to answer any questions relating to whether their sporting skill could have been inherited.

I'm a cricket writer and sports fan and certainly no scientist. I asked Alun to take it easy on me and not blind me with genetic theory. This is a cleaned up transcript of our chat.

ME: Is it possible for sporting prowess to be inherited – can it be passed down through the generations from a cricket father to a cricket son?

ALUN: The short answer is yes, but for any individual it will never be all about the genetics. In most cases it will be a combination of those genes and what they do with that potential. I'm not just talking about the physical development either, although that's where my particular speciality is.

ME: Okay, I'm quite pleased you said yes, otherwise it would be a short conversation. Tell me more – how do you go about establishing what part the genes play?

ALUN: To establish and quantify how important genetics is, you do twin or family studies. That doesn't involve looking at DNA at all, you are not doing any gene sequencing or anything, you are looking at people and how they are related and then trying to assess something about them, some trait or characteristic, physical or mental or whatever it is. What career they have or whether they are good at sport has been done in these kinds of studies. And then you do some calculations about how people in your study are related to each other and come out with a percentage contribution of genetics at the end of that. That's the first bit and as a category that's called classical genetics, where you are looking at how people are related and coming up with this number.

ME: Can you tell me about any studies like that which you have been involved in?

ALUN: The next bit from that, which is what me, and people I work with in other universities, are doing, is molecular genetics. When the evidence shows there is a significant genetic component to these different things, we are then trying to find which genes and which specific genetic components contribute to that.

ME: Can you give me an example from sport?

ALUN: In exercise and sports genetics there are a few genes which are the more well known. All genes have a symbol, a five letter digit shorthand, and I'll pick probably the most well known one – ACTN3, which stands for Alpha-actinin-3 [also known as alpha-actinin skeletal muscle isoform 3 or F-actin cross linking protein]. Actually it's a gene that has the sequence within it, the information, for making one particular protein that you find in muscle and specifically it's in the fast twitch muscle fibres, the ones we use for short sprint type performances – weightlifting, a jump or a sprint – anything that's just lasting a few seconds. To be good at that you are reliant on those fast twitch fibres to be working well for you. And you need to have a significant number of them. So it's both those things – a significant number doing the job as well as they can.

ME: (At this point I'm extremely interested, struggling to sound clued up on the other end of the telephone and conscious that Alun has just thrown a lot of information at me – so for the next minute I ask him to repeat a couple of things to ensure I can write them down accurately later. Then Alun continues.)

ALUN: There's a genetic variation in S gene, so it's one letter, one nuclear tide, within the sequence of that gene that actually allows, or particularly stops, the conversion of information in that gene into one particular protein that's found in those fast twitch muscle fibres. Depending upon the letter you have got at that point in the gene it has quite a large biological effect and you've either got the protein or you haven't.

It sounds quite dramatic, that someone is missing this protein, but there are other proteins that can step in and do a similar job. You wouldn't be able to tell by looking at people, or even assessing how good they are as a sprinter, which version of this gene they are carrying. But once you are assessing a lot of people at elite level sport - whether you look at the fast players in a rugby team, elite sprinters, I did some work in Russia with speed skaters - the story is always the same. Those people who are successful at those short events, they almost always do carry the version of the gene that does make the protein.

In the current population, approximately 20% of people don't have the version of the gene. But at the elite end of those short events, if you are missing that protein it makes it a lot harder. It may not be impossible, but a lot harder.

So that comes down through the generations. The genes that each person has got, you've got two copies of this gene, one from mum and one from dad. So you can blame them or thank them depending upon how it goes.

ME: It's not possible to have a gene that's not handed down from mum and dad?

ALUN: Almost totally, for everything that we need to be concerned about that is true. The DNA that's in all of our cells, yes we get it directly from our parents. When the DNA is opened up and read like a book and is translated into the next generation a small handful of very minor errors do occur, so it's not completely the same as the parents – some mistakes in the reading of the DNA – but it's so small it's almost non-existent and it's insignificant. For most people, even good sportspeople, it's not even a consideration.

ME: Is there potential in the future for sports clubs, or countries, to be screening their players for genes like the one you've mentioned?

ALUN: There is potential for it, yes. It's a little bit of a controversial area. Even though that gene I described, the ACTN3 gene, and a few others, have some good evidence behind them, on its own, or on their own as a small group, what we certainly don't know yet are all of the genes that are effecting physical performance and mental capacity in different ways.

Really we only know a very small proportion of what, in time, should be known. We only know a little bit of it. The science is not very well developed yet, so even though we know a few of the important genes and genetic markers, there could be other ones we don't know about that could outweigh the ones we could test for now. So it makes trying to assess potential talent via genetics pretty pointless really, at the moment.

ME: But ultimately, a team could scan its academy intake for the appropriate five genes and further the careers of those who have the identified genetic talent?

ALUN: I think that would be a natural reaction, but presumably you are not just assessing their genetics, you'd be assessing their natural ability at the sport, their physical qualities, their strength, their aerobic fitness and all kinds of different things. Unless those things were absolutely identical, which would never happen, at this stage I wouldn't use genetics for making decisions about who was going to be selected for a training squad. I'd use the traditional things that are staring you in the face more.

The reason I'm saying that – even if we tested for the five genes in the example you gave and someone carried all five and someone else only carried three of them, there would probably be another 250 that we are not testing for, so we don't know who has got which of those 250 and you'd get much stronger evidence for other factors you can assess through traditional sporting experience.

ME: From what you've said, the genes that affect a child's sporting prowess are more likely to be associated with power and speed? Sports like cricket and golf, where there is a lot of technique involved, is proficiency at these less likely to be genetic?

ALUN: (pauses for few seconds) I've opened up a list of various different traits and characteristics that I've made on my computer that I sometimes use in presentations with scientific papers mentioned next to them and then that number I mentioned right at the beginning of our conversation – the size of the genetic component.

Height certainly is very strongly genetic, probably at least 80%. Other physical things like aerobic fitness, that's more like 50%. Muscle mass and strength is a bit higher at 60-70%. And there are a variety of other things on the list.

There is one on skill acquisition. It wasn't a particular sporting skill, it was quite controlled in a laboratory, but the ability to learn a new physical skill in a controlled setting using sets of twins, as a lot of our research is done that way, came out with an inherent ability of around 70%. So that is not about strength, size or height, it's about learning a new skill. There will be various genes that are involved in laying down the newer pathways so that memories are made and there will be others that are important for the fine control of the movement. There is a lot of biology and neuro-biology behind it and that's how you can explain that kind of figure.

Therefore I wouldn't say it's more on the physical side.

ME: Sons have talked to me about fast eyes and reaction times they believe they've inherited to become better cricketers. Is the ability to react quickly to a cricket ball genetic? Following a ball's flight and responding more quickly than others - might that be genetic?

ALUN: Yes I believe so. I haven't seen a twin or family study to make the size of the genetic component, but I am aware of the other kind of genetics, the kind that I do that focus more on the physical speed and strength areas. I have seen some studies that relate to reaction times and there are some early findings on that.

Which gene someone might have seems to influence someone's ability to respond quickly or process information quickly as well. So not just a reaction time but the ability to process information and respond quickly. So when you are talking about a cricketer's ability to face a bowler and respond to the ball that is bowled, then yes, like with almost everything else, there is a genetic component.

Every time we ever look at any quality, it always comes out as a bit of both – there's always a genetic component and then what you do with that.

ME: Earlier in this chapter I wrote about the chunk theory – with hours of practice and experience an elite player reads and responds to match situations more proficiently. If you are a cricketer that is genetically more adept at processing information, then that would make chunking something that comes more easily and potentially puts you ahead of others with 'lesser' genes?

ALUN: Yes, I think so. Obviously no one is born with a natural ability to be able to read a sports match and it appears on the face of it that it's an entirely learned skill, but you need the hardware. In the same way that someone might have a better mobile phone or computer than you and can do more with it, some people have better hardware so they can run the software that you add to it - to try and read those cues and respond quickly and effectively in high pressure situations and everything else – some people are going to be more able to do that because they've got that better hardware – and that's the genes.

ME: If your dad is Usain Bolt, you are going to be more likely to be able to run 100 metres quicker than someone whose father is a bricklayer?

ALUN: Yes. But it doesn't mean I'm going to be able to guarantee that this person is going to do that. If they never do any training or anything else they would probably be quite quick I would have thought, but that would be it. But if they can combine that with a lot of training, they are going to have a better chance than I would have, because my dad was a cross-country runner.

ME: So a six-foot-four-inch fast bowler who has the stamina to bowl all day long – the chances are the son, if he has the drive, motivation and determination to make cricket his career, has got a head start on the rest?

ALUN: Yes. Again it doesn't guarantee anything. My message is certainly not to diminish the effect of training and practice and everything else – those are essential – without those you've got nothing. But in terms of having a bit of a head-start, as you put it, or having a better chance than somebody else whose father didn't have that experience, but also didn't have the more clinical qualities. If a person's father is 5 ft 8 their chances of becoming a 6 ft 4 fast bowler are a lot less.

ME: Many sons have talked about following their fathers around when they were children. They'd watch his matches, they'd play their own games with friends, get fed balls by other players. Effectively they were getting in their 10,000 hours from a very early age in a very conducive environment. If you add in the genetics, the inspiration their father provides to want to play the game and that all goes into the same pot – it gives them a very good chance of success surely?

ALUN: Exactly. You've got the right sort of ingredients going in. It still doesn't guarantee anything but they've got all the right things in the mix.

ME: They will obviously need some luck and all the rest but to have the psychology to be a successful sportsman, is that a genetic quality too - the ability to be competitive, to face a tight match situation and come out on top?

ALUN: Yes. I'm not a psychologist, but genetic research on psychological traits, say mental toughness, that has a significant genetic component. In terms of more basic intelligence, IQ, there's a genetic component there. And with things where the psychological and mental correlates with the physical, we talked about reaction times and the ability to learn new skills, they have significant genetic components as well.

ME: If, however, you are a child of non-sporty parents – many have gone on and become professional sportsmen and have been very successful, so it's not the be all and end all, having the genes?

ALUN: No, but I suppose what you don't know is what genes those parents had. They may have had some of those helpful genes, but didn't combine that with other elements like opportunity or desire or inspiration. Perhaps those genes were passed down and it does help people, even though they are seen as the first in their family to do well in sport. They could still have some genetic advantages that have been passed down to them, but that hadn't been applied in the right way before.

I think it also depends on what kind of sport that is. You mentioned Usain Bolt, so pure 100 metre sprinting, pure running speed. I personally could have trained to be a sprinter my whole life and I would never have been a world record holder or even a good regional sprinter. I'm sure of that.

I'm not particularly good at snooker, but if I'd have tried that sport where it's a different set of technical skills, then maybe I could have mastered it. You've talked about the 10,000-hour idea and maybe something like snooker is a little bit more receptive to that than 100 metre sprinting. So if the parents hadn't got certain genes, the child would have more chance in a sport where practice makes a significant difference.

ME: I've started to draft my final chapter and I've been pleased that you've mentioned words like opportunity, inspiration and desire.

ALUN: My experience is in the genetics side, but those things are huge, possibly not easily definable in many ways.

I had some answers. Mark Butcher could well be right that he got his fast eyes and reflexes from his father. The opportunity is there for cricket sons too and the early inspiration to get those 10,000 hours in, whether they realised they were doing it or not.

There had to be something in the genes. If that was the case it was time to talk to a family where the cricket genes had been very active. I got in touch with the Hadlees in New Zealand.

CHAPTER THIRTEEN

WALTER, BARRY, DAYLE and RICHARD HADLEE

"Happiness is only real when shared"
Jon Krakauer

Richard Hadlee took 431 Test wickets in 86 appearances for New Zealand and is undoubtedly the finest cricketer those islands have ever produced. He was the first bowler to pass 400 wickets in Tests, sticking the NZ flag at the top of that particular summit just before Ian Botham did the same for England. It was an era of the flamboyant all-rounders, Botham, Imran Khan and Kapil Dev providing Richard with competition throughout the late 1970s and 80s.

In terms of consistency with the ball, the Kiwi had the edge. The statistics he cherishes on a CV loaded with exceptional deeds are his 36 five-wicket hauls and nine 10-wicket Test matches. On 102 occasions in first-class cricket he claimed five wickets in an innings. Sometimes that word 'consistency' is used to build-up and glamorise a person without flare. Not the case with Richard Hadlee, who simply did the exceptional most of the time and never allowed his standards to drop throughout a 17-year international career.

He became a firm favourite at Nottinghamshire for a decade, in which the county won the Championship twice. His most successful year was 1984 when he hit over 1,000 runs and took over 100 wickets. He was knighted in 1994, while still playing the game.

The Hadlee boys had come together in early 2017 to honour their father in a book called the *The Skipper's Diary* about the tour to England in 1949. It was a collection of photographs and documents presented around their father's comprehensive day-to-day diary of the eight-month tour.

That tour had been so pivotal in the development of New Zealand cricket that the Hadlee boys owed their father in more than the normal paternal relationship way. One can see the father in Walter's attributes as a captain. He took a team of also-rans and made them gallop. He had the ability to make an average Test cricketer think he was capable of taking on all-comers. Tactically he was calculated and quick to adapt. The Kiwis' bowling attack was not going to keep the English batsmen awake at night, so Walter ensured his field placings posed challenges and that every member of the side fielded brilliantly. England's Len Hutton believed "it was harder to find a gap in their field than in any I have ever played against."

Walter looked like a schoolmaster, he was a gentleman, he played the game in the right spirit, but mistake his friendly nature for a lack of backbone or willingness to win at your peril. In a 1951 Test, England batsman Cyril Washbrook had been adjudged lbw to a ball he had obviously edged onto his own pads. Walter didn't hesitate as he called Washbrook back to the crease to resume his innings. He wanted to win every game he played, but winning in the right way was of paramount importance.

Today's New Zealand side has a reputation for sportsmanship. That started with Walter Hadlee. Of the 1949 side, *Wisden* remarked: "By every action on and off the field the 15 players enhanced the already firmly established reputation for sportsmanship that belongs to New Zealand cricketers."

Walter was denied the best years of international cricket by the Second World War. His 1,439 runs at 35.97 on the 1949 trip would have been better if he'd not regularly lost his wicket to allow other members of his squad a chance to bat.

Unlike many former Test players, Hadlee never lost his appetite for playing cricket. As late as 1976-77 he was still appearing in seniors' matches in New Zealand; in 1986 he featured in a Golden Oldies Festival in Sussex; and in 1990 he briefly kept wicket for a Hadlee Family XI against a prep school in New Zealand.

In his first-class career he played 117 matches and scored 7,523 runs (including 18 centuries) at an average of 40.44. In his 11 Test matches he made 543 runs for an average of 30.16. He was awarded the OBE in 1950.

* * * * *

It would be easy to write a chapter on the Hadlee family centred on Richard's career, throwing in a few paragraphs about his father Walter, who captained his country, and giving passing mentions to his brother Dayle, who played 27 Tests and 11 ODIs, and brother Barry, who played two ODIs.

Of course, they were the Hadlee headlines, but I was fascinated by the dynamics of a household built on Walter's cricket-loving foundations where five sons grew up in an environment where cricket was sacrosanct and holding a bat and ball was a rite of passage.

Barry, born in 1941, was Walter's eldest boy and a batsman like his father. His career as an opener with Canterbury saw him retire with 4,540 first-class runs for Canterbury at 31.52. He'd been a late developer. Finding his most consistent form in the latter part of his career, with a career best 163 not out coming in his final season. He'd only played 16 one-day matches in his career, so his call-up to the Kiwi team was left-field. He'd played just one List A match in the previous three seasons and, in that, he'd been run out without scoring. But his inclusion, aged 33, in New Zealand's team for the ODI against England at Dunedin on 8 March, 1975, led to a unique occurrence.

Never before had three sons of an international playing father taken the field for their country as Barry lined up alongside Dayle and Richard. It has only happened once more, the same three brothers in Dayle's second and final ODI in England during the inaugural 1975 World Cup.

I spoke to Dayle Hadlee and asked him of his memories of that period where three brothers were in the New Zealand dressing room together.

"It was brilliant," Dayle replied. "Richard and I had already been playing for New Zealand for a period of time and Barry had been a bit of a fringe player, but to get selected and then to go with us to that World Cup was a very special time. Mum and Dad both went over and watched it. Every time we went to England on tours they always made sure they were there.

"You don't even think about them as being your brothers when you are in a dressing room. When you are playing cricket you are just team-mates, but once you walk off the field and get away from the game, then all of a sudden they become your brothers again. We often talk about it now though.

"The build up to that World Cup was interesting because in New Zealand our season finishes at the end of March and we had all of April and part of May to get prepared for that trip. And we had an Indian summer and we were still practising outdoors on grass pitches just before we went, which was very unusual."

Walter's second son, Martin, was a decent cricketer too and played club cricket in Christchurch.

"Martin was considered by many to be the best batsman of all of us, but when he was young he got conscripted into the Army as a territorial and that cost him a lot of time away from playing cricket and things didn't quite happen for him. He became an accountant to follow Dad and Barry into that line of work. He also does a huge amount of work for community groups, fundraising and being the director of many companies who work in tourism and community service. They won't touch my tax though," Dayle laughs, "I have to go elsewhere."

Dayle was the third of Walter's offspring, the next was Richard and the final boy was named Christopher.

"Chris was a very reluctant person who got pulled along to watch cricket at Lancaster Park and he spent the whole time drawing pictures and collecting bottles," Dayle recalled. "We felt very sorry for Chris. On a Saturday night we'd sit around the dining room table and Dad would ask each of us, 'how did you get on today, how did you get out?'

"There was always this inquisition, salt and pepper shakers were put around the table to show where the field placements were and what had happened. And when it came to Chris and Dad said, 'how did you get on today?' He'd say, 'well Dad, I got nought not out again', and there was never any discussion or further inquiry.

"When we went to Christchurch Boys High School, my father and then his four brothers had all played for the 1st XI and teachers came out to look at the nets when they were having this compulsory net thinking *here's the next one, I wonder what he's like*. He wasn't very good, so it was really very hard on him.

"He coped by going to play soccer and tennis," Dayle added, "and he's the only one of us who is actively still playing tennis and physical sport nowadays, so he's shown us all up. He became an architect and runs his own business now and he's a very good artist as well."

I asked Dale whether Chris had been affected by not being part of the cricket playing family? Chris was seven years younger than Dayle and five years Richard's junior. It must surely have been tough for the youngster to feel marginalised?

"It's interesting, because we all thought that was what he thought," Dayle answered. "Chris wrote a chapter in *The Skipper's Diary* about how he felt about it, and it was actually very positive. I think he felt proud for what his dad and brothers had done, but the game wasn't for him. But he observed more than we all thought he had. We all thought he went along because of a sense of duty and so he could get a chance to draw trees, buildings and those sorts of things, but he had in fact taken a bit more on board than we expected. He was quite smart, ahead of his time I think.

"He did write a little bit unfortunately about how Richard and I kept hitting him with cricket balls on the legs and we had no pads and that didn't help his enthusiasm for the game either. He'd come out and have a go and we would try and teach him how to play, but he just wasn't really suited for the game."

* * * * *

No family has ever given more to cricket in New Zealand. When Walter Hadlee died aged 91 in September 2006 the Kiwi nation had lost a man that had devoted his existence to the sport, turning them from a minnow nation with little hope to a competitive force on the world stage.

Richard is rightly proud of his father's achievements. "My father has probably made the greatest contribution to New Zealand cricket," he stated to ESPN Cricinfo in January 2017. "He first represented New Zealand in 1937, and in 1949 he was the captain of the team that toured England. When he retired in 1951, he became a selector. In 1965 he managed the New Zealand team on the tour of England, India and Pakistan. So his role grew considerably. He was on the board of New Zealand Cricket and chairman of the board. He became president of New Zealand Cricket, the overall figurehead of the organisation. He became a life member. He watched the development and growth of not only myself but Barry, who played in the 1975 World Cup, and Dayle, who played 26 Tests. We are very much a cricketing family. My father's contribution to the game has been quite extraordinary."

That 1949 tour of England became a watershed series for New Zealand cricket. Without a win in 16 previous Test matches, Walter would steer his young cricketing nation from unsteady toddler to an adolescent nation in one English summer.

New Zealand didn't secure their first Test victory in England, but they returned home buoyed by drawing each of the four Tests played, only a solitary tour defeat to Oxford University, and 14 wins. Admittedly the Tests had been played over three days so defeat was easier to avoid and the summer was hot and conducive to batting, but Hadlee led his team with an authority that gave his nation a genuine belief. The adolescent nation would soon be fully-grown and able to look any opposition in the eye.

Walter had been a student of the game from the age of ten, when he pored over cricket history books and would traipse down to the Test ground in Christchurch to watch matches and keep score. Later in life he would become a respected captain, administrator and an accountant - his strategic, analytical and shrewd brain, his genuine love of the game, honed on those Lancaster Park benches.

"I was very fortunate like my four brothers to grow up in a family cricketing environment," Richard told TalkSport in 2015. "My father Walter played for New Zealand, he captained New Zealand and toured England way back in 1949 and of course in those days they used to travel from New Zealand by ship. It used to take about six weeks, they'd have six months in England playing games and they'd have another six weeks on the way back via ship.

"I think with that background and that upbringing it was the destiny for virtually all of us, to play cricket, and fortunately three of us went on to play for New Zealand."

Walter had met Richard's mother on a ship to England as he embarked on his first international tour in 1937. Walter and Lilla would have five sons together.

"My mother was a big supporter of her boys, making sure our cricket whites were nicely washed and cleaned and ironed for our games at the weekends. She was kept busy.

"We all played sports and I think the backyard rivalry we had was very significant in our upbringing in the game of cricket, because we had a big place and a big section (area of land)," Richard recalled. "We had pitches in the back yard, with a net on it and usually Dayle and myself would be bowling to Dad and my older brother Barry. And that's why Dayle and myself basically became bowlers, because we did all the bowling and we'd get a five-minute hit at the end before having to go to bed at night time, so it's quite interesting how those roles played out."

Sitting the New Zealand School Certificate examination in 1957 was to give Richard a wake-up call and life lesson that would serve him well.

"That was as a 16-year-old and what you had to do was get a 200 pass mark in your four best subjects and I'll never forget when the results came about three months after the exams and mother presented to me on a silver tray the envelope with the results. The expectation was there and I opened it up and there it was, 195, I had failed.

"Maybe I'd expected or assumed as of right that I'd automatically pass and I thought I'd done the preparation, but clearly I hadn't. I'd failed and I thought that failure was clearly not a nice option – it was embarrassing, degrading, disappointing and the lesson learnt from that was to work harder and prepare better.

"I sat the examination again the following year. I had to do a repeat year on it, set me back a year obviously. The system changed a bit and you had to get a 50% pass mark in your subjects to get the credits and I sat six subjects and got a pass mark in all six. Lesson learned, move on."

As their father had been before, Dayle and Richard were regulars at Lancaster Park as youngsters.

"I was engrossed in cricket and simply because Dad played and my older brother Barry, he's 10 years older than me, we used to go and watch them play," Richard said. "I sold programmes, collected bottles and got tuppence for a refund on the bottle so you could buy an ice cream, move around the embankment and collect all these bottles and annoy people," his voice dances as he remembers. "As time went on I operated the giant scoreboard with a number of other youngsters while the Test match was in progress and I often looked out from that scoreboard over the playing arena when a Test match was in progress at Lancaster Park and often thought to myself wouldn't it be wonderful one day to be out there playing a real Test match. I was 16 at the time I thought that. It was only five years later that the dream became a reality."

For someone viewing Richard from a distance his rapid rise into becoming a first-class cricketer could easily have prompted the impression that he was a natural. The truth would appear differently and those thousands of hours of competitive practice with his father and brothers made his rise seem more rapid and easy than it was. He had been putting in the hard work since being a small child.

His father had instilled in him certain core values, which he adhered to throughout his career.

"The biggest thing he said to me, and I presume my four brothers, is that, 'Whatever you do, Richard, take pride in your performance, do your best, be happy with your performance even if somebody does it better. Doing your best and giving your 100%, no one can criticise you'.

"This pride became important as a motivating factor. Prepare well, train well, so you have a better chance of performing.

"Another thing he said, and it is a common saying really, is that 'If you can't be a cricketer, at least look like a cricketer'. In other words, dress well. Even at practice, which you do in whites. He was a traditionalist. In those days you put on your whites and practised in the nets. You feel the game by doing that. You feel part of it. So look like it. And if you look like it and feel it, you have a chance of performing on the field of play."

"He always took interest in what we were doing, whether it was primary or secondary school, playing club cricket, Canterbury or New Zealand. We all knew he wanted us to do well."

I'd read about Walter and looking at old photographs of a bespectacled, respectable man, had got the impression he was a little austere, but when every picture is in black and white it's tougher to appear charismatic. He was described as a quiet man, but was also pretty tough. Dayle talked to me about his father.

"He was very strict," he began. "Back in those days if we got things wrong we'd get the bamboo stick and if we hadn't been good with Mum and not done as we were told, she'd say, 'You wait until your father gets home'. It was that era really where corporal punishment was the short and quick answer to bad behaviour.

"We're a very close family and we have a great love of each other, but there was always that little bit of a fear factor because of that corporal punishment thing.

"He was a very loving father and incredibly supportive. He'd always go and watch us play and he gave us every opportunity to excel."

"We started off on a concrete pitch and then we moved house and my father laid a white clay soil pitch and that was one of the best clays around in the district, which was very hard and fast, so we were brought up on one of those pitches. We had a net with short run-ups, we had 54 windows in the garage behind the net and every one of them got broken. Mum gave up in the end - got fed up of repairing them because there were balls flying around in all directions."

Walter seemed to me to be a very driven man. The Hadlee boys didn't seem to have a lot of choice but to give cricket a go. The other cricket families I'd talked to had all said that father had stood back and allowed the son to find their way. With the Hadlees the pitch in the back garden and regular practice sessions were at the other end of that spectrum. Had Dayle felt pressured into the game? Was Walter a pushy parent?

Dayle was candid in his response. "When I was a seven-year-old, I was put into the 1st XI at school and I felt totally out of my depth and I came home and said 'Dad, I've given up cricket, I'm going to play softball'. Within a week Dad had been down to the school and had me thrown out of the softball team and put back into the cricket team.

"He was very focused on cricket. When I got selected for a New Zealand Under-23 side, I was only about 19 at the time, and I felt like I'd only got there because of my name. And I remember going home to Dad and saying, 'I'm going to change my name so I can get there under my own steam and not under your name'. That only lasted for five minutes," Dayle added laughing. "I remember when I went up to get my cap for New Zealand Under-23s in that game, I could hear people talking, saying things like, 'He's only got there because he's the son of the Chairman of the Board'. And that's why I wanted to change my name and get there under my own steam.

"If I trace it back further," Dayle continued, "Dad had played for New Zealand and he had all of this New Zealand cricket in his coffin [that's a kitbag for the youngsters reading this], and Richard and I used to go and get his pads and bat out and put his New Zealand cap on and try to emulate playing for New Zealand. I think for both of us, there was always an expectation that it was going to happen naturally.

"And Dad gave us miles of advice, which at the time we rejected because fathers don't know anything, but now I'm a coach, all of his words are being regurgitated out of my mouth. He was very keen on the technique of the game. There was one day where he had us lined up on the back lawn, which was about 90 metres long, and we had to get ourselves into our batting stance and go up and down the lawn practising how to use your feet from the stance."

Walter seemed to have provided the carrot and the stick - the inspiration to his boys to follow him into New Zealand cricket, but then a strong will to get them there. Pushy? Yes. Loving? Yes. Supportive? Very definitely. But, certainly not the type of pushy that I'd read about before, where the parent was trying to fill a hole in their own life. Walter had nothing to prove to anyone. He wanted the same for his boys.

* * * * *

Richard made his first-class debut in January 1972 after a freak lawnmower accident to Dayle saw him called up to replace his brother and join another, Barry, in the Canterbury side.

"I was playing in a B game for Canterbury and I could see that mother was walking around the boundary quite frantically," he remembered. "She had just heard the news that Dayle had done something wrong. Dayle couldn't play for the remaining three first-class games of that particular season and I was his replacement. I got pulled out of that game I was playing in to report to Lancaster Park the next day and opened the bowling for Canterbury.

Opportunity offered, chance taken. He took 10 wickets in those first three games and in the third at Trafalgar Park, Nelson, he hit the headlines with a hat-trick.

"The New Zealand cricket team to go to Australia was about to be announced. I didn't think I had any chance because I'd only played three games, but I was picked more on potential and promise than performance. It was a great thrill."

In addition to the many hours of practice the brother had shared, it was also evident that they had provided each other with fierce competition. It's likely that without the other, neither would have become quite the players they did.

"He showed signs in the back garden when we used to have our little mini-Test matches," Dayle had told TalkSport. "I was always, luckily, three years older than him so when I was 15 and he was 12 I could dominate him, but eventually the tide started to turn.

"We played a lot of cricket together in first-class teams for Canterbury and then for New Zealand," Dayle added. "He always had the talent, but it was only when he went to English county cricket that he learnt to refine his skills and that's when I realised that he was pretty special."

Dayle recognised the importance of that sibling rivalry in their development and remembers that period of their lives with great fondness. "It was good fun," he said. "I think when you wheel it back a little bit, Richard and I were the bowlers for my father and eldest brother, because they were both batsmen in our backyard nets. To take that through to international cricket was very exciting for both of us.

"Richard became so consistent that all of a sudden New Zealand started winning Test matches, they had an unbeaten record at home for a number of years and it was through his efforts and people like Martin Crowe and a team of pretty solid performers around them that they did really well.

"Richard, when he went to county cricket and started hitting a 1,000 runs and taking 100 wickets in a season and doing things consistently over a long period of time it made people realise that he was extra-special.

"I'm extremely proud of him. I think we were always very competitive against each other when we first started. There was a period of time when he was playing for a different club team in Christchurch to me and we were after each other all the time in those games. But then as time went on and we both matured I think we hoped each would do well and when I gave up I was always very keen to see that he was the leading player in the team."

Richard responded to Dayle's words with complete agreement: "He's right about the competitive nature between us. Even when we played for Canterbury and New Zealand together, if he got two wickets, I wanted three wickets. If he was batting No 7 and I was at No 8 and he got 20 runs, I wanted 40 runs to reverse the batting position.

"I felt that we complemented each other pretty well and that strong desire really helped our performances.

"When Dayle got his New Zealand cap and sweater in 1969, I wanted to get on the next tour to England in 1973 and get my cap and sweater. So there was a bit of motivation there.

"He was hugely influential in my career. He has turned out to be one of the best fast-bowling coaches in world cricket today with his knowledge and experience," Richard continued. "He would be fielding at mid-off or mid-on and say to me, 'You haven't got your rhythm, have you?' I would say, 'No. Struggling a little bit'. He would say, 'Get that front foot down a lot quicker than what you are doing, so that you have a base to land on and support the body as you come up and over'. A little tip like that makes a huge difference. All of a sudden you are standing taller, the ball is bouncing more, you get a wicket and you're away again.

"So he was very supportive and encouraging. I could probably notice things as well when he was struggling, so we could help each other."

Dayle told me that he saw the difference in Richard's game immediately after he had played for Nottinghamshire in England.

"When he went to England in the first year he was a player that on his day was dynamic, but those days were very inconsistent, hot and cold," Dayle told me. "When he went to England he learnt the art of bowling and having a technique which was sustainable and very compact. He came back as a totally different bowler. And when he went on to a shorter run he became even better.

"I used to be at mid-off or mid-on when he was bowling and I could see if he wasn't bowling well, if he was bowling too short or too wide, it was nearly always because his head was back and his front foot hadn't landed at the right time. I'd just have a quiet little word to him and that would fix him up and away he'd go again.

"I think people like Mike Hendrick had quite an input with Richard because he taught him the importance of the front arm, and what Mike taught Richard, he's passed on to me and I teach my players now how important that front arm is."

Dayle had played 26 Tests and 11 ODIs for New Zealand and his final tally of 351 first-class wickets at 25.22 and 228 one-day scalps at 18.33 stands the test of time. He could have achieved more, and played county cricket himself, had his career not been blighted by injury.

"I was offered a contract for Leicestershire and I turned it down because I wanted to pursue my career as a school teacher and I was just coming back from a stress fracture at the time and didn't think I could get through a season," Dayle stated. "I was also offered a contract to play in the Lancashire League for Rawtenstall and turned that down for exactly the same reasons. If I could have a career that was injury free, rather than having three stress fractures, I'd have liked the opportunity.

"I was never envious of Richard. On a Monday morning the first thing I'd look for in the newspaper was the county results to see how he'd done. I followed his career very closely and was very proud of what he did."

Dayle had recognised the frailties in his body early and planned for a career in coaching when he finally hung up his boots.

"I had a stress fracture when I was around 21, picked up playing against Australia and I couldn't play, so I thought I could keep in the game by being a coach," he told me. "When I came back into the game then coaching and playing went parallel and I still coach today."

"I went for three-and-a-half years to Dubai and together with

Rod Marsh and Mudassar Nazar as coaches we set up the ICC Global Cricket Academy," Dayle continued. "I had started the New Zealand Cricket Academy in around 1996, so I was the director of the first national academy and then I became the Black Caps bowling coach. Then I went to Dubai and since then I've been back in New Zealand as consultant pace bowling coach for Canterbury and New Zealand cricket."

* * * * *

Walter is unique in the cricket world. He is the only former international to have sired three sons that went on to play international cricket. India's Lala Amarnath matches him in the Test arena with two sons that played Test cricket, in Surinder and Mohinder.

It is easy for cricket lovers to eulogise over the impact the Hadlee family had on New Zealand cricket and beyond, but that possibly over-eggs the importance of cricket and neglects the importance of family in its own right.

"We are aware of what people say, but cricket is only a small part of life and it doesn't dominate our thinking in any way," Dayle answered when I asked him what it was like to be a part of a cricket dynasty? "There was a time when we used to play for New Zealand and yes, it was really important, but life moves on in different directions. There are other families like the Crowe family who are pretty special in our scene as well, and the Bracewell family, others who've had a major input in what's happened in cricket."

Walter had married Lilla in 1940 and together had five sons. It's easy to focus on their cricketing achievements and forget the men. They had all given to their sport and, in turn, taken what they needed to, but regardless of their stature in that game, as Dayle had said, it's just a small part of life, although it doesn't seem like it some times.

Dayle summarises where the Hadlee boys are now: "We're all close and none of us call each other by our names, but talk to each other by our initials, so Richard's RJ, I'm DR, Barry is BJ, Martin is MG and Christopher is CW and even my father was WA.

"We're all in Christchurch and we get together just before Christmas, we have the brothers and their wives Christmas party and that goes around each others' houses. We had a weekend away to a mountain resort and had a golf weekend together and we stay very close."

Dayle had told me that all five were happy and tight as a family. In that regard Walter and Lilla did a fine job. This book centres on the relationship between fathers and sons, but never forget how important the mums are to the cricketers and families they produce.

"It's brilliant," Dayle concluded. "It was my mother's birthday a couple of days ago and Barry put out the message that it would have been her 100th birthday. We'd all realised that and got in touch with each other and talked about Mum and how important she had been to us all.

"She was amazing. I remember at her funeral, Barry said she was the propeller under the ship. She was the one you couldn't see. The ship goes along the top and she was the propeller driving it underneath."

CHAPTER FOURTEEN

GEORGE, RON and DEAN HEADLEY

"Every true thing has already been said, but each new generation must find a way to say it in their own words"
Marty Rubin

When the batting exploits of your Granddad had earned him the tag 'The Black Bradman' you know he must have been extraordinarily good. When your father too has played Test cricket for West Indies what are your chances of playing at the highest level when no other instances of direct descendant three-generation families exist? When you are picked to play for England and your first major overseas tour is to the Caribbean you also know your travels are going to garner significant attention.

When I'd spoken to David Lloyd he had mentioned Dean Headley as an aside. As the team manager on England's tour in January 1998, Dean who was concerned that the number of media requests he was bound to receive might become a burden and distract him from his cricket had approached Lloyd early in the trip. Lloyd recalled how he'd agreed to shield him only for Dean, "a deep thinker", to decide a few days later that he was happy to talk to the media about his family background after all.

Dean had created history the summer before when he had made his Test debut for England against Australia at Old Trafford in early July. It was the first instance of three generations of Test cricketers from the same family after his grandfather, George, and father, Ron, had previously played for West Indies.

There has only been one subsequent example. When Bazid Khan played his only Test for Pakistan in 2004, he followed his father, Majid Khan, who had played for Pakistan and his grandfather, Jahangir Khan, who had represented India.

So Dean knew his inclusion in England's touring party to the Caribbean would create intense interest, especially with the first Test scheduled for Kingston, Jamaica – the place where George had made his name.

"Your management and your coach are there to go and talk to

and I can imagine having that conversation with Bumble, but I can't necessarily recollect it," Dean told me. "The West Indies is a strange one for me because you get welcomed and you don't get welcomed.

"In some ways West Indies is quite nationalistic and fractioned in their setup, so you've got Jamaicans, Bajans, whatever," he continued. "George actually was half Bajan, but the Bajans don't claim George. George's father was from Barbados, but no Bajan ever talks about him. The rivalry between Barbados and Jamaica is quite fierce and the interactions between the islands and the relationships that they have are quite competitive."

It's not hard to imagine why Dean had concerns about the level of media interest in his tour. His Grandfather was a genuine legend. In 22 Tests he had scored 2,190 runs at an astonishing average of 60.83. This was at a time in West Indies cricket when his runs were vital in an otherwise fragile batting line-up. Of his 10 Test hundreds eight were made against England.

He was the first player to score a century in each innings of a Lord's Test, in 1939. After the Second World War he was not quite as potent.

He was destined for a career in dentistry, but there was a delay in securing a passport to the United States. In the meantime he had scored 78 and 211 in matches in Jamaica and his island kept a hold of their new star. He gave a passionate cricket nation a black hero. He inspired a fresh generation of talent.

In 1932, in a single month, he hit his career best 344 not out, and then 84, 155 not out and 140 against England in Jamaica. Sir Leonard Hutton, who saw him play in his 1939 pomp said that he had never seen a batsman play the ball later, a real mark of quality.

His statistics are exceptional. I'd always felt it said something about the sons, or in this instance the grandson, if they knew about their forefather's achievements. Dean did, and then some.

"It's the longevity that he did it over too," he said. "It's not as if he had a little bit of a purple patch. His career was 22 Tests starting from a Test debut in 1930 through to 1954.

"They brought him out of retirement after not playing first-class cricket, so if you take those two Tests against England out of it, he probably would have averaged about 70 in Tests. He was the youngest ever Test player for West Indies. The West Indians used to joke and call Don Bradman 'The White Headley,' which is quite an accolade.

"What people often forget about George is that he was playing at a time when West Indies wouldn't carry a player around to all the islands. They'd play people on their home island, so Bajans in Barbados, etc. So he was probably the first black player that they carried around everywhere. He was the first black man to captain West Indies. Frank Worrall was the first official black man named captain, but George was the first to captain in a Test match."

Dean had spent some time in Jamaica prior to that first England tour and had learned back then that his presence in the Caribbean caused a stir, and that was before he had played international cricket. Aged around 20, he had lived in Kingston for three months.

"When I first went to Jamaica it was ridiculous," Dean highlighted. "I was on the TV. People were interested. I played in some Jamaica trial games, not to trial for the team, but they allowed me to play. It would come on the news: 'Jimmy Adams 130 not out, Delroy Morgan 50 and Dean Headley four not out overnight'. I just thought *why would you put that last bit?*

"There was always banter all over the Caribbean," Dean added. "It was never ridiculously nasty, but in Jamaica I got welcomed everywhere that I went, whereas in the other countries I'd get a little bit of jibing where people would say stuff like, 'Obviously he couldn't play for West Indies because he's not good enough'.

"I would walk down the street and people would wind down their car windows and shout, 'Alright English man!' and it was good fun. I spent a lot of time with Michael Holding at his gas station chewing on sugar cane sticks. It was really nice to immerse myself in the culture."

Perhaps that was where Dean had picked up his intimate knowledge of George's career. I'd spent a bit of time in the Caribbean myself and knew how West Indians liked to talk long, loud and animatedly about cricket. Dean would have had his ears filled with many a memory.

"On that England tour we caught the back end of the great West Indies era. I thought we were a little unlucky in that series where rain saved them at Barbados and we started a Test match that we never should have started in Antigua on a wet wicket and lost five wickets on the first evening and that was the end of the Test match. I think we competed and that was the story of my England career in that we were always nearly there but never quite, not in my time.

"For me I didn't really feel the pressure of my father and grandfather," Dean continued. "I think it's the way that you are brought up. I was very aware that I had a famous Dad and Granddad, my uncle ran in the Commonwealth Games for Jamaica as well, and I've always been around quite famous people so, for me, it was normality.

"Lots of other people make a big thing of *the son of* or *grandson of* tag rather than yourself so you let them get on with it," he explained. "You learn pretty early that you can't affect people's opinions. There are people who have an opinion of me who don't know me, never met me, they might have seen me and they'll say that I'm arrogant or express whatever opinion. You've never met me - I don't really care! You can try all you want to get people to like you but ultimately you just need to be yourself and hopefully that's a half-decent person. Steve Bull, the England psychologist at that time, always used to say we should 'control the controllables', not worry about stuff we couldn't affect.

"There was a lot of banter in the bleachers in West Indies. I enjoyed the tour and it was great having your first major tour where your family was from."

* * * * *

As I spoke to Dean I became conscious that he referred to his grandfather as George throughout. The only time I heard him say the word Granddad was when he was telling me that he had only ever had one day with him.

"I met him only once when I was 11," he remembered. "A couple of my mates still have the pictures they took with him. It's weird because I was meeting my Granddad. I wasn't meeting this great player. I only met him for a day, so there are a lot of people that talk about him and know him better than I did, even though he was my Granddad."

Dean was 13 when George died in Jamaica, aged 74, so he was two generations removed from one of the all-time legends of West Indies cricket and largely lived on third hand information about the man.

But his father, the next generation, had felt the heat a little more. The pressure was on him far more as the son of George.

"He felt more pressure than I did," Dean began. "I think all that Dad really wanted to do was to prove to George that he could play cricket. He had a brother too called Sydney, who recently died, who was described by Michael Holding as the best schoolboy cricketer he's ever seen. George sent my father to England in order to be educated so he was on his own as well.

"It's a weird one because they are family members and that's why I'm glad with the way I got brought up, where cricket was never the key thing, like it might have been for Dad. I didn't play just cricket, I played every sport going, because I liked sport. My dad didn't really watch me when I was a kid because he made a conscious effort to keep away from me.

"My Dad was very interested in how I was getting on, yes, very much so," Dean continued. "But I can't think of many games where he came to watch Kent play and he didn't watch every day I played Test cricket in England or anything like that. He was proud of what I did and he'd be sitting there chewing his fingernails as nervous as hell."

Dean has three children, two boys aged 15 and 10 and a daughter.

"People ask me whether they are going to be good enough and I don't care really," he said. "At the end of the day, ask them. Do they want to be good enough? It's not for me to make their choices.

"The only thing I want my children to do is to have some sort of sport as part of their life because I think it's good for them. My eldest son plays rugby and high-level hockey. My other boy plays sport and I've got a daughter who doesn't play sport at all. The boys like their cricket but they don't do any extra training than other kids. I don't take them for one-to-ones or anything like that.

"I don't really watch my children play sport either, mainly because I'm coaching other people's kids. We're certainly in a culture now where parents feel that they have to be their kid's biggest supporters. I think people think it's strange that I don't go and watch my kids. I'm quite happy to drop my kid at a game, leave and come back and pick them up later, but very few parents do that.

"It starts with the sentence, 'I'm not one of those parents'. They are calling this generation the snowflake generation because no one tells them that they have failed. Then they get to the outside world and their first manager says they don't like what they are doing and they don't understand, get crushed or defensive.

"The kids from the snowflake generation are breakable because they've never really been criticised. I think it's hard for parents. I'm very much a dad who says 'go fly and see what happens' and of course I expect my children to fall down sometimes. I think you learn from that.

"If my son is playing cricket and he's messing about, I will tell him and ask him why, but I'd do that for rugby, hockey or whatever he is playing. I don't care if he makes a mistake, but the biggest thing I care about in my children's lives is how they go about things. I want them to work hard – it's the attitude rather than the outcome. They will fail sometimes but overall they'll be stronger."

* * * * *

Dean's father Ron was an elegant left-hand opening batsman and a fine fielder about whom, *ESPN Cricinfo* writes, "was always doomed to suffer by comparison with his father, the legendary George. It is, therefore, not too surprising that he played most of his career in England."

Yet from Dean's earlier explanation, Ron had been sent to England for schooling, had remained in the country, and had always retained a determination to prove himself, to his father, as a cricketer. Ron had joined Worcestershire in 1958 and was with the club when they won back-to-back Championships in 1964 and 1965. He captained the side in 1971 and won the John Player Sunday League.

His roots remained firmly Jamaican however, and he returned in 1965/66 season to play for his home island and again in 1973/74. Perhaps it wasn't anything sinister like trying to stay out of his father's shadow that made him stay in England. Falling in love can change anyone's priorities.

"He met my mum in England," Dean told me. "She's white English and he stayed here all his life and has hardly spent any time back in Jamaica.

"He loves it when he goes back, but his home is here in England. He'll probably go back every ten years and when he goes back he's in his element. He might have lived in England, but he's definitely West Indian!"

Ron got his chance at Test level in 1973 when he was called into the touring West Indies squad, which had been depleted by injuries. The tourists needed an opening batsman and they called in the Worcestershire man who had hit his career best 187 against Hampshire at New Road two years before.

Ron made his debut against England at The Oval in the July first Test. He made eight and 42 as Roy Fredericks' opening partner as West Indies won easily. In the second Test, a draw at Edgbaston, he scored one and 11 and in his only ODI appearance scored 19 as Fredericks destroyed England with a century. That was his international career, but in playing Tests the Headleys had already become only the second family to boast father and son Test cricketers.

A move to Derbyshire came about in 1975 and Ron played two seasons there before retiring. He had scored 21,695 first-class runs at 31.12 and scored 32 centuries. It may not be quite the CV that his father posted, but it's to be hoped George told his boy that he could indeed play the game of cricket.

I asked Dean whether, as a mixed race youngster growing up in a country where the male line was associated with Jamaica was at all confusing when he was trying to work out his own identity.

"I think if you'd asked me when I was 12, I supported West Indies," he answered. "I loved the West Indies. It wasn't hard to support them because they were so good at the time.

"No, I didn't find it confusing," Dean continued. "I lived in predominantly white areas. In Stourbridge it was a predominantly white school I went to. I didn't get brought up seeing colour.

"When apartheid officially ended in 1993, I went to South Africa in the October and I just couldn't get my head around it," Dean admitted. "Phil DeFreitas, Min Patel and myself were going into restaurants and I remember walking into Blues Restaurant in Camps Bay, Cape Town and the knives and forks just stopped. But that wouldn't deter us from going anywhere, not to prove a point and not us saying that we'd got the right, but we didn't not have the right.

"People forget, I supported West Bromwich Albion," he added. "I am a good friend with Cyrille Regis and Brendon Batson. Brendon moved to Stourbridge and there's camaraderie, Brendon gets to know about Dad and my dad gets to know about him, they become quite good friends.

"It was a difficult time racially, but I think people make too much of it now and that creates racism. If a kid calls me a name it's because he wants to hurt me, it doesn't mean he's a racist."

Ron had three children. Dean has two older sisters, Tina and Dawn.

"They both played sport and Tina was very good," said Dean. "She was one of only five girls to get the highest award for athletics in the Midlands."

* * * * *

I asked Dean if he'd ever had a chat with his father, or sought his advice, about becoming a professional cricketer.

"I don't think you choose to become a professional cricketer, I think the sport chooses you," he replied. "This is where I think parents have got it all wrong. Just play the game as well as you can and hopefully someone taps you on the shoulder one day and says, 'Do you want to earn your living from this?'

"I don't understand people who say their son's main sport is rugby, so he wants to be a rugby player. I couldn't give two hoots what he wants to be. The fact is if nobody *wants* you to be, you *can't* be. For me, certainly up to the age of 16, you want to be trying to play as many different sports as possible.

"I went to the Royal Grammar School in Worcester from the age of 14. At my school we had 11 people who had played minor-county, first-class or Test cricket as teachers. In those days they could teach for two terms and disappear to play cricket in the summer term, they'd end county cricket in September, miss the first week back at school and then start teaching again. It was a good private school and the head teacher wanted sport to thrive there and wanted good sportspeople there.

"And then, one of my best mates at school was Paul Fearnley," added Dean. "I was at his house having a barbecue one evening and his father, Duncan Fearnley, asked me if I wanted to play for Worcestershire. I said that I couldn't play unless someone asked me, so he said, 'Well, I'm asking you'.

"A lot of people thought I'd end up as a batsman, but I grew horrendously between the ages of 16 and 18 and lost my batting a little bit. The way that people made me bat in my career was in a very negative way. I should have averaged 28 or 29 in my career instead of 16 or 17 and that was because I used to bat for a long time because people used to say keep in for the batsman the other end.

"I'm not a big subscriber to that. In those days you didn't bat the situation and have the freedom to express how you could play, you took instructions. I think that held back English cricket. You see a different England player these days look to take it to the bowlers. You can't play this game with fear."

He spent time with Worcestershire in their second team, before moving to Middlesex in 1991 and then settling down to play for Kent from 1993 until his retirement due to a back injury in 2001.

"I got sacked at 18 by Worcestershire after one season and they said they felt I didn't want to play and that I was injury prone," he said. "I'd grown six inches in 18 months and my body wasn't ready. As a kid I was bowling lots of overs and there was no management of players' bodies in those days. I would just take the ball whenever my captain asked me, and that might have been detrimental to my career in the end. Sometimes things that happen to you shape you. My whole career was based on work ethic.

"I saw a friend called Jonathan Wright, a good cricketer that played a bit for Worcestershire, about seven years ago, and he said to me, 'I don't mean to be disrespectful Dean, but I saw you at 18 and you were struggling with injuries, with bowling and whatever and then the next thing I knew you were playing in the Middlesex side in 1991. I can't get my head around how quick you've gone from that to there'.

"I firmly believe that we look at people at the wrong age," Dean suggested. "We are missing out on a hell of a lot of late developers. We look at cricketers at 16 or 17 who can't mix it with men later on. You look at them when they are youngsters and think they can really play but there's something within them that stops them and they peter out. Your best times in cricket, for the majority of people, come with maturity between 25 and 34 being your peak years. That mental capacity to be able to cope, adapt and change – that's what makes it a great game and a very difficult one to master.

"A lot of it with cricket is the ability to cope with failure," he continued. "When I played my first Championship game for Middlesex I got a wicket with my first ball. I took 5-46 against Yorkshire and Angus Fraser came up to me and said, 'Well bowled, it's all downhill from here'.

"Everyone knows Gus is dour, but he's got a very good dry sense of humour. Gus added, 'Seriously, this is as simple as it gets. Your career will be defined by how you react when the chips are down and you're having a bad day and whether you can make your average day a bit better. And that means not giving up. Those days you have lots of. These good days you will have a few of'.

"I had 25 five wicket hauls, but there's been a lot of times I've walked off the field with no wickets and the difference is whether you have 20 overs 0-50 or 20 overs and 0-100."

Dean equalled a world record in September 2006 when he took his third hat-trick of an English summer, the third coming against Hampshire at Canterbury. Only Charlie Parker in 1924 and Joginder Rao in 1963/64 had achieved the feat before.

"Lots of times I've been on hat-tricks and it's because the majority of my wickets are bowled, lbw, caught keeper or to slip and that leans itself towards putting pressure on batsmen early. I bowled pretty straight."

Now retired, Dean teaches and coaches at Stamford School in Lincolnshire. I asked him if coaching gave him the same satisfaction as playing had.

"I don't think it will give me the same, but it's interesting how you can affect people and it gives you a real sense of pride when you see your cricketers progressing. Zak Chappell is one to look out for – he's a phenomenal player and he's on Leicestershire's books now. I'm not running a hard-line setup, we want them to enjoy it and realise that sport is a good thing to have in your life."

And is it a big thing for Dean to be part of the first three-generation Test family?

"There's only been one other ever and I think you'll struggle to find similar in any other major sport," he answered proudly. "You might find it in some minor sports like show jumping where the money dictates success to a degree.

"Can you imagine what the odds are of that happening to me? I think I've got more chance of winning the lottery twice. The question I always ask myself is which one would I have preferred," he laughed. "I don't know how it happened in our family. The others were batters and I ended up being a bowler, but then a lot of people thought I'd be a batsman, as I've said.

"We've got a good relationship," Dean added about himself and his father. "We probably differ on where we think the game is, but that's always healthy. The game is a completely different game to what I played and miles away from the game he played. The game has moved on."

And pride in his family's achievement?

"Yes absolutely," Dean replied instantly. "The stats say it all. There have been about 5,500 Test cricketers ever and you've got three from the same family, three generations from the same bloodline. That's phenomenal and something to be very proud of."

CHAPTER FIFTEEN

BASIL, DAMIAN and BRETT D'OLIVEIRA

"In my stars I am above thee; but not afraid of greatness
some are born great, some achieve greatness,
and some have greatness thrust upon 'em"
Malvolio in 'Twelfth Night' by William Shakespeare

Basil D'Oliveira's century for England against Australia at The Oval in 1958 had ramifications far beyond that grassy patch in South London.

'Dolly' had been dropped after the first Ashes Test but recalled for the Fifth Test, the 16th of his career. He ended day one unbeaten on 23 and would tell his wife Naomi of his determination to bat all of the following day. Although he didn't quite fulfil his promise, he kept out the Australian bowlers for over five hours before being the ninth man out for 158, his highest Test score and second century. England reached 494 en route to a win by 226 runs. It was surely enough to book Basil's place on England's winter tour to South Africa.

When the squad was announced a day later D'Oliveira's name was conspicuous by its absence. The MCC had bowed to political pressure from South Africa's Prime Minister John Vorster. Despite denials at the time, it has since been shown that the South African Cricket Board, the South African government, the MCC and the British government were in cahoots, had ongoing dialogue and had agreed that D'Oliveira's exclusion suited all parties.

D'Oliveira's omission caused a public outcry, but then a rather convenient injury to Tom Cartwright gave the selectors a second chance to do the right thing. D'Oliveira was added to the squad prompting South Africa to cancel the tour.

He was a cricketer who simply wanted to play, represent his country, score runs and take wickets. If he'd been left alone to do purely that he would simply now be remembered as a fine South African cricketer.

But sadly the world is more complicated than it should be. Basil was playing Test cricket for England because of South Africa's apartheid system of racial segregation. Introduced by the

National Party when it had come to power in South Africa in 1948 it meant Basil, the son of Indian and Portuguese parents, was classed as 'Cape Coloured'. As a non-white citizen his rights and freedoms were limited and he certainly couldn't hope to play Test cricket for his native country.

When South Africa cancelled the England tour due to the inclusion of a Cape Coloured player, the ripples caused would later become a larger wave that would ultimately see apartheid abolished in 1994.

The D'Oliveira Affair had woken people up, and in many cases made them aware, of the abhorrent racial landscape in South Africa and sporting and political sanctions soon followed. Although their enforced isolation cannot take sole credit for altering a nation's fortunes, the plight of D'Oliveira's situation became a catalyst for change. His 158 at The Oval were certainly the most influential runs he ever scored.

Basil had involuntarily become a poster boy for the anti-apartheid movement, unable to play any part in the sporting life of a country people had thought to be civilised. He'd become a pivotal figure in the change that followed in South Africa and earned respect worldwide for his grace, conduct and humanity. In South Africa he is revered like royalty.

Alec Douglas-Home, a future Prime Minister, but then Secretary of State for Commonwealth Relations, was keen to keep the cricketer quiet. He told him to: "Keep out of politics and if you continue to score runs you'll be more effective." That self-serving advice ultimately served Basil well. He remained a cricketer rather than a tub-thumping campaigner and it enabled him to show how important sport was to him, still highlighting the ridiculous nature of a system that would not allow him to take part.

Basil had grown up in the Signal Hill area of Cape Town and would climb the trees outside of the Newlands Cricket Ground to watch matches. As his own cricket developed he'd captain South Africa's non-white side and was a member of the country's non-white football team too.

He made the biggest move of his life in 1960 when he swapped Cape Town for Middleton in the Central Lancashire League thanks to the support of the well-known commentator John Arlott. Basil spoke of his surprise at seeing white people doing menial work and waiting on him in restaurants. In 1964 he signed for Worcestershire and became a British citizen. That was just the start.

He was 34 when he made his Test debut, the age when most people are planning for life after the game. He'd play the last of his 44 Test matches in 1972 when aged 40 and his final first-class match came eight years later. His age was always up for debate, as we'll hear.

One of the most touching stories I'd read had involved Basil's infamous omission from the England touring party. Here is his account in his own words:

"As I waited in the dressing room at New Road after a Worcestershire v Sussex game, to hear if my name had been announced for the forthcoming tour to South Africa, I kept waiting," he wrote.

It was customary in those days for radio cricket commentator Brian Johnston to read the selected players' names out in alphabetical order. When Johnners reached Edrich, with no mention of Basil, the realisation hit home. He'd been unfairly denied his dream tour back to his homeland.

"I kept waiting and when I wasn't mentioned I was dumbstruck," Basil continued. "You could have heard a pin drop in the room. I don't know how long I stood there but the first thing I recall was Tom Graveney swearing bitterly and saying 'I never thought they'd do this to you Bas'. Tom saw the state I was in and took me into the physio's room where I broke down and sobbed like a baby.

"Tom let me get away early and as I stepped outside the pavilion I saw Damian. 'Never mind Dad, you're still the greatest'. I didn't feel it. I was like a zombie. The stomach had been kicked out of me."

Damian was the older of his two sons and 24 years later he'd make his own Worcestershire debut. It was the start of a career that spanned 14 seasons and would see him, again as his father before him, convert to coaching when his playing days ended.

"It's difficult to get away from it, his intentions when he came over to England were just to play cricket and '68 was a by-product," said Damian, when his father died in 2011 after suffering from Parkinson's Disease in later life. Not talking to his son about that period in his life was not the only thing Basil kept quiet about.

"You could never get anything out of him, like his age," said D'Oliveira of his father, who did not have a birth certificate. Although Basil was officially 80 when he died, it could easily have been 83, making previous ages written about his retirement dates even more incredible.

"I'm not even sure my mum knows his real age, perhaps we will never know," said Damian, one of two sons. "We've heard there will be a memorial service on Newlands for him - we forget how big a name he really was."

For Damian the New Road ground would be his second home as a child, player and coach. As a youngster he'd watch his father play, then as a player himself he was a useful all-rounder, before becoming a respected coach until cancer ended his life prematurely, aged 53, in 2014.

"I never thought about cricket as I really wanted to be a footballer," Damian had written on the D'Oliveira family's website. "I had trials with West Bromwich Albion and Arsenal and only started playing cricket at the ripe old age of 15, after dad suggested l play because I had nothing else to do in the summer.

"I was offered a trial at Worcestershire in 1979 for six weeks at the start of the season. At this stage I decided to give up wicket-keeping and wanted to bat, unfortunately the 2nd team wicket-keeper was away at university and I had to keep, this meant me batting down the order.

"I was not taken on the staff following the trial and I was gutted. Mike Vockins, the secretary at Worcestershire, called me and asked if I would be interested in having a trial to go on the Lord's ground staff (MCC Young Cricketers). I had a trial in January 1980 and there were 160 applicants for four available places. I got lucky and was offered a place that I took up in March 1980.

"I had two seasons on the MCCYC Staff and the second year l spent most of the year playing for the Worcestershire 2nd XI and I had a good season finishing top of the batting averages.

"I was contracted as a player from 1983 to 1996 when I was appointed 2nd XI Captain/Coach. In 2001 I also adopted the role of Academy Director which I still do to this day and my official title is Assistant Coach & Academy Director."

In later life one of the promising players that Damian was responsible for bringing through the age groups and into the professional ranks was his youngest son Brett.

Damian said: "Brett's aware of the pressure but hopefully can carry his name on. That's probably our one regret, that Dad didn't get to see him play."

Unlike his grandfather over half a century earlier, Brett embarks on a career in the game with his surname already fondly cemented in the hearts of Worcestershire and world cricket. The Basil D'Oliveira Stand watches over the family's third generation.

While any professional cricketer must contribute to the team in order to get picked, when your name is as loved as Brett's is at New Road, supporters are likely to be more lenient as professional teeth are cut. The coaching staff may not be as nostalgic and Brett himself has no intention of coasting through life on the deeds of his grandfather and father.

"It's a well-known name and not for my doing," Brett told me. "But it's great to be around that. It's a massive honour, and not just for me but everyone in the family, that our name is so recognisable. That's down to my Granddad, and partly my Dad as well, so to still see that knowing that they've passed on, it's nice to recognise that definitely."

I told Brett that other cricketing sons had mentioned hearing the phrase 'You're only here because of your Dad' in their younger days at cricket clubs. Had he?

"Not so much at Worcester, but I can definitely relate to where he's coming from and it has been said before," Brett responded. "Not to my face, but from stuff I've heard and through rumours and various people around me have said they'd heard it, but I think you're always going to get that with a recognisable name like Sidebottom, Compton or D'Oliveira. You're always going to have your father's name in the background and there's always going to be a comparison with what was before you and debates about are you as good and can you be better. Because it's from such a young age you have to learn to deal with it and you knuckle down and get on with it.

When I ask Brett how instrumental his father had been in bringing him through as a cricketer, his voice changes and I could feel the warmth.

"Yes massively," he said. "It's very cliché when you say I'd like to thank my Dad for everything, but that really is how it is and I can't say it any better than that really. Everything that I've got to achieve and hopefully will achieve is a lot of his doing. Just simple things, like on school holidays he'd take me round with the second team, I was always at the games, and from such a young age I was always playing cricket on the outfield and just took it from there really. I fell in love with it and didn't look back."

I'd also read that Damian had worked tirelessly with his son to transform him into a leg-spinner. It was paying dividends as he continues to improve for his county.

"I used to bowl seamers and I got into Midlands teams bowling seamers and opened the bowling," Brett replied. "When I got to the age of 13 or 14 he sat me down and said, 'Look if you are really serious about cricket', which I was, 'you are never going to be six foot, you're never going to be express pace, so have you thought about changing to spin – what about leg-spin?'

"At that time he'd recently been away with Terry Jenner, who was Shane Warne's spin coach, and he'd done a camp with him and he came back off that and had a lot of ideas. I trusted his guidance and went with it and haven't looked back, touch wood.

"Never once did it cross my mind that I wasn't going to try and play cricket professionally. There were other sports that I loved playing like football and golf and I played a lot of basketball at school and really enjoyed that, but in terms of going professional, it was always cricket for me. I probably wasn't good enough with the other three anyway, so it made my decision for me."

I commented that if he wasn't tall enough he might need a couple more inches in height for basketball too and he laughed and suggested I re-evaluate my statement to five or six inches.

I turned our attention on to Basil and asked Brett what he had been aware of when younger about what his grandfather had gone through.

"I was very young when he was coming out of the back end of that and it was quite tough to understand from a young age. But the more I grew up and the older I got the more I understood it. So I didn't really know too much of it when I was growing up.

"I've got two older brothers and I think they understood it a bit more, but it was always taken in our stride as a family and he was always just like Granddad to us, so we didn't really realise his significance.

"It's incredible really," Brett continued. "You don't sometimes realise that it's part of your family and he was always just Granddad, who would buy you an ice cream or have a laugh and a joke with him in the lounge or wherever it might be. It was never the case that he was this big star and he never ever came across like that to me as a grandson.

"When I speak to other people he never showed his true colours until after he'd had a beer," Brett added. "That side of him was always kept in the background. It's a great part of the family and the legacy is incredible. It's touching when people ask you to speak about it.

"I was away in Cape Town this winter and some of the press and stuff that comes across there is incredible as well. People over there can't wait to come and share some stories with you. It's quite interesting really and you hear some great things. I've got a lot of family over there and they tell me a lot of things as well and it's always nice to hear the stories."

And it's down to Brett's Granddad, in part, that South Africa is a different place these days.

"Yes definitely, although if I'm totally honest, like you get everywhere, there's still some trouble with that sort of stuff, but on the whole it's ten times better now than it clearly was, so for him to have a hand in doing that is pretty incredible when you think about it.

"I speak to my Nan a lot about it, as she's still around, and she was right in the mix of things, but saw it from a different angle. She says that he didn't realise what he was doing and what sort of effect and impact it would have on the world, but now when you look back it is pretty incredible."

Did Brett ever speak to his Granddad about it all?

"I didn't, just for the simple fact that I was probably too young at the time and I didn't get it or understand the whole meaning of it and the reason why it had all happened," he admitted. "I sort of knew that there was something going on, but it was the elephant in the room that no one spoke about. He was very easy to get on with and very easy to talk to, but we just never really spoke about that."

I recounted the tale I included earlier in this chapter about Damian's young, innocent words of consolation to Basil when he'd been left out of the touring party.

"I've been told that story a couple of times and I've not asked my Nan about that, but I'll have to ask that question. It sums it up in a nice little story."

We then spoke about Damian's relationship with Basil and whether it had been as supportive as Brett's had clearly been with his own father.

"They had a completely different relationship to what I had with Dad," he responded. "I was very close and my Dad was very hands on with me, whereas my Dad and grandfather were obviously very close, but their emotions and feelings were expressed at home and when they were at cricket they'd walk into opposite nets. My Dad would go into the first net and my Granddad wouldn't watch my Dad, he'd go into the second net and deal with other players. I think it's probably easier not to coach your own son, or Dad might not want to hear what Granddad had to say about his game. But when they got home they'd discuss what my Dad could do better, what he should have done or what he maybe could try out.

"Granddad was coach at Worcestershire so it was the same things as my Dad to me when I was around the same age. But their relationship of how they worked together was completely different. At home as a family they were very similar."

I mentioned what Alec Stewart had said about Micky being a father at home and a boss at The Oval.

"It's difficult to find the balance I suppose, but that was the same for me really," Brett said. "As soon as we got to the club my Dad would walk off into his coaching department or his office and we didn't really speak to each other until we got to the net. He would simply then give me tips on cricket and then once we got in the car or got back home he'd talk about what we could try or what we could do better.

I suggested it must be hard for the coach with his son when he wants to be seen as impartial.

"There was definitely that sort of stuff in my head, that I didn't want to be shown any favouritism at all," Brett recalled. "I didn't want the easy route, so sometimes you feel that you need to do a bit more, you feel like you need to do a bit extra. In actual fact when you ask the rest of the lads at the club they probably forget that your Dad is actually the coach and it doesn't really matter, you're just one of the team in the end.

"It's the same with George Rhodes at the club now," Brett added. "Obviously Steve is his Dad and he's head coach at Worcestershire and George's boss basically. He's asked me a few questions about things because I think he found it a little bit harder when he started out. But now you do forget, as a team-mate of George's, that his Dad is actually the boss. I think that's a real credit to George as it shows how hard he actually does work.

"Having to work that bit harder doesn't do you any harm and is a good thing and maybe that's why my career is starting to take off as I put those hard yards in early on. You never know really."

Brett enjoyed a promising 2016 season. He was promoted to open the innings in the Championship and for the first half of the season scored plenty of runs. He was selected to play for England Lions. I suggested that if things go to plan then international cricket could be a possibility and then the national media would be asking Basil D'Oliveira questions left, right and centre.

"It's inevitable isn't it? I think if my career goes to plan and it goes the right way and I do play for England, which is what I want, yes, it will be talked about in the media. It already happened a bit when I represented the Lions and I did an interview and the first questions were 'How would your Granddad feel now?' and 'can you be better than your Granddad?'

"It can be frustrating but at the same time it's also a massive honour isn't it? Not every person in the world is like that, so it is special.

"You're only as good as your last game and that's how I've started to look at it and I think, if I'm totally honest, I had a good first half of the season and for the second half I wasn't great and I didn't really achieve what I wanted to achieve," he said. "But I definitely made a step in the right direction last year and it's about maintaining that now and that's the hard bit, being consistent. Joe Root scores every other game and that's why he's the best player in the world at the minute."

I'm nothing if not predictable. I asked Brett my Fred Bloggs question. Would he be playing cricket professionally if his name were Brett Bloggs?

"I'd like to think so because I genuinely do love my job and I love playing cricket and I love watching cricket and everything to do with cricket," was his heartfelt response. "Maybe if my family's interests had been in the construction business would I be a builder – I don't know. I'd like to think that I'd have found cricket somewhere.

"I think if your family are involved in something then the pathway to get to that place or to get involved in that sport is obviously ten times easier than Fred Bloggs walking the street. It just naturally is. I'd say it's in the genes. I think you do get handed down some kind of gene that allows you to catch or throw a ball a bit better than someone else who might go to the same school as you.

"I think the opportunity of playing cricket becomes a lot easier. I used to follow Dad around and he was always there for me. For someone who hasn't got a Dad that plays cricket it's probably harder to find that opportunity."

I told Brett about the 10,000-hours theory. Surely if you do get exposed to the game so young, as he had, then the practice is far more than 10,000-hours by the time you reach the age of 18?

"Exactly, and that's what I mean by opportunity. I had those opportunities every other day to follow him around, those opportunities to play on the outfield."

Will there be a fourth generation of D'Oliveiras at New Road?

"I'd like to think so," he laughed. "Sometime in the future, not just yet. I'm not quite ready for that yet. I do hope there is. I'd love that sort of tradition to carry on and for a fourth generation to carry the name on in the game.

"I'd be very much like my Dad I think," he added. "He was very laid back about it and he allowed us to make our decisions.

"Marcus, my eldest brother played to a fairly high standard for Worcestershire and like Dad was an MCC Young Cricketer, but didn't go any further with it. My middle brother Dom also played age group county cricket for Worcester, but their interests weren't really in cricket when they got older so they just play for fun now.

"They could have had the opportunity to go on, or at least give it a go, but they both spoke to Dad and said they wanted to do something else and he was very relaxed about it and said 'that's fine, there's no pressure on you to do anything'. So I think I'd be a lot like that and say 'if you want to do it then great, if you don't hopefully you find something that you do enjoy doing'.

"Dad definitely didn't push me at all and it was very much my own doing. I loved going to the games and it went from there and snowballed."

When you speak to some players you end the interview genuinely wishing them well. Brett's a player who has been through a lot with the death of his father and seems mature, likeable and has his head screwed on. I hope his snowball becomes an avalanche.

CHAPTER SIXTEEN

MAURICE, TIM and CHRIS TREMLETT

"Have no fear of perfection – you'll never reach it"
Salvador Dali

The trumpet of the Barmy Army sounded *The Last Post* as the giant paceman stood at the top of his run. His feet performed their customary shuffle, around eight little steps before the body was asked to steam in one more time. Muscle memory, the run of 14 large strides, the jump, turn, arms in synch and the ball delivered towards tailender Michael Beer. The Australian's feet shuffled back as his bat jabbed down uncertainly. The ball found the inside edge and ricocheted into his stumps.

The short-leg fielder Ian Bell was the first to reach the six foot seven inch giant, lifted in triumph as the trumpet's sound was replaced by raucous chants of 'easy, easy, easy', from the travelling English support. The bowler, now engulfed in a huddle as his team-mates jubilantly wrapped their arms around each other, had realised his dream. At 11.56am in the Sydney Cricket Ground on 7 January 2011 England had won the fifth Test by an innings and 83 runs to take the five-match series 3-1 and Chris Tremlett was an Ashes winner.

Chris is the third generation of the Tremletts to have played first-class cricket and the second, after his grandfather Maurice to play Tests for England.

His father Tim had enjoyed a 16-season career as an all-rounder with Hampshire, where he had remained after retirement as a coach and now their director of cricket. He wasn't far away from international cricket himself, particularly in the mid-1980s. He took 75 wickets at 21.60 and scored 450 runs at 30.00, including his only century, in 1985. It was perfect symmetry that his hundred came against Somerset at Taunton, where Maurice had played his county career.

He was rewarded with an England B tour to Sri Lanka, but never progressed any further. If he had, the Tremletts would have been the only three-generation family to have played their Test cricket for the same country.

When I spoke to Tim he said: "If you like I was the weakest link. I played for England B, which was effectively the England Lions back in the mid-1980s, my father had played three Test matches and Chris went on to play 12 Tests.

"You are always trying to become as good as you can be. Ideally you try to become a better player and my father encouraged me as much as possible. I guess I got as far as my ability allowed. I think my stats would say I was a very good county player.

"I was confident enough in myself not to let it bother me too much," Tim said. "I did go on a couple of tours to Zimbabwe and Sri Lanka. I did okay in one-day cricket and realised that I wasn't quick enough as a bowler to succeed on flat Test match pitches.

"I was certainly aware of my father's stats and it was something you aspire to. But I think when my father played, when I played and when Chris played the game is always evolving."

Tim remembered a speech that Chris delivered when he was leaving Primary School.

"I remember him standing in front of the class and the teacher asked them what they were going to do," Tim explained. "Chris said he was going to play professional cricket, or play golf in the Ryder Cup. They were his two ambitions, but at that age he was saying that without really knowing which direction he was going to go, although he knew he was good at sport. When he was 16 he had a better idea of what he wanted to do."

Almost 25 years and a career as a professional cricketer had passed between that speech and my phone chat with Chris, but he was soon back inside the head of his younger self.

Chris remembered: "From an early age it was in the blood. When I was at school I'd tell my friends that I was going to play sport for a living. I'm very thankful that I got to do that, because when you say it at an early age it doesn't mean you are necessarily going to do it. You don't appreciate the hard work you've got to go through to actually make it. The dedication and hard work you've got to do to stay there is a lot more than you think when you are an 11-year-old.

"Cricket was the one sport that stuck out amongst the other things," Chris told me. "I used to attend a local club every Tuesday and Thursday and I always remember being better than everyone else, which was always a bit of an ego boost. When the awards ceremonies came about each year I'd always win Player of the Year, so I knew cricket was my strength.

"At the same time I did try golf and other sports throughout school and college. I always tried my hardest at golf, but I just wasn't as good as I was at cricket and getting picked for Under-11s and Under-12s at Hampshire gave me the confidence to think I could make something of it.

"I got picked for the Hampshire Academy with Mark Garroway and Tony Middleton and soon I was playing in the 1st Team," Chris continued. "From that regard it all came about very quickly, making my Hampshire debut when I was 18.

"I never really sat down and said this is what I want to do and mapped out my path with my Dad. He relayed things that I might have to do and things that I might have to sacrifice along the way to make it. When I was 16 I wanted to go to Ibiza with my friends, but at the same time during the cricket season it was very difficult to do that.

"It was always handy having Dad around to discuss things and without making those sacrifices I wouldn't have had the career I had. He always gave me very measured advice along the way to nudge me and help me."

Tim exposed Chris to cricket at an early age and one trip in particular served as a source of inspiration for the youngster.

Tim explained: "When Hampshire reached the NatWest final in 1991, he would have been nine, so I took him along. It was on purpose I guess so he could lap up the atmosphere at Lord's. The fact Hampshire won probably helped. Whether that had an effect on him or not, I don't know."

It did. Chris remembered it well.

"I remember going to Lord's, going up into the changing rooms, being told by the people on the door that I wasn't smart enough, but Dad managed to sneak me up into the dressing room. Those kind of memories stick in my mind. It was pretty special.

"Obviously my Dad, I'd never tell him, but he was always a big inspiration. Whenever I'd go down to the County Ground to watch him play on a Sunday I'd think I want to do that as a career like my Dad. And that day at Lord's it was very special to witness that kind of stuff and even though it's 20 years ago I still remember it today."

* * * * *

Maurice died in 1984, aged 61, but left behind a distinguished career with Somerset and England and two further generations of Hampshire cricketers in son Tim and Grandson Chris.

When Maurice uprooted the Tremlett family along the south coast to Southampton when he had retired in 1960, Tim was still a small child. Although he didn't know it at the time a change of scene would have longer-term benefits.

"I think it certainly helped that he had played for Somerset," Tim admitted. "I was only four when we moved to Southampton, therefore it was a different expectation in Hampshire."

The change of scene at a county with fewer preconceived notions offered a less pressurised atmosphere in which Tim could find his feet and blossom.

"It was something that I wanted to do from an early age. Dad had always encouraged us to play as many sports as possible, so it wasn't just cricket," Tim told me. "By the time I got to 15 or 16 I knew that playing cricket was exactly what I wanted to do.

"Then there were players about who had played with and against my father so there was a certain level of expectation, but I think that came from within myself, trying to emulate what my father had done.

"When I was finding my way at Hampshire, I had got selected in the team and then I got left out in around 1978," continued Tim. "I played in a Championship match in Weston-Super-Mare, ironically against Somerset. I played reasonably well, but the next game was in Cheltenham against Gloucestershire and I got left out. It was fair enough looking back, but I was obviously very disappointed at the time.

"I didn't know that my father actually wrote to Richard Gilliat who was the very good captain of Hampshire. Richard didn't let me know. It was a private conversation between the two of them. But I did find out about that much later in my career. If I'd known that I would have been totally embarrassed by that sort of situation. I didn't know the exact contents of the letter, but basically he felt that it was unfair that I'd been left out of the team."

Tim grew up in a household that also included a sister, eight years his senior, and a younger brother. His sister played tennis and golf, while his younger brother was a decent cricketer, progressing as far as the Hampshire 2nd XI. Sport played a huge part in his upbringing with a friendly rivalry existing between the siblings.

"My mother was always very supportive as well," Tim informed me. "She was a very good swimmer and had a very good chance of swimming in the Olympics, but she was only 14 or 15 when the war came along. That wrecked her swimming career. She swam in the army during the war.

"We were always playing sport. You could only play cricket during the summer and once we were old enough we'd all be out playing golf together – we were all single figure handicap golfers. We'd much prefer to be out playing football or rugby or doing something else competitively rather than sitting down watching television. My parents didn't really like us doing that anyway.

We had a table tennis table in our front room, which my mother wasn't too impressed with, but my father bought it one Christmas and that was something else we used to do as a family. He even bought a shove halfpenny board and we used to play that. We'd eat fairly early as a family and then have a game to decide who was going to do the chores.

"We didn't appreciate it at the time, but my brother and I would always end up doing the washing and wiping up because Dad never let us win," Tim added ruefully. "He would never let us win at anything and that competitiveness grew inside us at a very early age. I think it's very important."

Maurice died before he had the chance to see Chris play. Chris was only three when his grandfather died.

Chris said: "I have a couple of really random memories of him, but obviously I didn't really know him at all. To have three Tremlett generations at the ground together would have been nice. Obviously Dad got to see me play throughout my career and it would have been nice to have Granddad do the same, but it's one of those things. It's been nice to keep that tradition going in the family and three generations is something that is pretty rare."

I asked Tim about his father Maurice. Would he have loved to watch Chris and been a useful man to have had around?

"He would have been very good," Tim replied. "He was very astute, knew the game and was a very good coach. He was the first professional captain at Somerset. He had great stories about when he was growing up and when he got into the Somerset side initially he'd talk about the players at the club who mentored him.

"If you speak to a lot of the old Somerset players they regard him as a very good captain. He was a very good coach to me when I was growing up. He was good technically, but more talking about the game and working the game out.

"He would have certainly enjoyed watching Chris and would have got a lot of enjoyment out of it, as I have done."

Maurice had retired before Tim got to see him play competitively, although he recalled watching him turn out in benefit games and charity matches.

"It would have been different for Chris because I was still playing when he was very young and I was coaching by the time he was old enough to take everything in," Tim asserted. "He would have been exposed. I had three boys and Chris was the one that showed the most natural athletic prowess to become a cricketer. But he was tall from a very early age so he was good at basketball and volleyball etc.

"My youngest son was never quite as athletic as Chris, although he played a number of sports and my middle son was interested in horses and was never going to play cricket," Tim had told me. "Like my father had done with me, I encouraged Chris towards cricket, but I didn't push him there and he was about 16 when he thought he could make it a career."

When I asked my next question I was unaware of the tragedy that had hit the Tremletts. I asked whether he'd held his baby sons and thought *I wonder if this little chap will play cricket?*

"Unfortunately my middle son was killed in a car crash and really you just hope they are going to be fit, healthy and happy. If one of them had gone on to play cricket then that was fine.

"My middle son, the one that got killed, was a very talented horseman and was doing really well locally with his horse riding. My younger son went on to play junior schools cricket and played to Under-13 level for Hampshire schools. He was very talented, but he wasn't as athletic. He had a number of major operations on his feet when he was very young. In a way he had many other interests as well and through his work and his interest in cars he's given me a lot of enjoyment and has succeeded in his job."

Had Chris discussed becoming a professional cricketer much with Tim?

"A little bit, yes," Tim answered. "He'd been away in Jersey with the Hampshire Under-16s and when he came back I think it was then that he thought that he would be good enough to play cricket.

Chris came up through our Academy, but I didn't try and get too involved, but I did speak to the coaches and just said what I thought about his cricket.

I took a backward step because I certainly would have been Chris's fiercest critic. When he went away with England we would keep in touch but after he had that very good tour to Australia I wouldn't, because I hadn't played Test cricket and wouldn't know the pressures of what that involved. He had England players and coaches around him to help him deal with that."

Chris said: "It was good to have my Dad around to give me advice, but I think even when you are taking advice from your father you naturally kind of argue and being quite stubborn people we'd always argue about stuff. Obviously I would listen, but I'd maybe not let him know that I was listening as much as I was."

Post retirement, Chris had thrown himself into life on civvy street and his busy work schedule had made it tough for us to grab some time on the phone. I finally managed to schedule a phone call as he battled through Stansted Airport's departure lounge. Interviewing him as we battled the noise of the PA system his words very much echoed those of his father's. Again, for the Tremletts, the deeds of the father had become a motivation for the son.

"I've never really looked at my Granddad's stats, but my Dad's stats show the kind of cricketer he was," he said. "Obviously we played in very different eras, they played a lot more games per year and it's very difficult to judge yourselves against each other.

"I was a very different kind of bowler to my Dad who wasn't as fast as me. He was a hit the line and length type of bowler, run in all day, run into the wind and do a job for the team. Whereas, certainly on my younger days, I was more of an aggressive, hit the deck type of bowler. I was taller and more of a strike bowler. Certainly when Shane Warne was at Hampshire that was my role in the team, to bowl short three or four over spells and try and take wickets.

"I didn't think about stats too much," he added, before admitting, "I knew how many wickets he'd taken in his career so it was nice to overtake him in that regard. In terms of other stats like averages and stuff, I wasn't that fussed about, but going on to play for England and winning the Ashes I suppose I've got one-up on him there.

"With going further to international cricket and that kind of stuff, I think I was always trying to do and prove things my own way and for me, my motivation was to try and be ahead of my Dad – try and get more wickets than my Dad, have a better record than my Dad and have certain people saying 'you're a better cricketer than your Dad'.

"There was definitely that family competition. My Granddad's not around anymore to have that banter with, but with my Dad we have banter at home – 'I played X number of Test matches more than you', 'I took more wickets than you and then retired', but it's funny and a bit of a laugh."

* * * * *

I'd never seen Maurice play, not even on archive footage, but when looking at photographs it was striking how similar the three Tremlett generations are facially at similar ages. All were tall too.

"I've probably got a bit more height than my Granddad or my Dad," Chris stated. "As far as I can remember as a three-year-old picking up a cricket bat was very natural to me and was the one sport that sticks out in my mind when I was a very young kid and was the sport I was better at growing up through school and the county age groups.

"It was the one sport I always seemed to be naturally talented at. I tried playing a lot of other sports at different ages, but cricket was always something that was very natural to me and whether it was in the genes or not, I can't tell you that, but it was the easiest sport for me to play and the one I was a lot better at than all of the other sports I attempted."

Tim's job with Hampshire meant he got to watch his son's

progress from close quarters. It wasn't always easy.

"It's very nerve wracking," Tim said. "It's probably different because I played. I always had a good view when he was playing here at Hampshire.

"I got equally as nervous watching him bat or bowl and when the team were playing away from home, or he was playing for England, I'd work out exactly when he would be involved in the game. You can't do anything yourself. In a way you can work out what's going to happen in a passage of play, but nonetheless cricket doesn't always follow that pattern. Everything is outside of your control."

Some people might suggest that having a well-known surname might open a few doors. Chris Cowdrey had told me that aspect had possibly offset some of the negatives the name brought with it.

Chris Tremlett told me: "When I was younger I actually saw the name as a bit of a disadvantage. I remember there were a few kids saying, 'you're only here because your Dad was coach at Hampshire'. So I had to try to prove them wrong and establish myself in my own way and not just use my Dad's name. I had to try and let my performances do the talking.

"Obviously going through the ranks and playing professional cricket and international cricket, you can't get by with having just a name. You have to prove it," Chris contended. "But when I was a bit younger it was a bit tougher. It never seemed to me to be an advantage.

"It wasn't so much sledging on the pitch, it was more from kids I was around. Some kids can be a little bit nasty at times and they can pick holes in people. I was in the team because I had some talent, but I don't think as a 13-year-old that I was head and shoulders above everyone else.

"Even as a youngster I think it does give you that extra bit of determination and, having my Granddad and my Dad playing, I think it gave me the motivation to go out there and prove myself."

I had to ask the Fred Bloggs question. Would cricket have found Chris had he not been called Tremlett?

"It's hard to answer that really," Chris admitted. "Now I'm retired I don't think about cricket as much. Cricket was always natural for me as a youngster so whether it was because my Dad stuck a bat in my hand or whether it would have happened anyway, who's to say?

"Having it in my genes obviously helps and having Dad's influence along the way, watching him play at the County Ground, those things happening to me did motivate me to want to play cricket. I think there was something in my genes that made me want to be like my Dad and Granddad.

"Dad never forced me," Chris continued. "He was always playing cricket with me and my brothers in the garden but he certainly didn't force us to play. It was something that we loved to do and he would give us tips along the way. My parents wanted us to do what we wanted to do. I wasn't playing cricket because Dad wanted me to do it, I did it because I wanted to do it. That's something that's very important."

Maurice played for 13 years, Tim and Chris for 15 years, so the length of career may have been in the genes too. The Tremletts appeared to have a shelf life in the cricket aisle.

"I'm lucky to have played as long as I did as I had a lot of injuries and operations and there were times when I did contemplate retiring and throwing in the towel because my body had let me down on so many occasions, but yes we had a similar length career," Chris said. "It's funny how it unravelled and came to an end as I thought I would play for a couple more years, but there was a kind of switch in my head that said that the body had had enough and it coincided with Granddad and Dad's retirement of around 15 years.

"I'm happy with the career I've had and the timeframe, it was a respectable length of career, but personally I knew it was the right time to retire and I have no regrets."

Will there be a fourth generation of Tremletts?

"Who knows? I've not had any kids as yet, but I'd like to have children at some stage down the line, but I won't be a Dad that looks to force a bat into my child's hand when they are two-years-old," Chris answered. "But if they want to play cricket I'll give them some coaching and point them in the right direction, but I think it's important that your kids do what they want to do and not what you want them to do."

Those Ashes ambitions burned bright inside Chris. He'd played three Tests for England and wanted more. He had been toiling on the Rose Bowl wickets and decided he needed to reinvigorate his career ahead of the 2010 season. He'd played 10 seasons with Hampshire, a county that meant so much to both himself and his father. How big a wrench was it to sign for Surrey?

"It was a tough decision," Chris recalled. "I just felt very comfortable at Hampshire as I'd been there for quite a long time but if I wanted to achieve my ambitions of playing in an Ashes series in Australia I felt I needed to move. Surrey came along with an offer and I spoke to Rod Bransgrove [Hampshire's chairman] and relayed my thoughts.

"I didn't really want to move in terms of the people at Hampshire, but I needed to change people's perceptions of who I was at the time. I needed a bit of a kick up the backside and to prove people wrong. In hindsight it worked out really well and got to do what I wanted to do. At the same time Hampshire was obviously my main club so there was a lot of sadness leaving, but I think from a personal point of view it was the right thing for me at the time. I don't have any regrets doing it. I played in and won an Ashes."

And the move undoubtedly worked. That Ashes success is the highlight of a career that could have been more had injuries not held him back. But 53 Test wickets at 27.00 with a best of 6-48 against Sri Lanka in 2011 screamed quality. He ended his career with 459 first-class scalps at 28.66 with a career best 8-96. He was also a potent weapon in one-day cricket.

Granddad would have been proud.

CHAPTER SEVENTEEN

AROUND THE WORLD IN 56 FAMILIES

"Never keep up with the Joneses, drag them down to your level"
Quentin Crisp

There have been only 49 families where fathers and sons that have both played at Test level, including those where the son played for a different country. If you count the instances where more than one son followed their father into Tests that rises to 51. If the parameters are changed again, the list of fathers and sons who have both played at international level, including the one-day formats, rises to 56.

In addition, four further examples exist of players from the same bloodline who are two generations or more apart, playing at international level, basically grandfathers or great grandfathers. And if you count each Chappell grandson separately that number rises to seven.

England lead the charts with 13 examples of fathers and sons in Tests, another of a son following a Test playing father into ODIs and two examples of grandfathers and grandsons playing Test cricket.

Next comes New Zealand, bolstered by the Hadlees, then India as the other double figure countries in this respect.

Surprisingly, given the longevity of Australia on the international stage, they have had only two examples of father and son Test cricketers, a further of an ODI son and then two examples of grandfathers and great grandfathers producing a Test player a couple of generations, or more, down the line.

Of the major nations, no examples exist from Bangladesh or Sri Lanka, but their relative infancy in terms of Test cricket accounts somewhat for that.

Here are all examples, by country, and ordered by the date the second generation made their international debut - 56 households and 122 rather extraordinary cricketers.

* * * * *

AUSTRALIA: FATHERS & SONS in TESTS

1   **Edward Gregory** (1 Test, 1877),
     Syd Gregory (58 Tests, 1890-1912)

Edward, or Ned Gregory, played just one Test, but it was the first one ever played. He also has the unfortunate distinction of being the first player out for a duck in Tests. He played a major part in Australian cricket in those early days, but possibly his biggest gift to his nation was his son. His brother, Dave, Australia's first captain, and two other brothers played for New South Wales. Ned's life belonged to cricket in Sydney. He built the first comprehensive scoreboard at the Sydney Cricket Ground and was the ground's custodian. He died in his cottage on the ground in 1899, aged 59.

Syd Gregory almost had no choice but to pick up a bat after being born on the SCG site in 1870. He played 52 of his 58 Tests against England as an attacking right-handed bat. He made four centuries and captained his country in 1912 and was the best cover fielder of his generation. His best tour came in England in 1896 when he scored over 1,400 runs in all matches and finishing top of the averages. He died in 1929, aged 59.

2   **Geoff Marsh** (50 Tests, 1985-1992),
     Shaun Marsh (20* Tests, 2008-Present),
     Mitchell Marsh (20 Tests, 2014-Present)

Geoff Marsh, a dogged right-hand opening batsman played his first Test in December 1985 at No 3 but soon formed solid opening partnerships with David Boon and then Mark Taylor. He was more free in One-Day Internationals scoring 4,357 runs at just under 40 with nine centuries and 22 fifties, contributing to Australia's success at the 1987 World Cup. Geoff took charge of the Australian side as coach in July 1996 and won series in West Indies, the Ashes and in Pakistan and the 1999 World Cup. He then became an Australian selector before coaching a troubled Zimbabwe side and then Sri Lanka in 2011.

Geoff's two sons, Shaun and Mitchell, both play Test cricket. Shaun made his debut in Sri Lanka in September 2011 and Mitchell followed against Pakistan in Dubai in October 2014. Both sons had spent much of their youth following their father around as he played for the Australian side. Shaun played his first ODI in 2008 and scored a century on Test debut in Sri Lanka in 2011. A back injury and poor form on his return led to intermittent appearances thereafter. Mitchell is a pace bowler and lower order hitter who claimed the all-rounder position during the 2015 Ashes tour. His game is ideally suited to one-day cricket and he scored his first ODI century against India in Sydney in 2016. He was a member of the 2015 World Cup-winning squad. Geoff's daughter Melissa is a basketball player for Perth Lynx in the Women's National Basketball League.

AUSTRALIA: FATHERS & SONS in INTERNATIONALS

1   **Trevor Laughlin** (3 Tests, 1978),
    Ben Laughlin (5 ODIs & 3 T20Is 2009-2013)

Trevor, a right-arm medium-pacer and left-handed middle-order hitter, got a Test chance when more established players headed off to play World Series Cricket. In his three Test appearances, two in West Indies and one against England, he scored only 87 runs in five innings and his six wickets were expensive, despite taking 5-101 in his second Test. He did better in his six ODIs, but when the Packer players returned his chances ended.

Trevor's son Ben enjoyed a good 2008/09 season with Queensland Bulls and after Australia suffered an injury crisis amongst its bowlers he was selected to tour South Africa and the United Arab Emirates with the Australian limited-overs team. His six international wickets were expensive and, like his father, when the established stars returned, he found himself surplus to requirements.

AUSTRALIA: GRANDFATHERS & GREAT GRANDSONS / GRANDSONS in TESTS

1   **William Cooper** (2 Tests, 1881-1884),
    Paul Sheahan (31 Tests, 1967-1974)

William, born in Kent, England, was eight when his parents moved to Australia and 27 when medical advice to take exercise led to him taking cricket seriously. He bowled leg-spin and made his Test debut against England in Melbourne in the 1881/82 New Year's match. He took nine wickets in the game. He was wicketless in his only other Test appearance. He captained Victoria, became a State Selector and was vice-president of the Victoria Cricket Association. He died in Melbourne in 1939, aged 89.

William's great grandson, Paul Sheahan, made an entertaining 81 on Test debut against India at Adelaide in December 1967. His 31 Tests saw him score 1,594 at 33.91 with two hundreds, 114 against India at Kanpur on the 1969-70 tour and 127 against Pakistan in Melbourne in the 1972/73 season. He played only twice more having not fulfilled his early promise. His final Test came at the age of 27 in January 1974, 93 years after his great-grandfather had played his first. He became a teacher and headmaster at Melbourne Grammar School.

2   **Vic Richardson** (19 Tests, 1924-1936),
      Ian Chappell (75 Tests, 1964-1980),
      Glen Chappell (87 Tests, 1970-1984),
      Trevor Chappell (3 Tests, 1981)

The first family of Australian cricket were the Richardson/Chappell clan. Grandfather Vic Richardson played Tests between 1924 and 1936 and would be followed three decades later by Ian, Glen and Trevor Chappell.

Vic represented South Australia at cricket, baseball and golf and was accomplished at tennis, lacrosse, basketball and swimming. He scored 10,714 first-class runs at 37.59, including 27 centuries with a top score of 231 against the MCC tourists in 1928. He famously hooked England's Harold Larwood for six en route to his highest Test score of 138 in Melbourne in the 1924/25 series. He played all five of the infamous 1932/33 Bodyline series and was Australia captain for the five-Test series in South Africa in 1935/36 which his team won 4-0. After retirement he became a radio commentator.

Vic's eldest grandchild, Ian, would become Australian captain between 1971 and 1975, skippering his country in 30 matches, winning 15 of them and never losing a series. He was a wholehearted team man who commentator John Arlott described as a "cricketer of effect rather than graces". He scored 5,436 Test runs at 42.42 with 14 hundreds, the best of which, 196, coming in only 246 balls against Pakistan at Adelaide in the 1972/73 series. He played a key role in establishing Kerry Packer's World Series Cricket after many confrontations with the Australian Cricket Board. He took his forthright opinions into the television commentary box upon retirement as a player.

The next family member to become Test captain was Greg, the premier Australian batsman of his generation. He took the captaincy reins from his brother in 1975 and was in charge for 48 matches, winning 21 and drawing 14. He made 24 Test centuries including one in his debut Test against England in Perth in December 1970 and another in his final Test against Pakistan in Sydney in 1984. He also scored a hundred in each innings in his first Test as captain. He made 7,110 Test runs at 53.86 with a highest score of 247 not out against New Zealand in

Wellington during the 1973/74 tour. He added 133 in the second innings to record the highest individual aggregate of 380 runs in a Test (since beaten by Graham Gooch at Lord's in 1990). He became a successful coach after his retirement, including a spell as national team coach to India from May 2005. Greg's most controversial moment involved his younger brother Trevor. With New Zealand requiring six from the final ball of an ODI in Melbourne Greg instructed Trevor to bowl the ball underarm to ensure victory. Ian would write in his newspaper column: "Fair dinkum Greg, how much pride did you sacrifice to win $35,000."

Trevor Chappell was a right-handed batsman and medium pacer who found most success in one-day cricket. He made his debut for South Australia in 1972-73, before relocating to Western Australia in 1976-77 and again to New South Wales in 1979-80. He also joined World Series Cricket. He played three Tests during the 'Botham's Ashes' series in England in 1981, but failed to secure his place with only 79 runs in six innings. He scored 110 for Australia against India in the 1983 World Cup. He retired in 1986 and after playing a few seasons of grade cricket he coached the Gordon Women's Cricket Club and was subsequently engaged by Sri Lanka as a fielding coach and had a spell as Bangladesh's national coach.

* * * * *

ENGLAND: FATHERS & SONS in TESTS

1   **Fred Tate** (1 Test, 1902),
     Maurice Tate (39 Tests, 1924-1935)

Fred Tate's story is a rather sad one. He played a solitary Test at Old Trafford in 1902, a thrilling game that saw England lose the match to Australia by three runs and, with it, the series. He is remembered for dropping a crucial catch to spare Australian captain Joe Darling and then, with England needing eight runs to win, Tate as last man, edged a four before being bowled fourth ball after missing with wild slog. A tearful Fred is said to have vowed that his young son would come through and avenge him.

Fred's Sussex career was more impressive, spanning 19 seasons, which saw his off-spin claim 1,331 first-class wickets at 21.55 with a career best of 9-73. In retirement he coached Derbyshire and ran a Derby pub until 1937. He died in 1943, aged 75.

He had three sons, two of which would play cricket. Cecil played 11 first-class games for Derbyshire and Warwickshire between 1928 and 1933 without causing any ripples. The son he had promised in 1902 turned out to be Maurice. For Sussex, he'd begun as a hard-hitting batsman and off-spinner, but in 1922, ten years after making his debut, he clean bowled Sussex captain Arthur Gilligan in the nets with a much faster ball. "Maurice, you must change your style of bowling immediately," was the skipper's response and an impressive pace bowler he became.

In three seasons between 1923 and 1925 he took over 200 wickets and scored over 1,000 runs. Famously Maurice became only the eighth bowler to take a wicket with his first ball of his Test career. Making his Test debut in 1924 he took 4-12 and Gilligan 6-7 as South Africa were dismissed for a mere 30 at Edgbaston. When he toured Australia in 1924/5 he took 38 wickets at 23.18, a record for an English bowler on an Ashes tour. Despite being a batting force in county cricket, Tate hit his only Test century against South Africa. His first-class career total of 2,784 wickets at 18.16 is the 11th highest ever and with 21,717 runs at 25.01 he is one of only nine people ever to get a career double of 20,000 runs and 2,000 wickets. He also claimed three hat-tricks and was named *Wisden* Cricketer of the Year in 1924. He died in 1956, aged 60.

2   Joe Hardstaff Sr. (5 Tests, 1907), Joe Hardstaff Jr. (23 Tests, 1935-1948)

Joe senior played all five of his Tests in Australia in 1907/08, scoring 1,384 runs on the tour and finishing third in the Test averages. Joe junior was a more stylish batsman whose Test debut came against South Africa in 1935. Joe junior only played the one Test that summer, the third, while Joe senior, by then a respected umpire, had stood in the first and fifth matches, the last of his 21 Tests in that capacity. Joe junior played 23 Tests either side of World War Two, including two tours to Australia in 1936/37 and 1946/47. He was one of many terrific talents who lost his prime cricketing years to that conflict. Who knows what he could have achieved, although a record of 1,656 runs at an average of 46.74 proves his quality. His highest Test score, a brilliant unbeaten 205, came against India at Lord's in 1946.

3   Charlie Townsend (2 Tests, 1899), David Townsend (3 Tests, 1935)

The Townsends were a cricketing dynasty with six family members over four generations played first-class cricket. Charlie Townsend was a prodigious talent, particularly as a youngster. An amateur all-rounder, whose big leg-spinners on sticky wickets and stylish left-handed batting made him a potent dual threat.

He played 199 first-class matches alongside WG Grace and his brothers, for Gloucestershire between 1893 and 1909, although his last first-class game was in 1922. He played two Tests against Australia in 1899.

In 1893, aged 16, he took a unique hat-trick against Somerset at Cheltenham when every victim was stumped. His best seasons were 1895 when he took 131 wickets at 13, 1898 when he scored 1,270 runs and took 145 wickets at 20 and then in 1899 he hit 2,440 runs at 51 and claimed 101 wickets. His highest score of 224 not out came against Essex in 1899, one of nine centuries he hit that summer. He was rewarded with being named a *Wisden* Cricketer of the Year in the 1899 edition.

His effectiveness as a bowler was gradually diminishing and becoming more expensive by the time he was chosen to play two Tests against Australia and he returned the relatively meagre stats of 51 runs at 17 and three wickets at 25. His main interests had been turning towards his work as a solicitor and his appointment as the Official Receiver in Stockton, yet he still managed to fit in cracking 129 out of 169 made in two hours at Cheltenham against the Australians in 1909.

The Townsends were a multi-generational side. Charlie's father Frank had played alongside the Graces at Gloucestershire and his son David would also play for England. David made three Test appearances in the Caribbean in 1934/35 and was the last man to play for England without ever playing county cricket, instead gaining selection with runs for Oxford University. Like his father, he turned his back on the game to pursue a career in law.

4   **Frank Mann** (5 Tests, 1922),
     George Mann (7 Tests, 1948-1949)

A Middlesex stalwart whose career spanned the Great War, Frank Mann captained MCC in South Africa in 1922-23 where he played all his five Tests, winning the series 2-1 as well as 14 of the 22 tour matches. He went on to become an England selector. His son George captained England in South Africa in 1948-49, winning plaudits for his attitude both on and off the field, but after two Tests in 1949 he stood down, unable to commit to the tour of Australia in 1950/51 due to his growing business commitments. Like his father, he went on to be president of Middlesex, but George also became MCC president in 1983/84 as well as chairman of the Test and County Cricket Board (the forerunner of the ECB).

5 Jim Parks Sr. (1 Test, 1937),
Jim Parks, Jr. (1954-1968),
Bobby Parks (nearly, 1986)

Jim senior was selected for his one Test appearance after an amazing summer in which he scored 3,003 runs and took 101 wickets with his medium paced bowling. Jim junior later recalled that after the death of his mother, "Dad just threw himself into his cricket to forget his loss." Parks made 22 and seven and took three for 36 at Lord's and was unlucky not to get further opportunities. He had debuted for Sussex in 1924 and lost the latter part of his career to the war years. His younger brother, Henry, played 483 first-class matches for Sussex as a batsman. In the 1960s Jim senior coached Sussex. He died in Sussex in 1980, aged 77.

At 17 Jim junior scored his maiden first-class hundred and further runs for Sussex saw him debut for England against Pakistan at Old Trafford in July 1954. Sussex lost their regular keeper Rupert Webb to injury in 1958 and captain Robin Marlar nominated Jim to fill the breach. For the initial game against Essex he was forced to borrow some gloves from his opposite number, Brian Taylor. Like his father he had become an excellent fielder so the transition was smooth and led to his move behind the stumps during the 1960s for England too. He scored 1,962 Test runs at 32.16 with two centuries. He moved to Somerset ahead of the 1973 season and played his last three seasons there. In retirement he worked as a marketing manager for Sussex, managed the Old England cricket team and in 2013 was elected President of Sussex.

A third generation, Bobby, also played Test cricket, albeit only for one day against New Zealand as a substitute for Bruce French, who had been injured by a Richard Hadlee bouncer. It was Bobby's only exposure to international cricket, but he was a very capable gloveman whose first-class career spanned 14 seasons for Hampshire and Kent. After his retirement he became an accountant, coached at Hampshire and also with the France national team.

6 Leonard Hutton (79 Tests, 1937-54),
Richard Hutton (5 Tests, 1971)

That I never got to speak to Richard Hutton is my one regret from writing this book. At some stage you feel it's the right time to stop pestering. Richard, like Liam Botham and other sons of genuine greatness had a huge task in following Sir Leonard who was a Yorkshire Colossus.

I'd read bio pieces on Richard and pretty much every single one begins in similar fashion to this from *ESPN* Cricinfo: "Richard Hutton was a good county all-rounder, who was never quite able to escape the shadow of his illustrious father." Another piece suggested: "Richard Hutton was probably the one most blighted by the weight of expectancy. The fact that he was rather good at the game actually made things worse, since many seemed to believe that since he had some of his father's talent, he ought to be even better." I would love to ask Richard, 'how does that make you feel?'

His statistical record is very good. In all first-class cricket he scored 7,561 runs at 36.50 with a career best of 189, one of five hundreds. He also took 625 wickets at 24.01 with a best analysis of 8-50. It is generally considered that the mark of a very good all-rounder is if their batting average is higher than their bowling average. From that perspective Richard was exceptional.

He was selected for his five Test appearances because of his own pedigree, not the name of his father. His Test record too suggests he could have been afforded more opportunity. His Test batting average was 36.50 with a highest score of 81, which came against India in his final Test at The Oval, whereas his bowling average, again lower, saw his nine wickets come at 28.55. That's not too shabby.

Father and son were different. Len was a working-class lad from Pudsey, whereas Richard was sent to public school and attended Cambridge University. Richard played 16 summers for Yorkshire without ever escaping his father's shadow.

Len played 79 Tests for England, had a career that spanned the War from 1937 and 1955, scored 6,971 Test runs at 56.67, and became England's first professional captain in 1952. His highest Test score of 364 was a world record until beaten by Garry Sobers. He was knighted shortly after his retirement in 1956. In short he was a genius and many wouldn't have tried to follow him.

Len's brother-in-law was Yorkshire all-rounder Frank Dennis. Another son John played one first-class game for MCC. His nephew, Simon Dennis, played for Yorkshire as a bowler. One grandson, Ben Hutton, played 10 seasons of first-class cricket for Middlesex, and another, Oliver Hutton, played one game for Oxford MCCU.

There are quite a few cricketers in the Hutton clan, but unfortunately for Richard, there will only ever be one Sir Leonard Hutton.

7   **Colin Cowdrey** (114 Tests, 1954-1974),
     Chris Cowdrey (6 Tests, 1984-1988)
     See Chapter One.

8   **Micky Stewart** (8 Tests, 1962-1963),
     Alec Stewart (133 Tests, 1990-2003)
     See Chapter Five.

9   **Alan Butcher** (1 Test, 1979),
     Mark Butcher (71 Tests, 1997-2004)
     See Chapter Eleven.

10   **Arnie Sidebottom** (1 Test, 1985),
     Ryan Sidebottom (22 Tests, 2001-2010)
     See Chapter Two.

11   **Jeff Jones** (15 Tests, 1964-1968),
     Simon Jones (18 Tests, 2002-2005)

Jeff Jones was Glamorgan's left-arm pace threat for nine seasons through the 1960s. He was building a promising 15 Test career when a serious shoulder injury ended his career in 1968.

It was a similar tale for Jeff's son Simon who had played 18 Tests when injury saw him miss the final act of a sensational 2005 Ashes summer. Although he continued to play county cricket for Glamorgan, Hampshire and Worcestershire until 2013, he was never quite the threat he was before.

Jeff took 45 Test wickets at 40.20. Simon took 59 at 28.23 and also played eight ODIs. I spoke to Simon about the role his father had played in his career and whether he felt cricket was in his genes.

"Dad just said from day dot that, once I'd started playing sport aged about six, that he just wanted me to find something I loved doing and as long as I enjoyed doing it, he'd back me no matter what," Simon told me. "He was very supportive. Although it's nice to surpass his statistics there's that respect issue as well. I totally respect everything that he achieved in the game and barring injury when he was 26, who knows how many Tests he would have gone on to play? More than me I think.

"I played alongside him a few times when I was 12 or 13 in the local team. I've got two other brothers and the three of us and my Dad played in the same team, which was a great experience," Simon continued. "Obviously he couldn't do what he used to do because he was getting on a bit and the body was failing him slightly. To have him on the field with me at mid-on or mid-off giving me advice and to stick by me was obviously great.

"I went to Millfield School at the age of 15, so I was in a sporty school. I was always a bit more switched on than my brothers, I was the more aggressive of the three, I didn't like it when people got the better of me and I guess I was just more competitive. One brother is three years older and I've got a twin that is five minutes older than me. The pair of them were very good cricketers. They were both all-rounders, but lost interest in the game. I was always faster than the pair of them.

"I've seen footage of Dad play and every time I watched him, the way he bowled, the pace he bowled and some of the people, like Garry Sobers, he bowled at, it's great to see. I would have loved to have been at an age where I could have watched him play live and appreciated what he was doing. But he was quite late having us so there was no chance of that.

"At Glamorgan people always introduced me as Jeff Jones's son and I was known as 'son of Jeff' up until I turned professional at the age of 16. It didn't bother me one bit and when I started making a career for myself that tag slipped away slowly. It fills me with pride that people thought of him so highly and they'd put the two of us in the same sentence.

"From the age of 12 I was bowling fast so I made a reputation for myself," Simon answered when I asked him if he got any sledging because of his father? "I think if I'd been an average cricketer then people may have said more about my Dad, and I'm not being arrogant or big-headed there, but I've seen certain people who had Dads that were a lot better than them and it must hurt them like hell.

"He was a left-arm bowler and I was right-arm. He batted right-handed and I batted left-handed. I don't know how that happened. I do think it's down to genetics. Dad bowled quickly, around 90mph, and so did I. The coordination has to be achieved through playing the game and training, but I think you do need to have that natural gift to play the game.

"I've read a few pieces on him that have described Dad as a 'strapping, skiddy, fast bowler' and that's exactly what I was. I'm 6'3" and he's 6'1" so I'm slightly taller than him. And the funny thing was we had very different actions as well. Dad was very much side on, whereas I was chest on, but I think that was down to the fact that my action needed changing around 17 to save my back. I think I was very much like my Dad. I look at photos of him when he was playing and he looked like me. It's a weird one isn't it?

"You get people watching cricket on the television and it looks a simple easy game, but I think when you are playing it, it is totally different. I think when your Dad has been there and done it, he understands the pressures you are under anyway. If you've been in a high-pressure situation you are more understanding than someone who has parents who haven't been there and achieved.

"Dad said to me, 'Simon, you are going to have more bad days than good days, so get used to it and learn to deal with them because I'll never put any pressure on you or have a go at you if you bowl badly. As long as you learn from that experience then I'm happy'.

"I've said to my eldest boy that as long as he puts 100% in, then once you lose the enjoyment, move on to something else. Life is too short. If you are doing something on a weekend then you've got to be enjoying it rather than feeling that you've been pressured into it. It comes down to man management as well," Simon contended. "I think you have to sit back and let people make mistakes. You can be the sounding board if they come to you.

"I've played at a couple of counties where coaches have gone ballistic and it can push a player away from them. You have to be realistic at times when a player is not having the best day of his career," Simon concluded. "So what, that's life. As long as your preparation and everything you've done before that game is sound you just have to take your hat off to someone else sometimes and say 'he was better than me today'."

12 Chris Broad (25 Tests, 1984-1989), Stuart Broad (102* Tests, 2007-Present)

Chris played 25 Tests for England with considerable success, including scoring three centuries in successive Tests during the successful 1986-87 Ashes tour. In 1983 he had left his native county Gloucestershire for Nottinghamshire, stating that their lack of ambition had not assisted his international aspirations. He made his Test debut soon after, in July 1984 at Lord's against West Indies. He scored 139 in the Sydney bicentenary Test a year later but was in hot water, after being bowled, for crashing his bat into the stumps in frustration. Under the guise of loss of form he was dropped the following summer after another show of petulance at Lord's. He played only two more Tests and ended with 1,661 runs at 39.54 with six hundreds. He scored a further 1,361 runs at 40.02 in 34 ODIs. He saw out the end of his career at Gloucestershire. He did commentary for BBC television and is now an ICC match referee.

Chris's son Stuart, who has inherited his father's feistiness and determination, made his Test debut against Sri Lanka in Colombo in December 2007. His new ball partnership with Jimmy Anderson was the most successful in world cricket in the 2010s.

Despite passing 100 caps and being third behind Anderson and Ian Botham (who he should pass in 2017) in England's all-time wicket-taking charts, he will be remembered most for one remarkable morning at Trent Bridge against Australia. He took 8-15 as Australia were bowled out for 60 before lunch on the first day inside 19 overs. He took 5-37 in the fifth Test against Australia to secure the Ashes urn and his man-of-the-series display against India was topped by a spell of 5-5, including the first Test hat-trick at Trent Bridge. His batting had always been dangerous as his only hundred, 169 against Pakistan at Lord's in 2010, after England had been 102 for seven, suggests. He'd entered the game as a batsman, but shot up to six feet five inches and transformed his game at Leicestershire to become a bowling all-rounder. He moved from Leicestershire to Nottinghamshire in 2008.

13   **David Bairstow** (4 Tests, 1979-1981),
      Jonny Bairstow (38* Tests, 2012-Present)
      See Chapter Four.

ENGLAND: FATHERS & SONS in INTERNATIONALS

1   **David Lloyd** (9 Tests, 1974-1975),
      Graham Lloyd (8 ODIs, 1996-1998)
      See Chapter Five.

ENGLAND: GRANDFATHER & GRANDSON in TESTS

1   **Maurice Tremlett** (3 Tests, 1948),
      Chris Tremlett (12 Tests, 2007-2013)
      See Chapter Sixteen.

2   **Denis Compton** (78 Tests, 1937-1957),
      Nick Compton (16 Tests, 2012-2016)

Cutting Denis Compton down to a few paragraphs is difficult and feels slightly disrespectful because he was a great cricketer and footballer, but more than that he was a personality who transcended the sport, a little like David Beckham has done over the last 15 years. He brightened a sombre post war Britain with his flamboyant play.

He was almost good enough, as his 622 first-class wickets testify, to forge a career as a spinner, but that was a secondary string to his bow. He joined the Lord's staff aged 15 in 1933 and debuted for Middlesex in 1936 and in June he notched his maiden century in 135 minutes against Northamptonshire. Three months later he made his Arsenal debut, scoring the first goal in a 2-2 draw with Derby County.

In 1937 he scored 1,980 runs and made his Test bow against New Zealand at The Oval. Len Hutton arrived around the same time - contrasting players and everyone had their favourite. In 1939 the pair added 248 against West Indies at Lord's in quick time as Denis headed to 2,468 runs that summer. He served during the war, but also found time to play some first-class cricket. His final total was 5,807 Test runs at 50.06, but who knows what that record could have reached had he not lost six of his prime seasons to the conflict? He was the country's leading scorer with 2,403 first-class runs in 1946, and scored a hundred in each innings in the Adelaide Test in February 1947. He made 753 of the 3,816 runs he hit in 1947 in the Tests.

Knee trouble gained from a collision with the Charlton goalkeeper reduced his potency slightly towards the end of his career, but most mortal players would have taken the runs and talent of a Compton even reduced by injury. He notched two big Test hundreds in 1948 against Bradman's invincible Australians and walloped 300 in three hours against North-Eastern Transvaal team a few months later.

As the Lord's stands now testify, he was a Middlesex man and synonymous at Lord's alongside Bill Edrich. He signed a deal with Brylcreem, slicked down his previously wavy hair and will forever be referred to as the Brylcreem Boy. In November 1955 he had his right kneecap removed and it now sits in the Lord's Museum. He played another two seasons and hit 143 in his final game for Middlesex in 1957. It had been a remarkable career. He was in demand in retirement, writing for the *Sunday Express* and commentating for the BBC. After his death, aged 78, in 1997, his memorial service at Westminster Abbey created more applications for tickets than any in 30 years.

Anyone following Denis had a task-and-a-half. His brother Leslie had played 275 first-class games for Middlesex as a wicket-keeper and he also played football for Arsenal. Denis's sons, Patrick and Richard, both made South Africa their home, playing a handful of matches for Natal. Reports are that they could have made a career if they'd so desired, but the looming shadow of their father's deeds could have put most people off.

Richard's son, Nick, however played for Middlesex and Somerset and represented England in 16 Tests. I interviewed Nick for around eight minutes for this book before a boiler failure aborted our chat and I was never able to get him back on the phone. I'd begun by suggesting that the *ESPN Cricinfo* short bio of him was a bit dismissive of his talents. It starts: 'Grandson of the legendary Denis, Nick Compton had quite an act to emulate. He might not share his relation's ability to entertain with the bat - few ever have - but he has made his own career as a strong-willed top-order batsman with a correct technique that has been highly regarded enough to win England Test caps."

Nick told me, "I think there are two questions. There's the grandfather connection and his record, prowess and everything speaks for itself. My father and uncle might have played a few first-class games and were very talented but they certainly didn't have a career and they made a choice not to pursue a cricket career. Without making the legacy more than it needs to be, my father and uncle could have been very good from what I'm told, but they didn't play or try and get better at it.

"My grandfather was over here and my father was taken over to South Africa at an early age and didn't have the fatherly support," Nick explained. "I don't think he had the drive and ambition or anything like that. I think partly they didn't want the life. They didn't want to go down that route and lacked the ambition.

"I guess the whole grandfather thing, the way you've said it, when I think about it you are probably right. But I've never thought *how dare they say that*? It kind of goes with the territory and you get bored of it over time.

"I don't agree with it if I'm honest," Nick had continued. "The one thing that does upset me is how I'm conveyed as this dour opening batter."

Nick was in between stints in the England side and obviously felt hard done by. He told me he had all the shots but had figured a way to succeed, bat long and score runs. And the evidence was there to suggest he was right. Over 11,000 first-class runs at 41.21 more than suggest he knows how to play the game. But he was obviously frustrated that his efforts to solidify the top of England's order had engendered criticism of his scoring rate at a time that Twenty20 cricket was seeing runs plundered at rapid rates in Test cricket too.

Nick struck me as a man who was comfortable with the Compton name and proud of his own game. It's likely the criticism would have come whether his name had been Compton or something else. When he got the second chance at Test level he craved, it didn't work out. He'd played nine Tests in his first incarnation and scored 479 runs at 31.93 with two centuries. He'd been one of the few tried by the selectors to have forged a successful partnership with Alastair Cook at the top of the order. I shared Nick's assertion that he had earned more of a chance. When he was recalled for the tour of South Africa in 2015/16, and for the first part of the following summer, he played seven further Tests scoring 296 runs at 24.66 with just one fifty. I'm sure if I spoke to him again he would admit that wasn't good enough.

His Grandfather was known to enjoy life away from the game. Nick had already ventured into television and modelling. He is well equipped to succeed away from cricket when he finally calls it a day with his county Middlesex.

I hope his boiler got fixed.

* * * * *

INDIA: FATHERS & SONS in TESTS

1   **Iftikhar Ali Khan** (6 Tests, 1932-1946),
     Mansur Ali Khan (46 Tests, 1961-1975)

Iftikhar, better known as the Nawab of Pataudi senior, played three Tests for England between 1932 and 1934 before captaining the Indian team in three further Tests on their 1946 tour of England. He made 102 in Sydney in his debut Test innings for England in 1932 and played his last match for England in 1934. 12 years later he played three Tests for India to become the only cricketer to play Test matches for both India and England. He died playing polo only five years after retirement at the age of 41.

Iftikhar's son was Mansur Ali Khan, known as Nawab of Pataudi junior, who became captain of India at the age of 21, a few months after a car accident permanently impaired the vision in his right eye. He became arguably the best Indian captain ever leading his team to its first overseas Test victory against New Zealand in 1967. He scored 2,793 runs at 34.91, including six centuries. His highest score of 203 came against England at the Feroz Shah Kotla in Delhi. Of his 40 Tests in charge, India won nine. After retirement he became an ICC match referee and editor of a sports magazine. He died in Delhi in 2011, aged 70.

2   **Lala Amarnath** (24 Tests, 1933-1952),
     Mohinder Amarnath (69 Tests, 1969-1988),
     Surinder Amarnath (10 Tests, 1976-1978)

On his debut, India's first ever home Test in Bombay, Lala became his country's first centurion. His innings failed to prevent defeat to England, but it barely mattered to the Indian people who immediately took him to their hearts. He was also his country's first captain and would later become a selector, manager, coach and broadcaster. That initial high was as good as his batting got, although he could be brilliant on his day. He swore at team management after being dropped down the order in a tour match at Lord's in 1936 and was sent home. It led to a 12-year gap between his third and fourth Test. He toured England again in 1946 when his leg-break bowling was his biggest weapon. He captained India again, on their first tour to Australia, but Bradman took them apart, but against West Indies in 1948/49 he almost led his country to their first Test win in Bombay. He was no longer captain, but still in the side, when India beat England in Madras in 1951/52. He scored 878 Test runs at 24.38 and took 45 wickets at 32.91.

Lala was instrumental in his three sons becoming first-class cricketers. The youngest boy, Rajunder played only first-class cricket, 36 matches for Haryana. But the older two played Test cricket. The eldest, Surinder, emulated his father by making a century on his Test debut, 124 against New Zealand in Auckland in January 1976, but in nine further Tests he failed to reach three figures again. The initial success only added to the expectation after a stellar pathway through schoolboy matches. He ended with 550 runs at 30.55.

Mohinder surpassed them all. Two years Surinder's junior, he debuted against Australia in Chennai in December 1969 and, although he didn't register a century on debut, he scored 11 Test hundreds and was also a key member of the one-day side, which won the 1983 World Cup. He won back-to-back man-of-the-match awards for two wickets and 46 runs against England at Old Trafford in the semi-final and his 26 and 3-12 against West Indies in the Lord's final. His 4,378 Test runs came at 42.50 and his medium paced bowling took 32 wickets. His best season was 1982/83 when he returned to the side after a three-year absence to score 1,182 runs in 11 away matches against West Indies and Pakistan, including five hundreds.

3   **Vinoo Mankad** (44 Tests, 1946-1959),
     Ashok Mankad (22 Tests, 1969-1978)

Vinoo (a childhood nickname that stuck) was a true great of Indian cricket. He scored 2,109 runs at 31.47 and took 162 wickets at 32.31. He made five centuries and twice took eight wickets in an innings. He shared a world record opening stand of 431 with Pankaj Roy against New Zealand in Madras in 1955/56 with his contribution a career best 231. His 8-55 and 4-53 against England in Madras in 1952 played a huge part in securing India their first win over the mother country. At Lord's in 1952 he hit 72 and 184 and bowled 97 overs in the match as he collected 5-231. It was a mammoth effort in a losing cause, but that was largely his role as the star of a side that only won five of the 44 Tests he played. Vinoo died in Bombay in 1978, aged 61.

Vinoo's son, Ashok played for India as a batsman, but his Test career did not match his exploits in the first-class game. He was in and out of the Test side and failed to register a century, his six fifties and an average of 25.41 nowhere near the 12,980 first-class runs, 31 centuries and highest score of 265 he forged for Mumbai. Ashok died in 2008, aged 61. Two of his brothers, Rahul and Atul Mankad, also played first-class cricket.

4   Datta Gaekwad (11 Tests, 1952-1961),
Anshuman Gaekwad (40 Tests, 1974-1984)

Datta made his debut in England in 1952, but never established a regular place in the India side. Despite that he was appointed captain for the tour of England in 1959, but India lost all five matches. His highest Test score was 52 against West Indies at New Delhi in 1959 and his batting average of 18.42 didn't match the 36.40 he averaged in first-class cricket for Baroda, for whom his highest score was an unbeaten 249 against Maharashtra in 1959/60.

Datta's son Anshuman did more to find his feet at international level, but largely through attrition and bravery. His Test highest score of 201 against Pakistan at Jalandhar in 1882/83 took over 11 hours and was then the slowest double century in first-class cricket. He stood up to the West Indies pace battery to score 81 in Jamaica in 1975/76. On that tour he required surgery on a punctured eardrum after being struck on the ear by a Michael Holding bouncer. He scored a century in his final first-class game in the 1991/92 season and then became a selector and national coach. Anshuman's son Shatrunjay played Baroda and Kolkata Knight Riders in a 12-year career that ended in 2014, in which he made one first-class century.

5   Pankaj Roy (43 Tests, 1951-1960),
Pranob Roy (2 Tests, 1981)

Pankaj experienced peaks and troughs, but when he was good he was every bit an international force. On first-class debut in 1946/47 he reached three figures and scored two hundreds in his debut Test series against England in 1951/52. In England the following summer he made five ducks in seven innings. Then runs returned, including partnering Vinoo Mankad to a world record opening stand of 413 against New Zealand in Madras in

1955/56. He captained India in one Test, in England in 1959, but India lost the series 5-0. He died in Kolkata in 2001, aged 72.

Pankaj's brother, Nemailal, played 12 matches for Bengal spread over a decade, and his son, Pranab, played two Tests for India against England but, other than an unbeaten 60, didn't impress as an opening batsman. He floundered in English conditions in 1982 and wasn't required again. He was successful during a 14-year career for Bengal, in which he scored 4,056 runs at 40.96 with a highest score of 206 not out against Assam in 1983/84. Pranob's cousin, the son of Nemailal, was Ambar who played four Tests for India in 1969.

6   Vijay Manjrekar (55 Tests, 1952-1965),
Sanjay Manjrekar (37 Tests, 1987-1996)

Vijay played his first Test in the 1951/52 series, aged 20, against England at Calcutta and on the return tour in 1952 made 133 in his first Test innings in England. He'd come in with India 43 for three and reeling against the pace of Fred Trueman at Headingley, but shared a stand of 222 for the fourth wicket. In an era when India were susceptible to fast bowling he stood firm. He made 118 the following winter against West Indies, made 386 at 77.20 against New Zealand in India in 1955/56 and 586 at 83.71 against England in India in 1961/62, a series that included his highest Test score of 189 in Delhi. He scored the last of his seven Test hundreds in his final Test innings, against New Zealand at Madras in February 1965. In the Ranji Trophy he scored 3,734 runs at 57.44 for six different teams. Vijay died in 1983, aged 52.

Vijay's uncle, Dattaram Hindlekar, had played four Tests for India, and his son, Sanjay, followed him into the India Test team. He was known to work obsessively at his game and as the son of a Test player a huge amount was expected of him. He had never seen his father play but those who had made constant comparisons. His four Test hundreds, one a double against Pakistan, were technically brilliant, but he couldn't deliver more. He was faced with having to develop his game in a new era where he played 74 ODIs. His 2,043 Test runs at 37.14 didn't come close to his 55.11 average in first-class cricket for Mumbai. If he'd not been a cricket son he would go down as a fine player, but you won't find a write-up of his career where he's not described as unfulfilled in the shadow of his father - the perils of following in the footsteps. In retirement he moved into television commentary.

7   Hemant Kanitkar (2 Tests, 1974),
Hrishikesh Kanitkar (2 Tests, 1999-2000)

Hemant's first-class record for Maharashtra is impressive. Over a 15-year career he averaged 42.78 with a highest score of 13 centuries was 250 against Rajasthan in 1970/71. But his two Tests the wicket-keeper batsman failed to cause a ripple despite scoring 65 in his first Test innings against West Indies in Bangalore. He managed 46 runs across his other three innings and didn't get selected again. Hemant died in Pune, aged 72, in 2015.

Hemant's son, Hrishikesh, played two Tests and 34 ODIs as a left-handed middle-order bat and off-spinner. He was skippering the India A team in West Indies when an injury to Ajay Jadeja saw him flown to Australia for the Tests. He was no match for the Australians, scoring 74 runs in his four innings. He didn't succeed in the ODIs there either and never played for his country again.

8   **Yograj Singh** (1 Test, 1980),
     Yuvraj Singh (40* Tests, 2000-Present)

There are few sons who surpassed their father's deeds on the scale that Yuvraj Singh did. His father played 1 Test and 6 ODIs for India, contributing only 11 runs and five wickets across both formats. Yuvraj went past his father and is still going, recognised as one of the best all-rounders his country has produced, particularly scintillating in the one-day arena, where his hard-hitting left-handed batting and accurate left-arm spin have made him a highly priced acquisition for Indian Premier League franchises. 40 Tests, 296 ODIs and 58 T20Is have been peppered by 17 centuries, almost 12,000 runs, 249 sixes and 148 wickets. His match-winning partnership with Mohammad Kaif in the 2002 NatWest Trophy final against England helped India chase down 326 at Lord's. He hit England's Stuart Broad for six sixes in an over during the 2007 ICC World T20 as India claimed the trophy and was named player of the tournament at the 2011 ICC Cricket World Cup. In ODIs he has scored 8,539 runs at 36.80 and averages 33.92 in Tests with 169 at Bangalore against Pakistan in December 2007 being the highest of three centuries.

9   **Roger Binny** (27 Tests, 1979-1987),
     Stuart Binny (6* Tests, 2014-Present)

Roger was an all-rounder, remembered most for his one-day performances, but he had an uncanny ability to pop up in Test cricket when his country most needed it. He scored an unbeaten 83 and shared a 155 run seventh wicket stand against Pakistan in Bangalore in 1983. He took seven wickets as India beat

England at Headingley in 1986 and his Test best 6-56 came against Pakistan at Calcutta in 1987. But he goes down as the man who played a key role in India's triumph at the 1983 World Cup where he took 18 wickets. In first-class cricket he grabbed the headlines when he scored a career best 211 not out in an unbroken 451 for the first wicket with Sanjay Desai against Kerala in 1977/78. He later turned to coaching the Under-19 Indian side that won the 2000 World Cup. He became a national selector in 2012.

Roger's son, Stuart, was an all-rounder from the same mould as his father. Performances for Karnataka earned him selection for India's ODI tour to New Zealand in 2013. He took 6-4, India's best ODI analysis, against Bangladesh in Mirpur. He toured England in 2014 and made his Test debut at Trent Bridge and helped earn a draw with 79 in the second innings, but England won the series and that was his only notable contribution. He played further Tests in Sri Lanka in late 2015 and then against South Africa, but it's been in ODIs and the Indian Premier League with the Rajasthan Royals and Royal Challengers Bangalore that he's made his name.

INDIA: FATHERS & SONS in INTERNATIONALS

1   **Sunil Gavaskar** (125 Tests, 1971-1987),
      Rohan Gavaskar (11 ODIs, 2004)

Sunil ranks as one of the best Indian players ever and one of the greatest Test batsmen in history. His technique was impregnable, his concentration immaculate and his contribution to cricket in India unparalleled. He was the first player to pass 10,000 Test runs and until Sachin Tendulkar deposed him, his 34 Test centuries set the benchmark. He ended with 10,122 runs at 51.12 and a highest score of 236 not out against West Indies in Madras in 1984. In that series he'd already gone past Sir Don Bradman's record for most Test hundreds. After retirement he became a commentator, journalist and administrator.

In India, as a batsman, if you are going to choose anyone to be compared with, Sunil was not that man. But his son, Rohan, had no choice. He scored 6,938 first-class runs at 44.19, mostly for Bengal, but his international opportunity came in ODIs where he scored 151 in 11 matches and fell by the wayside.

* * * * *

NEW ZEALAND: FATHERS & SONS in TESTS

1   **Giff Vivian** (7 Tests, 1931-1937),
     Graham Vivian (5 Tests, 1965-1972)

Giff, a left-handed all-rounder, was 18 when he made his Test debut at The Oval in 1931. On the tour he took 64 wickets and scored 1,002 runs, including centuries against Oxford University and Yorkshire. At Wellington in 1931-32, against South Africa, he scored his only Test century to go with the 73 and four for 58 in the same game. He was appointed New Zealand captain at 22 and played his last three Tests in England in 1937 when he hit three fifties but a back injury ended his career with a Test average of 42.10 and 17 wickets at 37.23. He became an administrator and Test selector in retirement. In all first-class cricket he'd scored 4,443 runs at 34.71, including six centuries, and taken 223 wickets. Giff died in 1983, aged 70.

Giff's son, Graham, a left-handed batsman, made his debut against India at Calcutta in 1965. It was also his first-class debut. He'd impressed in the nets, but his father's name cannot have hurt. His second innings 43 was his highest Test score. He couldn't master English conditions on the 1965 tour and his performances in West Indies in 1971/72 were below par. Deteriorating eyesight prompted his 1979 retirement when he went into business as a supplier of artificial turf.

2   **Walter Hadlee** (11 Tests, 1937-1950),
     Dayle Hadlee (26 Tests, 1969-1977),
     Richard Hadlee (86 Tests, 1972-1990)
     See Chapter Thirteen.

3   **Mac Anderson** (1 Test, 1946),
     Robert Anderson (9 Tests, 1976-1978)

William McDougall Anderson, or Mac, played 12 seasons for Canterbury and scored 1,728 runs at 36.80. In his one Test match against Australia, New Zealand's first after the War, the left-hander opened the batting and became Ray Lindwall's first Test wicket as he scored only 4 and 1. In retirement he became a New Zealand selector.

Mac's son, Robert, was a right-hander and toured England in 1973, but had to wait until the Pakistan tour in 1976/77 to make his debut. He played all three Tests, made 92 on debut, his highest Test score, but was then dropped. He returned for England's 1977/78 visit and toured England in 1978, but managed only 29 runs in six Test innings.

4   Lance Cairns (43 Tests, 1974-85),
    Chris Cairns (62 Tests, 1989-2004)

Lance ran in with a big heart, bowled off the wrong foot, could dip the ball into the right-hander and could also wallop a cricket ball out of the ground with agricultural intent. He took 130 Test wickets at 32.92 with a best of 7-74 against England at Headingley in 1983. He played 78 ODIs too, a game tailored for him, and added 89 wickets and many more sixes in that format.

Lance's son Chris was a more polished version of his father. Troubled by frequent injuries throughout his career, he still goes down as the best Kiwi all-rounder to have played the game. He became only the sixth man to achieve the Test double of 200 wickets and 3000 runs in March 2004. He ended his Test career at Trent Bridge in 2004 with 3,320 runs at 33.53 and 218 wickets at 29.40. It was an appropriate venue as he played for Nottinghamshire between 1989 and 1996 and added 2003 for good measure. Chris retired from ODIs in January 2006, with 215 appearances and 4,950 runs at 29.46 and 201 wickets at 32.80. Unfortunately for Chris, a six hitter like his father, his career came just too early to fully prosper from Twenty20 cricket.

5   Wynne Bradburn (2 Tests, 1964),
    Grant Bradburn (7 Tests, 1990-2001)

Wynne was called into the Test side to play South Africa in 1964 a little out of the blue as, although in decent form, he hadn't registered a first-class century at the time. He made 32 in his first Test and 2 and 14 in the second and never featured again. He made his highest first-class score for Northern Districts in the following season with 107 against Auckland.

Wynne's son, Grant, played five more Tests than his father and 16 seasons for Northern Districts as an off-spinner. He had two short stints in international cricket. The first in the early 1990s when he played three Tests and the second when he was recalled in 2000/01, aged 35. He did little of note in either incarnation, but when he retired had played more matches than anyone, including his father, for Northern Districts. In retirement he ran a sports shop and continued at Northern Districts as a coach, winning the Plunket Shield in 2012. He then coached New Zealand Under-19s and Scotland.

6   Zin Harris (9 Tests, 1955-1965),
    Chris Harris (23 Tests, 1992-2002)

A right-hand batsman, Zin reached fifty twice in 18 innings, both in South Africa in the 1961/62 series. He scored 74 in the first Test at Durban and 101, one of only three first-class centuries, in the third Test in Cape Town.

His son, Chris, also played Tests for New Zealand and another son, Ben, played seven seasons of first-class cricket for Canterbury and Otago. Chris was a right-hand middle-order batsman and medium pacer, ideally suited to one-day cricket, particularly as a finisher as his 62 not outs in a Kiwi record 250 ODIs testified. He was also the first Black Cap to 200 wickets, ending on 203 at 37.50. A shoulder injury prevented any further internationals, but he began coaching and continued to successfully play club cricket. In first-class games for Canterbury and county cricket for Derbyshire and Gloucestershire he scored over 7,000 runs at 45.54. His foray into Test cricket didn't replicate that standard however, his batting average of 20.44 and 16 wickets at 73.12 being a disappointing return.

7   Rodney Redmond (1 Test, 1973),
Aaron Redmond (8 Tests, 2008-2013)

There are one Test wonders and then there is the wonder of Rodney Redmond, an attacking opening batsman who played his only Test against Pakistan at Christchurch in 1973. Usually players who end with a solitary cap did not fit the bill, but Rodney hit 107 and 56 and would not have lost his place had it not been for failing to acclimatise to contact lenses on the 1973 England tour and only played first-class matches. He retired after the 1975/76 season and now lives in Perth, Australia. He averaged 81.50 in Tests!

Rodney's son, Aaron, played as a leg-spinner for Canterbury before moving to Otago to open the innings. He was selected to tour England in 2008. He scored 54 runs in three Tests, but in Australia made 83 in Adelaide. His time had come and gone and he looks set to end his Test career with 325 runs at 21.66 in Tests and 152 runs at 25.33 in six ODIs.

8   Brendon Bracewell (6 Tests, 1978-85),
Doug Bracewell (27* Tests, 2011-Present)

Brendon Bracewell was one of four brothers who played first-class cricket. John was the most successful playing 41 Tests before becoming a successful coach, Douglas played six seasons for Canterbury and Central Districts and Mark played one first-class game for Otago. Brendon, a fast bowler, toured England in 1978, aged 18, after just three first-class games, but he enjoyed success with nine wickets in three Tests. That he played only three more Tests was due to injury. He ran the Northern Cricket Academy in retirement.

Brendon's son, Doug, took match figures of 9-60 in only his third Test in Hobart as the Kiwis claimed their first win in Australia for 26 years. He played in the Under-19 World Cup alongside his cousin Michael, who plays first-class cricket for Otago, but Doug progressed to ODIs before making a Test debut against Zimbabwe in Bulawayo in 2011. He took six wickets in that game and currently sits on 72 Test wickets at 38.83.

9 Ken Rutherford (56 Tests, 1985-1995), Hamish Rutherford (16* Tests, 2013-Present)

It took Ken a while to make any impression on the international stage. A pair on Test debut in 1985 against West Indies in Port of Spain was followed by 12 runs in his next seven innings. When he was on song he was exceptional as an innings he played in 1986 illustrated. He made 317 at Scarborough Festival, including 199 between lunch and tea and his third hundred coming in only 33 balls. He captained New Zealand from 1992 to 1995 when he was dropped. 2,465 Test runs at the modest average of 27.08 was a poor return on his talent. He made three Test centuries but never made more than 107 and scored 18 further fifties that weren't converted to centuries. He played 121 ODIs where he scored two hundreds and averaged 29.65 with the bat. Post retirement he became Ireland's coach for two years and then, already with a reputation for liking a bet, he worked as a bookmaker in New Zealand, Singapore and South Africa, while also doing some television commentary.

Ken's son, Hamish, was far quicker out the international blocks than his father, scoring 171 on Test debut against England in Dunedin in March 2013. The left-handed opener had already played T20Is in Kiwi colours after impressing in domestic cricket for Otago. He lost his Test place in 2015 after 24 innings which saw him score only one fifty, his average after 16 Tests dropping to 26.96.

10 Rod Latham (4 Tests, 1992-1993), Tom Latham (29* Tests, 2014-Present)

Rod made his only Test hundred against Zimbabwe in 1992 in his second match. In his fifth Test son Tom bagged his first century against Pakistan in Abu Dhabi to level the stakes. Tom told reporters: "He's always been on about how he holds a Test hundred against me. So now we've both got one, which is nice. It's pretty special, it's something me and him will have together." Tom had debuted against India in Wellington in February 2014 and continued his good form, adding another five centuries in his first 29 Tests with a highest score of 177. The bragging rights have gone to the young gun in the Latham household.

NEW ZEALAND: FATHERS & SONS in INTERNATIONALS

1   **Walter Hadlee** (11 Tests, 1937-1950),
    Barry Hadlee (2 ODIs, 1975)
    See Chapter Thirteen.

2   **John Reid** (58 Tests, 1949-1965),
    Richard Reid (9 ODIs, 1988-1991)

John was an attacking batsman, a superb fielder and a bowler of immense variety. Teenage rheumatic fever prevented him from pursuing a promising rugby career. His best season came in South Africa tour in 1961/62 when he scored 546 runs in five Tests at 60.64 and scored 1,915 tour runs with seven centuries. He scored 3,428 Test runs at 33.28 with the best of his six hundreds being 142 against South Africa in Johannesburg. In retirement he was a coach, a New Zealand selector and an ICC match referee.

John's son, Richard, made his first-class debut for Wellington in 1979/80. He scored 1,789 first-class runs at 24.84 with one century, but his attacking instincts mimicked his father's and it was one-day cricket where he achieved greatest success. His first ODIs were in 1987/88 against England and he was recalled during the 1990/91 season to play the World Series finals in Australia, during which he achieved his highest ODI score of 64 in Melbourne. In retirement Richard worked in marketing for sports company Nike before becoming chief executive of Canterbury Cricket in 2001. After six years in the post he moved to take a similar role with Otago rugby.

* * * * *

PAKISTAN: FATHERS & SONS in TESTS

1   Nazar Mohammad (5 Tests, 1952),
Mudassar Nazar (76 Tests, 1976-1988)

Nazar Mohammad played one Test series, against India in 1952, but became Pakistan's first Test centurion. His son Mudassar played 76 Tests, scoring 4,114 runs, which featured ten centuries, six of them against India (including 231 and 199). Nazar's maiden hundred, against England in 1977/78, came in 557 minutes and was the slowest ever scored in Test cricket.

2   Hanif Mohammad (55 Tests, 1952-1969),
Shoaib Mohammad (45 Tests, 1983-1995)

Hanif Mohammad's marathon 970-minute innings that yielded 337 for Pakistan versus West Indies at Bridgetown was the longest knock in Test history. He completed century stands with four different players, one his brother, Wazir Mohammad. Hanif scored hundreds against all Test opponents outside of Pakistan. Brothers Mushtaq Mohammad and Sadiq Mohammad also played for Pakistan and a fifth brother, Raees Mohammad, once performed twelfth man duties for the national team.

Hani's son, Shoaib Mohammad, averaged 44.34 in Test cricket, had inherited his father's epic concentration, but didn't reach the heights of his dad. The Mohammads accumulated 218 Test caps between them, which was a record for appearances from one family until Steve and Mark Waugh surpassed it with a combined 296 Tests for Australia.

3   Jahangir Khan (4 Tests for India, 1932-1936),
Majid Khan (63 Tests, 1964-1983),
Bazid Khan (1 Test, 2004)

Jahangir Khan may have played his Test cricket for India but, after Partition in 1947, he was a key figure in developing cricket in Pakistan as an administrator and selector. His son, Majid, captained Pakistan, as did his nephews, Javed Burki and Imran Khan, and his brother Baqa Jilani, had played Test cricket for India. And his grandson, Bazid, played one Test for Pakistan, thereby making the Khans only the second example of a three generation Test family after the Headleys for West Indies and England.

Jahangir was a blue at Cambridge University, as was Majid, and his elder son, Asad, was a blue at Oxford University. A seamer and attacking right-hand bat, he made his India Test debut, aged 22, at Lord's in 1932 where he took three for 60 from 30 second innings overs. On the tour he hit 448 first-class runs at 19.47 and claimed 53 wickets at 29.05. If you've ever visited the Lord's Museum you'll have seen the stuffed sparrow. When Jahangir had been playing for Cambridge against MCC at Lord's he bowled to TN Pearce who defended and then noticed the bails had been dislodged and the sparrow was lying next to the stumps, while no one was able to confirm how it got there. In 1936 he hit his highest score of 133 for Cambridge and his eight for 33 for the Muslims against the Europeans at Lahore in 1929-30 was his best bowling.

Jahangir's son, Majid, was the cousin of Pakistan players Javed Burki and Imran Khan, who was ultimately tasked with dropping him in 1983. He formed a successful opening partnership in Tests with Sadiq Mohammad. He scored 3,391 Test runs at 38.92 with a highest score of 167, one of eight hundreds. He also played 23 ODIs and scored 786 runs at 37.42 with one hundred. In retirement Majid became an influential administrator in Pakistan cricket.

When Majid's son, Bazid Khan, played a solitary Test for Pakistan in 2004, the trio became only the second direct descendent three-generation cricket family. Much had been expected of Bazid with his lineage. He played for Pakistan Under-19s when only 15, but it wasn't until 2004/05, when he averaged over 70 for Lahore, that earned the first of five ODI caps the following season. In all he made 163 international runs, but spent his career on the periphery.

* * * * *

PAKISTAN / INDIA: FATHERS & SONS in TESTS

1   **Syed Wazir Ali** (7 Tests for India, 1932-1936),
     Khalid Wazir (2 Tests for Pakistan, 1954)

Syed Wazir Ali and his younger brother Nazir Ali both made their Test debut in India's inaugural Test match against England at Lord's in 1932. All his Test appearances came against England, comprising two tours of England in 1932 and 1936 and a home series in 1933. In 1932 he scored six hundreds in England and made 1,725 runs and on the second visit, despite being troubled by a finger injury for much of the trip, scored an unbeaten 155 against an England XI in Folkestone. His Test average of 16.92 was nowhere near his first-class form, where he averaged 38.77, hit 22 hundreds, with a best of 268 not out. He died in Karachi in

1950, aged 46.

Syed Wazir Ali's son, Khalid Wazir, played Test cricket for Pakistan. At 18 he toured England in 1954, but found no success in his two Test appearances as a batsman. He didn't play first-class cricket again.

* * * * *

SOUTH AFRICA'S FATHERS & SONS in TESTS

1   **Frank Hearne** (6 Tests, 1889-1896),
     George Hearne (3 Tests, 1922-1924)

Frank played in six South Africa v England Tests, the first two for England on their 1889 tour and the last four as a South African player from 1892 to 1896. Previously a Kent player, he'd remained in South Africa on health grounds at the end of the England trip where he coached and opened a sports outfitters in Cape Town. He played for Western Province and made his South African debut against an England team that included his two brothers, George and Alec, who both made their only Test appearances in Cape Town. He scored 168 Test runs at 16.80.

Frank's son, George made his Test debut for South Africa in 1922 and toured England in 1924. His 59 Test runs came at an average of 11.80. Both father and son lived until the age of 90. Frank died in Cape Town in 1949 and George died in Transvaal in 1978.

2   **Dave Nourse** (45 Tests, 1902-1924),
     Dudley Nourse (34 Tests, 1935-1951)

Arthur "Dave" Nourse, was born in England, but went to South Africa with the Army as a 17-year-old and ended up making 45 consecutive Test appearances for them. As a belligerent left-hander he made 15 Test fifties and one century, 111 against Australia at Johannesburg in 1921/22. He played first-class cricket until he was 57, hence the nickname 'The Grand Old Man of South Africa'. He set the record of the most runs scored in South African domestic cricket, including an unbeaten 304 for Natal against Transvaal in 1919/20.

Dave's son, Dudley, played 34 Tests for South Africa. Father and son played provincial cricket together at the end of Dave's career. Dave died in 1948, aged 69. Dudley made his Test debut against England at Trent Bridge in 1935 and his last game at The Oval in 1951. The war saw him miss his best international years. In all, he scored 2,950 Test runs and nine hundreds at 53.81. He once batted for nine hours through the pain of a broken thumb to notch 208 at Trent Bridge in 1951. It was the first double hundred by a South African and as captain he led his team to their first Test win for 16 years. Dudley made 91 in the first Test and 231 in the second against the touring Australians in 1935/36. The double ton remained a Test record in Johannesburg and was, at the time, the highest Test score for South Africa. When serving in the Middle East during the war he cracked nine successive sixes in a match in Alexandria. When he retired in 1952/53, Dudley had scored 12,472 first-class runs at 51.37, with 41 centuries. He died in Durban in 1981, aged 70.

3   Len Tuckett (1 Test, 1914), Lindsay Tuckett Jnr. (9 Tests, 1947-1949)

Len, a right-arm pace bowler, is most remembered for featuring in two century stands for the 10th wicket in the same game for Orange Free State against Western Province in 1925/26. A partnership of 115 in the first innings with LG Fuller and a stand of 129 in the second innings with F Caulfield established a world first. He played against England in one Test match in 1914. He died in 1963, aged 77.

Len's son Lindsay toured England in 1947 and played the last of nine Tests during England's 1947/48 tour of South Africa. Another player whose career was affected by war, he was 20 when the Second World War broke out, he would become President of the Orange Free State Cricket Union and a Test Selector. He died in Bloemfontein, aged 97, in 2016.

4   Johnny Lindsay (3 Tests, 1947), Denis Lindsay (19 Tests, 1963-1969)

Johnny debuted for Transvaal in 1933, but played his only full season before war broke out in 1937/38. It wasn't until the age of 38 in 1946-47 that he was chosen to tour England in 1947 and lost his spot after the third Test. His last first-class game was for North Eastern Transvaal against the touring MCC when, despite Denis Compton making 300 in three hours in a total of 484 for four, he did not concede a bye. He died aged 81 in Transvaal in 1990.

Johnny's son Denis played 19 Tests in the 1960s. His career highlight came against the Australian tourists in 1966/67 where his carefree batting style collected 606 runs at 86.57. He also grabbed 24 catches in a 3-1 series win, South Africa's first over Australia. He was the difference between the teams, scoring 69 and 182 to rescue the 1st Test from a forlorn position and his more controlled 137 in the 3rd Test had the same effect. His international career was cut short by South Africa's period in the international wilderness due to the apartheid regime. He would later serve as an ICC match referee. Johnny died in Johannesburg in Transvaal, aged 66, in 1990.

5   Peter Pollock (28 Tests, 1961-1969),
Shaun Pollock (108 Tests, 1995-2007)

Arguably the best of South Africa's father and son combinations, Peter and Shaun shared 136 Tests. Peter, the older brother of South African legendary left-hand batsman Graeme Pollock, was a pace bowler who took 116 Test wickets at 24.18 and added real teeth to the Test line-up in the 1960s. The Pollock brother combined at Trent Bridge in 1965 to double-handedly beat England as Peter took 5-53 and 5-34 and Graeme added 125 and 59. Peter, a 1966 *Wisden* Cricketer of the Year, took a career best 6-38 as South Africa won the first Test against New Zealand in December 1961. He was a trained journalist, a lay preacher and was the national side's convener of selectors in the 1990s. He was responsible for selecting his son, Shaun, for his debut Test against England in November 1995, but he was never accused of nepotism as his son's potential as an all-rounder was clear and he rapidly found his feet.

Shaun became the highest South African Test wicket-taker ever with 421. His 3,781 Test runs at 32.31 put him in his nation's top ten. Add 387 ODI wickets and you have the complete all-rounder. His partnership with fast bowler Allan Donald during the 1990s was one of the most feared ever. While Donald was blood and thunder, Shaun was incredibly accurate and could move the ball both ways. His career best 7-87 summed up his character as he bowled tirelessly in the Adelaide heat on a pitch that offered him little. He became South African captain in late 2000 after Hansie Cronje fell from grace amidst a match-fixing scandal, but would be replaced by Graeme Smith in 2003 after winning 14 of his 26 games in charge. He played his final Test against England in January 2008 on his home ground in Durban. He is now a TV commentator.

6   Jimmy Cook (3 Tests, 1992-1993),
Stephen Cook (9* Tests, 2016-Present)

Jimmy had to wait for his Test debut in November 1992 after being denied a long international career by South Africa's exclusion from world cricket because of apartheid. Aged 39 he edged his first ball against India, bowled by Kapil Dev, to slip and would make only 107 runs at 17.83 in the three matches he played. It was not remotely reflective of the talent that had seen him amass 21,143 first-class runs for Transvaal and Somerset at 50.58 with 64 centuries. A career robbed by politics.

Jimmy's son Stephen was forced to wait too. His delay, because others like Graeme Smith were considered a better fit, only made him more determined to prove his technique and temperament when the chance finally came. He was 33 and had been a first-class cricketer for 16 years when he opened the batting against England at Centurion in January 2016. His father had told him, "You haven't got much to beat here boy. You've only got to last two balls and then you'll be fine." He lasted 218 balls, scored 118, became only the sixth South African to score a century on debut as his proud father watched from the stands. Nine Tests into his international career he has so far scored 615 runs at 41.00 with two further hundreds. Stephen has talked about developing a thick skin as the son of a former player: "I've been in a lot of different change-rooms and pretty hostile environments. I always say that if you make it out of your own dressing room, you can make it in the middle." He also said he was a graduate of a "school of tough love," where his father had impressed upon him that he could get out for any reason except being tired. Hard work and patience pays – perhaps those qualities run in the family.

* * * * *

WEST INDIES: FATHERS & SONS in TESTS

1   **Tommy Scott** (8 Tests, 1928-1930),
       Alfred Scott (1 Test, 1953)

Tommy played for Jamaica and in eight Test matches for West Indies. A batsman and slow leg-break bowler, Tommy Scott toured England in 1928, playing in two Test matches. When visiting Australia in 1930-31, he took part in all five Tests and in the first at Adelaide he finished the Australian innings by dismissing four batsmen in nine deliveries without cost. In first-class cricket he scored 1,322 runs, average 22.40, and took 203 wickets for 28.70 runs each. Tommy died in Kingston, Jamaica, in 1961, aged 68. His son Alfred played one ignominious Test in 1953 scoring only five runs and without taking a wicket while conceding 140 runs.

2 **George Headley** (22 Tests, 1930-1953),
Ron Headley (2 Tests, 1973),
Dean Headley (15 Tests for England, 1997-1999)
See Chapter Fourteen.

3 **Everton Weekes** (48 Tests, 1947-1958),
David Murray (19 Tests, 1977-1981)

Everton was the last of the famous 'Three Ws' of Frank Worrall, Everton Weekes and Clyde Walcott to be knighted in 1995. After debuting in Test cricket in Barbados against England in 1948 he excelled in India scoring 779 runs at 111.28. He established a world record of five successive hundreds, which could easily have been six, but for a debatable run out decision in Madras. He made 2,310 runs at 79.65 on the England tour of 1950, including a triple hundred against Cambridge, although in the Tests he made only 338 at 56.33. In New Zealand in 1955-56 he hammered 940 runs at 104.44 in eight first-class matches. A thigh injury saw him retire from international cricket, aged 33, with a final Test tally of 4,455 runs at 58.61 and a best of 207 against India at Queens Park Oval, Trinidad in 1953. At the time of writing he is 92 not out and living in Barbados.

Had it not been for Deryck Murray (no relation) and Jeff Dujon, David would have played far more for West Indies. There is little written about the relationship between Everton and David and one can only assume that David was illegitimate and lived under his mother's name. He made three Test fifties and a first-class double hundred, at Jamshedpur on the 1978/79 tour of India. He briefly got his chance to own the international gloves in 1980/81 but was struggling with a drug problem. After playing Tests in Australia on the 1981/2 he was left out of the one-day side and fell out with the management. Banned for life by the West Indies Cricket Board after partaking in the 1983 rebel tour of South Africa, many of the rebels struggled with their punishment and the public backlash. None more so than David, whose life sadly spiralled into drug addiction. David's son Ricky Hoyte played 32 first-class matches for Barbados.

* * * * *

ZIMBABWE: FATHERS & SONS in TESTS

1   **Malcolm Jarvis** (5 Tests, 1992-1994),
    Kyle Jarvis (8 Tests, 2011-2013)

Malcolm, a left-arm seam bowler, played in Zimbabwe's Inaugural Test match against India in October 1992 and was proud of the fact that, in his five Tests, he never finished on the losing side. He retired at 38 and was briefly Zimbabwe's fitness trainer. Malcolm's son Kyle was right-arm and quicker than his father. He played eight Tests taking 30 wickets at 31.73. He also added 24 ODIs and 9 T20Is but turned his back on Zimbabwe cricket in 2013 amidst the salary disputes and political wrangling that dogged cricket in the country in that period. He subsequently pursued a career in English county cricket with Lancashire.

2   **Andy Waller** (2 Tests, 1996),
    Malcolm Waller (11* Tests, 2011-Present)

Andy, who balanced life as a cricketer and tobacco farmer, was a fixture in Zimbabwe's one-day side as an entertaining batsman. He was in the side that played in the 1987, 1992 and 1996 World Cups, but had to wait until he was 37 to taste Test cricket. He'd acquired the reputation of being a one-day specialist, but a determined fifty on debut proved a few doubters wrong. He played the second Test against England, a game that would be his last in first-class cricket. The tobacco farm was reclaimed by the Zimbabwe government under Robert Mugabe's Land Reform Programme forcing Andy to move into cricket coaching. He coached Namibia before becoming coaching manager of Zimbabwe Cricket in April 2009 and also head coach to Mid West Rhinos. He was then briefly Zimbabwe's head coach before taking up a new role as national director of cricket coaching. Andy's son Malcolm followed as a middle-order batsman. He made his name with a fine 74-ball unbeaten 99 to enable Zimbabwe to chase down a record 329 against New Zealand in October 2011. That paved the way for his Test debut against the Kiwis a few weeks later.

CHAPTER EIGHTEEN

THE FINAL OVER

"Build me a son, O Lord, who will be strong enough to know
when he is weak, and brave enough to face himself when he is afraid,
one who will be proud and unbending in honest defeat,
and humble and gentle in victory"
Douglas MacArthur

As the man who jumped off the Eiffel Tower said when he was halfway down: "No problems so far."

But now I have to write my conclusions and findings. But before I began I re-read my introduction. Sometimes it helps to remember what you were looking for in the first place.

I wanted to talk to fathers and sons who had played professional cricket and hear their experiences. Specifically I wanted to know these sportsmen had coped with the pressures of expectation. I had wondered whether cricket was in the genes. And most of all, I wanted to know what it was like to follow one's father into the spotlight.

The first part, to speak to the players themselves, had been, on the whole, far easier than I'd imagined. I've often thought that cricket is one of the more enjoyable sports to cover as a journalist. The egos are there but they are rarely off-putting, the intelligence permits well thought out answers and the players tend to understand your role in promoting their sport.

There have been countless times, particularly when I've been interviewing cricketers on the radio, that a poorly constructed and hastily voiced question has gone unnoticed because the player has provided a great answer regardless. I've seen similar questions asked to football managers given extremely short shrift.

I've thanked the cricketers whose words you have read elsewhere in this book, but I genuinely cannot thank them enough – so thanks again!

* * * * *

As I'd been speaking to the players I'd jotted down a number of factors I'd realised were important to a person's chances of becoming a successful professional sportsman.

1. OPPORTUNITY

This is vital. Without opportunity a sportsman would never even have their feet in the starting blocks, let alone escape them. How many sporting champions have the world missed out on because they never had the opportunity to pick up a bat, racket or club?

You have probably walked past people in the street every single day who have no idea that if they had been introduced to cricket at an early age they would now have played 100 Test matches. For every Tiger Woods or Serena Williams, there are millions of people who didn't have an Earl Woods or Richard Williams to guide them and give them the opportunity.

Unfortunately, it's that last point that leads to pushy parents who believe their own child can be shoehorned into success. Not every one with opportunity will succeed, but without opportunity there is no chance. I'd subscribe to Dean Headley's view that sport is a positive factor and children should be encouraged to play as many as they can. If something world-class comes from that it's a bonus.

Having a cricket father effectively puts the sport in your compass and your mission if you choose to accept it.

I'd read a bit about how important the month someone is born in can be, particularly when determining success in a highly physical sport. A child born in September is likely to be physically more developed in his teenage years than his peer that was born in August. The UK school year begins in September. Coaches and scouts see the big centre forward that is stronger than another player in his year, but don't necessarily check birth certificates. As Dean Headley pointed out we often ignore late developers. But that fortune of birth date, nothing to do with DNA, creates opportunity or limits a person's chance of being selected for higher standard games. If moved up through the ranks the bigger lad plays against tougher opposition, improves, plays more and succeeds.

2. CULTURE and ENVIRONMENT

I've thought of this point as the 'Billy Elliot Factor'. If you've not seen the film, Billy is a young boy growing up in the north of England with dreams of becoming a dancer. Yet in the backdrop of an area where men were men and his stereotypically gruff coal mining father is embarrassed and cannot comprehend his son's choices. For Billy it came good. But if Mr Elliot had himself been a dancer it would never have been an issue.

This factor is linked to the first. Unless you want to take on your family as well as the world, it is positive to grow up in an environment that understands and promotes the choice to take cricket seriously. Imagine if Ian Botham had been born in France. His chances of becoming the cricketer he did would have been slim to nought.

3. BROKEN BARRIERS

When a father had previously played professional sport it opens up that world to his children. You often hear people say things like "he's the first person in our family to go to university" and it's seen as a major achievement because it's a breakthrough moment, but for many other households further education is the norm.

For most people the task of making it as a professional sportsman seems huge, but if you've grown up in a household where professional sport is your father's job and you've been in dressing rooms and around other elite players, the task of doing that too could be viewed as less daunting. It's on your family's radar and not a distant dream.

4. THE SPARK

Many sporting greats cite a moment when everything came into focus and they knew they wanted sport as a career and what they had to do to get it. American NBA player Shaquille O'Neal tells of a moment when as a young man he was good but coasting and taking short cuts, but one day his mother gave him a stern talk. She highlighted that Shaquille had an amazing opportunity and he should give it everything and take his chance. Did he want to settle for normality and slip into a culture of doing it tomorrow, or did he want to grab his chances today? It hit home and he devoted every living hour from then on to become one of the best basketball players ever. That was his spark.

I think back to Ryan Sidebottom's story of the coach who told him he didn't have what it took. He wobbled, but came back stronger and was determined to prove that coach wrong. That was his Shaquille O'Neal moment. Or maybe Shaq had a Ryan moment. Either way, experiences like that can be the catalyst for greatness.

Cricketers' sons gain inspiration by virtue that their father becomes their hero. Whether that creates a spark inside them is down to them, but if it's there, it's a huge determining factor on whether they are prepared to put in the hard yards to make it.

5. MENTAL TOUGHNESS

The positive mentality, a competitive spirit, or whatever you want to call it is vital if a sportsman is going to succeed. I'd heard from Alun Williams that this could be handed down in the genes. It doesn't just come in handy in a sporting context. When your team-mates, pundits or spectators are saying versions of 'you're only here because of your Dad' you need to be mentally strong. All of the sons I'd spoken to had said they had to deal with that in their young lives, before they'd proved their talent, and many felt they had to work harder to get what they wanted. If an individual has the qualities to cope and continue, they are halfway there.

6. DESIRE

Add to mental toughness a genuine desire to succeed and you have a potent package. Not all sons of cricketers have these two traits and they are probably the guys who go down a different route. Desire isn't just wanting to pick up a bat or ball and play, but to want to go all the way and make the many sacrifices required to go the extra mile. You can have all the talent in the world, but unless you really *want* it, you've got nothing more than an amateur club career anyone can enjoy, regardless of parentage.

7. LUCK

Former cricketer, Ed Smith, wrote a very good book entitled *Luck: What It Means and Why It Matters* in 2012. While he goes into great depth, the basic principle is that, to be successful, we all need our fair share of fortune.

When people say *luck evens itself out*, or *you make your own luck*, I've often thought that to be garbage. For example, if a batsman is incorrectly adjudged to be lbw when on nought, how do we know that wasn't going to be his day where he'd have scored a career best? A batsman dropped on nought who goes on to score a double century is rarely classed as lucky when people look back years later, but he was.

I think back to Matthew Syed's example of living in a house that allowed his dreams of becoming a table tennis player to reach fruition. Living one door down he'd have not had the opportunity to do what he did. That is luck and nothing more. But in Syed's case, when fortune presented itself he embraced it and worked hard to make it count for something.

Some people would say that cricket sons are lucky to have the fathers they do. And they are correct, because all of the previous factors I've listed can be positively influence by a successful father. But there are negatives too as many of the players have said.

Any successful sportsman requires luck to be on their side at times and this is one factor that a father cannot influence. Once their boy has taken guard and the quick bowler is steaming in they are standing on their own two feet. As David Lloyd has told me, it is the sons who score the runs and not the fathers. And equally it is the sons who get their own share of luck, or not.

8. PRACTICE MAKES PERFECT

The 10,000-hours theory hasn't been questioned. To become an elite athlete many hours of proper practice is required. Where a cricket son gets a head start is that they are picking up bats, watching games and becoming immersed in the sport from a very young age. In most cases they are not being intentionally targeted towards the sport. All parents seek ways to occupy their children and keep them from being troublesome. What better way than to give them a bat and ball while dad is making his living in the middle? And what that does, without exception throughout this book, is give them a head start. Chris Cowdrey talked about being better than his peers by the time he was playing at school. That engenders confidence and reinforces the feeling that this sport is for them.

When theorists looked at the 10,000-hours required they equated it to around 10 years. Take a cricket son who is playing with dad in the back garden and at matches throughout the summer from the age of five. By the time they are coming into age group teams, hitting county academies and being judged by coaches on whether they can make it as a professional player, they already have those 10,000 hours in their locker. Very few 'normal' children would be able to say the same.

9. GOOD GUIDANCE

All elite athletes will point to inspirational, effective and crucial individuals in their lives, who gave them coaching, mentored them and pointed them in the right direction when needed. Most of the cricket fathers had told me they had stood back from their son's development, but they had always been there when needed. They all knew the landscape, they'd been there, and they knew the best coaches - the best way to give their son the greatest chance. While Walter Hadlee is rare in creating a net and family coaching structure in the back garden for his boys, all of the parents had known, in their own way, the right way to give their son the best start and guidance.

10. THE GENES

Alun Williams has told me that most character traits and skills were being found to be genetic. Power, speed, height and attributes like that were handed down. The ability to learn new skills and be psychologically equipped had also been proved to be genetic.

While there isn't a cricket gene, and as Mark Butcher had commented, the techniques required to play cricket are unnatural in many ways, there are a series of genes that together are capable of assembling every trait and skill required to succeed on a cricket field.

As Alun had told me, the genes themselves are nothing without certain other factors, but they do provide an individual with a head start.

When I'd spoken to Simon Hartley, the sports psychologist, at the start of this book he had said that it was unlikely that I'd come up with any conclusions other than that people are different and deal with challenges in their own ways. While that is true the biggest conclusion I've made when writing this book is this:

To become a professional cricketer, or an elite sportsman, there are a number of important factors required. If you combine the factors one to nine, as listed above, and then add in a father's good sporting genes, then that person has the very best chance of becoming a sporting success. This guarantees nothing, but a head start is always handy. This conclusion is transferrable to any sport.

* * * * *

A few points stood out from the conversations I'd had with both former and current cricket players.

Having a famous father did create pressure and challenges for the son. It could also engender resentment.

Having a well-known surname did create expectation. When that name was coming through the age groups it attracted more attention and when spectators saw that name on scorecards they judged whether he was better than the previous generation and expected the youngster to be a carbon copy of their father. A cricket son's presence in the sport created more excitement than if Fred Bloggs was coming through.

Those youngsters that withstood the pressures of their surname felt they were ultimately stronger and better people/players for the experience. Having to work that bit harder to prove themselves did them no harm and in many cases had pushed them on past their peers.

The experience is the same, yet very different for everyone and how they cope with it varies. A Ryan Sidebottom was more sensitive to the challenges than an Alec Stewart. That doesn't mean Stewart is a better person than Sidebottom, in many ways it gives me more admiration for the Sidebottoms who felt they had more to cope with.

The cricket sons that now had children of their own are, in many cases more aware of their role in their offspring's future. Mark Ealham provides a good example with two children coming through at Kent. He is acutely aware of the potential pressures, has spoken to his father Alan about it, and given his role in their development considerable thought.

The Lehmanns had introduced the possibility that Darren could well step down from his position of head coach to Australia if Jake is selected. That showed the father and son relationship could potentially influence the career path of the father as well as the son.

Some fathers almost can't be followed. While nothing is impossible, the genuine greats like Bradman. Richards and Botham really are harder acts to follow than players with less illustrious pasts.

Greta Bradman's incredible rise to being a professional singer, but the challenges she had faced in getting there, proved that a famous name doesn't just affect the lives of sons that followed in the same profession. Her father John had changed his name. The entire family can be affected by having a really famous forefather.

I found Liam Botham particularly interesting as he obviously had the talent to play at the highest level, but for him that wasn't enough. He knew he was always going to be compared to his father Ian and rarely, if ever, write his own headlines. If he'd been almost anyone else's son he would have been delighted with the talent he had and had a very high chance of being hugely successful. The more I thought about his route into rugby the more I respected the heart searching that must have gone into that decision.

I'd found Dean Headley's take on pushy parents, the snowflake generation and that we are prone to ignoring late developers in sport fascinating.

And Basil D'Oliveira being caught up in apartheid politics through no fault of his own had made him, at least for a time, bigger than the game. But Damian and now Brett had coped with their surname admirably regardless.

While a key driver for sons is to better their father's statistics, there are many examples I'd found, like Ron Headley, where all the son wanted was to show he could be good at his father's job too. Finding one's identity in sport isn't all about success. In Ron's case he wanted his father to see that he was a worthy player. It can also be about being happy you have made your father proud. That could be a match-winning double century, or it could be that your father knew you had done your best. The ultimate success was feeling good about what you'd done.

When asked, all of the cricketers, in varying ways, had said they believed that cricket was in the genes. My chat with Alun Williams had proved them correct. Children inherit certain attributes and traits from their fathers, but they are merely ingredients in a bigger recipe. To cook up the full appetising dish those genes need to be mixed with opportunity, a productive environment, desire, practice, guidance and a little bit of luck to stand a chance of longer term success. But the cricket sons had a head start on most of their peers.

The cricket fathers that I felt got it most right were the ones like Arnie Sidebottom, Tim Tremlett and Damian D'Oliveira, who had stood back, allowed their boys access to cricket, but also to everything else the world had to offer. I liked to hear things, such as Brett D'Oliveira telling me that his father Damian had been completely at ease with his other sons' decisions to pursue alternative careers. Perhaps these cricket fathers had nothing else to prove.

At the end of the day there is more to life than cricket. The thing I took most from talking to Tim Tremlett was the death of his middle son in a car accident. Having a happy and healthy family is more important than a few runs and wickets.

* * * * *

Ultimately the sons of famous fathers have more chance of becoming successful in their sport than my old friend Fred Bloggs, but that doesn't in any way devalue their careers. On the contrary, I would suggest that, despite some advantages in opportunity and genetics, their achievements are even more admirable because they had more to cope with than most other people. Weight of expectation, both public and within oneself, are tough nuts to crack.

While Usain Bolt's only task is to run from A to B in the quickest time possible, the job of a cricketer is to conquer technique and take on the challenge of a sport where no two days are the same. No two overs are the same!

A cricketer is largely judged on how many runs they score, the wickets they take and the games they win. It is the sons that earn their own statistical records and trophy cabinets and not their fathers. It is their father's exploits that have inspired them to achieve.

Together the generations have combined to give the sporting world some of the most remarkable families. I'd venture further - it has given us some very fine men.

ACKNOWLEDGEMENTS

Thanks to my Mum and Dad for being my parents and giving me the love, guidance and support to be able to appreciate what it is like to follow on from very special people.

Thanks to my children. Kate, Emma and Sam you are very loved. As is Annette, who has the patience of a saint in putting up with me!

This book would not have been possible without the generous time of the cricketers I have interviewed or have pointed me in the right direction. Huge thanks go to Liam Botham, Alan, Ian and Mark Butcher, Nick Compton, Chris, Graham and Fabian Cowdrey, Simon Dennis, Brett D'Oliveira, Alan and Mark Ealham, Dayle Hadlee, Dean Headley, Simon Jones, Jake Lehmann, David and Graham Lloyd, Martyn Moxon, Kevin Sharp, Arnie and Ryan Sidebottom, Alec Stewart, Tim and Chris Tremlett.

The time they have given and the friendly, honest and thoughtful answers they provided are hugely appreciated. Every one of them has provided me with entertainment down the years and it's good to know the players you have admired for their cricket are just as good off the field of play. I wish you well for the future whether still playing or not.

Thanks also to Alun Williams and Simon Hartley, my experts, who made the complicated fit inside my uncomplicated brain.

Thanks to David Warner, Graham Hardcastle and Hattie Wright who have read the book and made suggestions and encouraging noises. And thanks to David Burrill, at Great Northern Books, for his support, guidance and deadlines. I always work better with them.

Thanks to you for reading. I hope you enjoyed it.